Another Cup of Tea
-The Teenage Years

David M Cameron

Copyright © 2021 David M Cameron

All rights reserved.

ISBN: 9798751091989

DEDICATION

For the many people who put up with me during my teenage years, and for Olwyn, as always.

CONTENTS

    Acknowledgments

1. The End of Primary School
2. Starting Roundhay School, or At Least Getting Ready
3. The Day of Judgement
4. Settling into School.
5. Smells, Explosions, Mayhem, and Madness
6. How Did We Survive?
7. He's Just a Very Naughty boy!
8. Two Jackets to Elland Road and Back
9. We're All in for the High Jump!
10. The Merrion.
11. The Changing Home
12. Freedom, Cinemas, Courting and Snogging
13. Naked Baths and Straight-Arm Tackles
14. Call That Running, Boy?
15. Scouting For Boys
16. Starting Youth Clubs
17. A Trip to the Dentist
18. Passion, Extremes and Hair
19. What Foolish Things
20. The Clock, the Cellar, and the Paint That Never Dried

21	Illicit Fags, Booze and the Finger Incident
22	The Last Bus Home
23	Let the Music Play
24	Singles, LPs, and the Cassette Tape
25	Let the Music Play Live
26	Pipers, Chablis, Pete's Cellar and the Poly
27	Puberty Blues
28	Fair Crack of the Whip for the Guruts
29	The Gledhow Lane Shootout
30	The Who Moment, and Adventures on Ilkley Moor
31	Coventry Capers
32	24 Mile Midnight Hike and the Fist Real Concert
33	The Unkempt Years
34	Chapel Allerton Hall Riot
35	Your Mother Warned You about Boys Like Us
36	Let the Music Play Live, Again
37	Beauty and Ugliness
38	The Judean, Spalding and a Five-a-side Trauma!
39	Texas Grill, Pinball, and the Jukebox
40	A Bit of Biffo!
41	Drugs, Sex and Rock-and-roll

42	Fancy Pants	
43	Summer Nights, and the Icy Kiss of Winter Frost	
44	Exams and the Dreaded Results	
45	Learning to Drive	
46	The Ups and Downs of Driving for Wraggs	
47	The Girl in the Shorts	
48	The Cow and Calf	
49	Dancing With Death	
50	Almscliffe Crag and Snowdonia	
51	What Strange Teenagers	
52	Ruining a Wedding	
53	Boating, Piracy and a Near Drowning	
54	Final Year and Growing Older if Not Wiser	

ACKNOWLEDGMENTS

My thanks to Olwyn Cameron for all her hard work and support.

THE END OF PRIMARY SCHOOL

Those who have read the earlier book, Cup of Tea Tales – The Early Years, will already know that growing up in Leeds in the 1950s and 1960s was full of fun, challenges and interesting people. My family was, as far as I was concerned, very normal, but I guess it was the standard, two parents, three children, family that is less common nowadays. My father was an engineer and Scottish, and my mother was from Leeds. I was the middle child with an older brother, Andrew, and a younger brother, Stuart. My mother worked, at least part-time, for all the time I can remember, and my father worked for a steel foundry, Cattons, in Black Bull Street in Leeds. I was lucky. I loved my parents and brothers and they would do anything for us. We weren't well off, but neither were we poor. We had originally lived in a two-bedroom semi, but when my younger brother appeared, we moved into a three-bedroom semi-detached house in Gipton Wood Crescent, near Harehills.

My stories were originally written as part of my blog, Cup of Tea Tales, and podcasts, but I was asked to convert them into a book and here is my second volume. This edition will cover my life at Roundhay School and the turbulent times of my teenage years. Society was experiencing major changes and upheavals during the 1960s and early 1970s and so was I as I passed from boyhood into manhood. For those who lived through these times, I am sure that there will be things that will bring back your own memories. No life is uneventful, despite being ordinary, and no family is without its own story, and this is mine. I am happy to share it with you and I hope you enjoy the journey.

After my mother got over the delight of my gaining a place at Roundhay School, there was a hiatus where life returned to normal and Mr Kelly, at Harehills County Primary, continued in his usual form. When he became frustrated, out came his, 'Angels and Ministers of Grace Defend Us!', a call to divine intervention to help the children under his charge. Funnily, that was as aggressive as I remember him being, but corporal punishment with the slipper did happen in the school. I do remember some of us questioning him once about why he had brown stains on his fingers and he told us it was from peeling a lot of apples. Even in our innocence, we didn't believe that one.

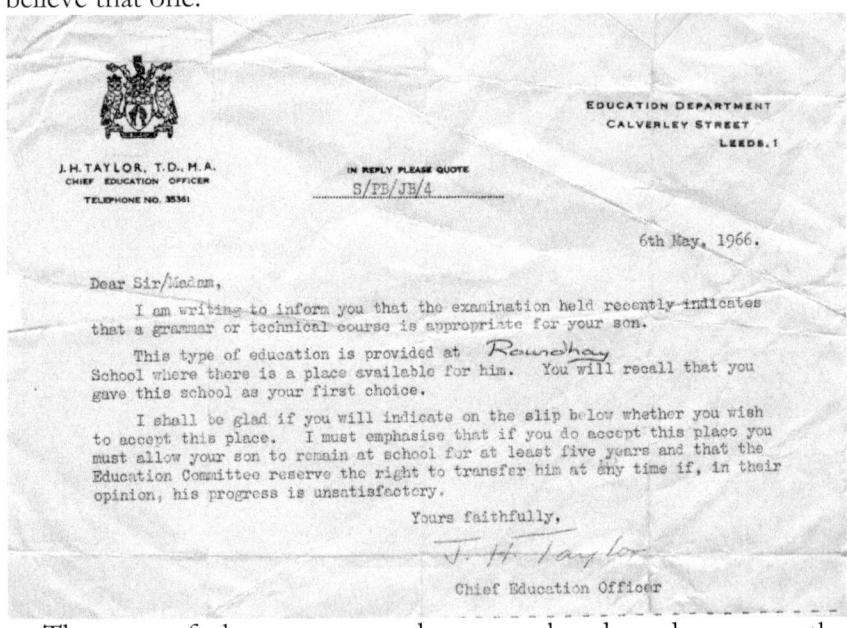

> EDUCATION DEPARTMENT
> CALVERLEY STREET
> LEEDS. 1
>
> J.H. TAYLOR, T.D., M.A.
> CHIEF EDUCATION OFFICER
> TELEPHONE NO. 35361
>
> IN REPLY PLEASE QUOTE
> S/PB/JB/4
>
> 6th May, 1966.
>
> Dear Sir/Madam,
>
> I am writing to inform you that the examination held recently indicates that a grammar or technical course is appropriate for your son.
>
> This type of education is provided at Roundhay School where there is a place available for him. You will recall that you gave this school as your first choice.
>
> I shall be glad if you will indicate on the slip below whether you wish to accept this place. I must emphasise that if you do accept this place you must allow your son to remain at school for at least five years and that the Education Committee reserve the right to transfer him at any time if, in their opinion, his progress is unsatisfactory.
>
> Yours faithfully,
>
> J. H. Taylor
>
> Chief Education Officer

The rest of the year seemed more relaxed, and we saw the introduction of ballpoint pens and the removal of the dip pens, blotting paper and inkwells. Anyway, there was some excitement at having the coloured pens, shaped very much like an ink pen: stubby at the point and tapering to a thin end. The ritual filling of inkwells, asking for blotting paper and occasional replacement nibs, disappeared overnight. I missed the ability to flick pellets of ink soaked blotting paper at girls sitting in the rows in front and using the pens as darts and throwing them into the bare floorboards where a good shot would have it stuck in the wood, swaying from side to side. Of course, this was never done when Mr Kelly was in the room.

Times were very different in the 1960s and, along with the

disappearance of the ink pens, a whole new world was opening up. Cliff Richard had appeared in the film, Summer Holiday, in 1963, which starts in black and white, but once the bus reaches Europe, it changes to full colour. I saw it with my grandma in the Dominion in Chapel Allerton. The change of colour in the film was mirrored in my life at this time. The old life was black and white and the new was bright and colourful. The pens were vivid red, bright green or yellow and the new desks that arrived weren't double desks with iron frames. There was a general sense of optimism that hadn't been there before. There was to be a brave new world, and we were to experience it head-on. I even remember one Friday afternoon a couple, man and woman, arriving at the classroom and they were researchers and wanted our opinions on several chocolate bars. Now this probably wouldn't be permissible nowadays, but it was ok then. The bars were all unwrapped, and we were not told what any of them were called. We were handed some to try, and we had to give them scores for our preferences. One was very much like a Milky Way and another like a Mars Bar. It is possible it was the prototype Aztec Bar that was Cadbury's answer to the Mars Bar. The Aztec was launched for the Mexico Olympics in 1968, so it is possible. Anyway, that was a memorable day and but unfortunately one that was never repeated.

As summer approached, the school picked a cricket team. Now I don't remember many opportunities for inter-school sports, but I think a new keen male teacher organised one. We had trials and some practices on a Saturday morning on the Soldiers' Field at Oakwood. We weren't up to much and the equipment was basic. The pads were old, torn and heavy, and we found them difficult to run in, but wearing them made you feel special. The bats were old, fairly battered, and smelt of linseed oil. I loved the smell and just writing this the odour is filling my mind. We used to play cricket at lunch and break times on the tarmac yard at Harehills, using tennis balls, with wickets that were painted on the caretaker's house wall. There was a slope down to the wicket and some kids could build up a real pace. I was just ok at batting and bowling and I turned up for the practice, which I seem to remember happened after school in the yard. Joy above joy, I was selected and turned up on Saturday for a proper practice with anticipation and pride. I batted and scored about seven runs, which I was quite pleased with. I think we were limited to only batting a couple of overs. The first game with another school came along and I have no idea if we won, but I scored twelve runs, so I was delighted. I think we only had one or two more matches, but I do remember my dad turning up to watch one that was after school. The match was somewhere near Crossgates, and this was on a proper cricket pitch. The time came for me to bat and I strode out, knowing that my dad was watching. I was nervous, but it was one of those days where everything worked out. I seemed to see the ball more easily, and I scored twenty, with one four. I was over the moon and my dad seemed quite impressed. I went home with him in his car rather than on the bus, and I think it was the only time he ever saw me play in a match. It still means a lot.

In the mid-sixties, boys wore shorts at primary school and, in fact, well into high school. I was no exception, and I had a rather baggy pair of grey school shorts. We didn't have many clothes, and we wore them until they became threadbare and patched. I often remember hand-me-downs from my brother or neighbours. Washing was something that was done once a week and not daily, as is now the case. I think I used to wear my school shirt all week. Anyway, I didn't own a pair of long trousers at the time and this was to prove interesting.

My mother received some complimentary tickets for the Silver Blades ice skating rink on Kirkstall Road, near the Yorkshire Television buildings. Now my mother could have won them, as she was keen on entering competitions and quite successful. I remember one year she won a year's free dry cleaning at Martins the Cleaners at Harehills. She received a book of vouchers and I don't think we ever looked so clean as we did that year. Never having been ice skating, it was an exciting opportunity and dad dropped off my mum, my older brother Andrew and me, and we went in and exchanged our shoes for some very uncomfortable ice skating boots.

The boots laced up to above the ankle, and the rink was a hive of activity. The cold hit you and the air had a vibrancy that gave sounds a higher tone, which shocked the senses. It was nigh on impossible to walk in the skates. My legs splayed out like a baby giraffe taking its first steps. I staggered to the nearest entrance onto the ice, and holding onto the rail, stepped out. Now the rink was full of capable skaters of all ages. They flashed by with unimaginable ease and grace. There were those who showed off by skating backwards, dodging between the laggards, impressing everyone, and particularly the opposite sex. It was just like the men on the waltzers at the fairground. Music blared, and in the centre of the revolving masses, a girl, clearly a figure skater, demonstrated what we could all aspire to. I wanted to be like them. How hard could it be?

It was at this point that I noticed the cold air around my knees, and then the horror struck me. I was the only boy in the place in short trousers. Everyone else was suitably attired in long trousers, even the girls, though some wore tights. The horror of my faux pas hit me and a sudden rush of heat spread all over me, sending the chill well into retreat. I looked at my mum. How could she have done this to me? Of course, she was oblivious. I stood there, horrified, but as I had no option, I stepped off from the edge and attempted to emulate all the others around. I saw that many of them were very shaky and collisions and falls were common. How hard could it be? I thought again, and I set off. One push off, a wobble and then disaster. The ice was hard, cold and wet and I was splayed on my back like an overturned beetle. Getting back on my feet was easier said than done, and a very ungracious crawl to the side followed. I pulled myself up and noticed that my brother seemed to be mastering the skill, even in a very basic way. I tried again and, bit by bit, I managed to get a balance and pushed and pulled myself around the edge. Finally, I plucked up courage to let go of the side and pushed off. I was skating. I shuffled myself along and over time grew in confidence and built up the speed. The problem was that no one had told me how to stop or turn. I went in a straight line across the rink, others almost diving aside to avoid me, and I shot at speed, pink kneed, pink faced and out of control, until I went smack into the opposite side and hit the ice again. Having gained some self-assurance, I continued on, noting that my older brother was annoyingly smooth and controlled. After half an hour, I reached the stage of managing a lap. My turns, though far from elegant, were beginning to be effective, and with pressure being exerted on the outer foot, I could gain directional control.

There was a master of ceremonies, or disk jockey for those old enough to know what a disk is, and at times he would clear the ice for speed skating or for the machine to go out and groom the ice. This was the time I sat with my brother and mum and had a drink. After the break, me and my embarrassing pink and almost bleeding knees ventured back out. It was a bit easier this time, and I felt better until a girl fell in front of me and I had neither the ability nor the knowledge of how to stop in time or swerve to avoid her. I hit her side-on and flew like a graceless dodo and landed face forward into the ice, spread-eagled like a star. This fallen star had, by this time, had enough. The girl was getting up and so I knew I hadn't cut her in half, like the lady in a box with a magician. The blades for beginners were fairly blunt, but I did wonder if they could cut through a finger if one were skated over. I got back to my feet and continued, because I felt I had to and I didn't want to be beaten by anything. At this point in my life, I had succeeded, to a reasonable level, in everything I had done, so I wasn't going to be defeated by this. Soon mum was indicating our time was up. I went around one more time and then managed to make the right exit, even if too fast, and smashed into the side wall. Out of breath, out of patience and knees out in the open, I was glad to get the skates off and return them and get my wonderfully comfortable shoes back. Dad was waiting as arranged, and on the way home, even my mum agreed I needed some long trousers.

This wasn't my only attempt at it, as we went back at least a couple more times. The next occasion was more successful and my knees didn't get another outing. Looking back, I think this might have been the first time that I had experienced real embarrassment and a sense of lack of control. There are many times since that I have experienced both, but at eleven years old, I suppose your development gives you a greater anxiety regarding how you are perceived. Of course, at my current age, I have lost many of my inhibitions and often delight in being embarrassing, much to the horror of my children and long-suffering wife.

STARTING ROUNDHAY SCHOOL, OR AT LEAST GETTING READY

After receiving notification that I was to attend Roundhay School for my secondary education, there was a period where nothing really happened. Summer was approaching and, from memory, it was one of those real summers when the weather was hot and rain was infrequent. This was the summer of 1966 and I remember my parents receiving a package of information regarding my attendance at Roundhay School. There was a list of uniform that was required and it named the shops in Leeds that could provide it. There were two main ones and Rawcliffe was the one we used. This was an exciting time for me.

Harehills County Primary School had no uniform apart from a choir one, and so I was intrigued about what I needed. The letter informed me I was allocated to Kelvin House. Again, Harehills only had colours, and a house with a name was something new. With this letter came the first real recognition that my life was to change. It is true that I had already changed from Stainbeck Preparatory School to Harehills, but I was only seven and it happened with almost no warning. Attending High School was very different. For one thing, there was a whole range of new subjects that were studied: science, in proper laboratories, woodwork, metalwork, and foreign languages, and each subject had a different teacher. This was real learning, or so I thought. There was also sport. Harehills, like most primary schools, dabbled in sport and science. There were nature tables and, in most cases, science was at the whim and interest of the teachers. Mr Kelly was quite keen and so we had seen eyeball dissections and other attempts to extend our experiences. Sport was again more a token, as it needed playing fields and meant a bus ride to the Soldiers' Fields. We had gym lessons under the building near the caretaker's house, but all I can really remember is lining up and trying to vault over the horse or box. Mr Kelly would assist, but he made his feelings very clear if you couldn't do it, and he always blamed lack of effort rather than natural aptitude. I also remember the green gym mats. They were heavy, required at least two to drag them out so that we could practise forward rolls, headstands and handstands. Mr Kelly's wit and sarcasm appeared to be kept for the plumper boys and girls. Luckily, I wasn't in that category, but I was in those without natural ability and we would receive occasional jibes.

Anyway, I digress. Real sport was something I longed for. Cross-country, rugby, cricket and athletics were on the list and I hoped I would be good at something. The uniform list showed that I required a blue (house colour) rugby shirt with a white band sewn on the inside. This caused my mother no end of stress, as she wasn't handy with the sewing needle.

The day arrived when we went shopping at Rawcliffe's in Leeds. I remember we had to go upstairs into a large room where a man assisted. He checked the list and started to collect the things required. He measured me up with an experienced eye and reappeared with the standard tie. He pulled out a tape measure, encircled my head and returned with the green and black cap, six and seven-eighths. It was placed on my head and it felt strange. I was impressed that it had a shiny enamelled badge with the words Virtutem Petamus. A matching cloth badge followed, that much to my mother's horror, she had to sew onto the blazer. The blazer then appeared, and I slipped my arms into it. The salesman encouraged my mother to get one at least a size or two bigger.

"It will last longer and allow him to grow into it," he told her.

My mother needed little encouraging, as money was quite tight. So it was that I was provided with a blazer that would probably still be too large for me now, but I was overcome by all the fuss that was happening around me and more and more items were gathering on the counter. I was to wear grey shorts and so I avoided the need for any inside leg measurement, which was a relief to me and possibly a disappointment for the assistant, but I needed knee-length socks with coloured stripes where they turned down at the top. Rugby also required special striped socks and black shorts. Very dashing! The last items were a gabardine raincoat and a leather satchel. My satchel was fairly basic, unlike some boys who had very flash ones with their initials in gold lettering.

"Now remember that every item has to be named," the man told my mother, "We have a service to make name labels. Would you like to order some?" I think my mother was getting overcome with the whole process at this point, so she readily agreed. I am not sure that this would have been the case if she had understood that she had to sew each label into each item of uniform.

The labels had to be collected later, but we left the store with quite a collection and headed home on the bus. I became quite nervous at this point. This was the moment I realised it was for real. There were only a few weeks to go before the next chapter of my life and growing up. Looking back, this was probably the first time I suffered from anxiety. It is only recently that I have become aware I am a sufferer and probably most people who know me have never suspected. Within the school information package were the dates for the next school year, the times of the day, and information on corporal punishment and detentions. The school had Saturday morning detentions at this time, and there were also prefect detentions. This struck me as barbaric and went against my sense of fair play. If I was getting stressed, this was nothing in comparison to my mother. She was struggling to sew the badge neatly onto the blazer, and had several attempts to get it straight and the stitches neat and invisible. I discovered later that the other store, more expensive, had the badges already sewn into the pockets. I think my mum would have paid any price if she had known.

A week or two later, the labels arrived, and further anguish for my mother followed. Each label had to be sewn into socks, shirts, blazer, sports equipment and she tormented herself as she completed the task. She couldn't be seen as the one mother in the school who failed to get the labels neat and level. Finally, I was just about kitted-out. The remaining items were a fountain pen, medium nib, a bottle of blue-black Quink Ink and a geometry set. Now, we had done a bit of technical drawing with Mr Kelly, so I was used to compasses, but there were other items such as set squares, dividers and protractors that were a mystery to me.

It was with pride that I was told to don my uniform for a photograph. Out into the garden I went, and a photo was taken in blazer and cap and then another in the rugby shirt and sports gear. What a splendid sight.! My mother was ecstatic that the sewing was completed and that her number two son would not be let down on his first day. It was the only time that the uniform would look pristine, as first day was 'open season' on new boys' uniforms. This was a tradition that the older boys took to with a passion!

THE DAY OF JUDGEMENT

In 1966, there wasn't much fanfare when you left school. There were no fancy balls or special ceremonies, just a clearing out of your desks, a few words from Mr Kelly and then a few goodbyes with classmates and the usual walk home. There really wasn't much more to it than that. The summer holidays beckoned, and that was more pressing than starting high school. When you are eleven years old, time is very much in the present, whereas now time seems to fly by quicker with each passing year. Waiting a week or two for something to arrive is no big deal, but when I was young, the wait would seem endless.

The holiday was not particularly memorable. I am sure that we would have gone on a holiday somewhere, but I can't place which one it was. It was most likely a stay in a cottage on the East Coast, as I don't think we went further afield to Bournemouth and Torquay until the next year or so. As September approached, I began to focus more on my new school. I had walked through Gipton Woods and across the Soldiers' Fields to get a good look and, I must admit, it was a very imposing building and grounds. Harehills seemed so small and insignificant in comparison. Cricket grounds stretched before the main building and there were intriguing huts to the left and set back a little. It seemed vast. Many classroom windows faced the fields, and the driveway led through the low stone wall and a couple of cars were parked outside the front even though it was the holidays. I realised the walk was about thirty minutes from my house in Gipton Wood Crescent and as walks went, it was a delightful one. The wood was magnificent, ever changing with the seasons, and I knew it well from playing there many, many hours since moving to Gipton Wood Crescent. Oakwood had a lovely village feel, which it still has, and it was then just a short walk to school. It was a walk that many would envy and nowadays one that few children would make. Parents tend to take children to school and drop them off, at least in the first year or two of secondary schooling. I found the walk a good time to gather my thoughts for the new day ahead.

As time to start school approached, I began to get a little anxious. I was excited, optimistic and eager, but also nervous and apprehensive. I was concerned about the rumours I had heard about older boys bullying the first years and I was anxious about prefects. Justice being handed out by older boys struck me as potentially very unfair and, through experience, still does. Some used their status as an opportunity to make others suffer. Mind you, so did more than one or two teachers. The start seemed so far off and then suddenly, without warning, it was upon me.

My mother had suffered her sewing ordeal, my satchel was packed with mathematical instruments, my shoes and my face had been scrubbed to be shiny, and new socks pulled up, blazer spotless and vivid green and, to top it off, my school cap with impressive enamelled badge. I felt sick! I walked out through the back door of our house carrying a kiss from my mum and a message of good luck. I didn't know anyone else in the street that was going and so I headed off down the road, conspicuous in my pristine uniform. This would be the first and last time I ever looked this way.

I can't say I took much notice of the journey that morning as I walked through the woods and past the shops of Oakwood. I must have passed the newsagents, with the cigarette vending machine outside, Jones of Oakwood, with its electrical goods and the butcher's that used to have pheasants hanging from hooks, vile piles of tripe, real lolling cows' tongues and the occasional rabbit. I crossed the zebra crossing at the Belisha Beacons, past the opticians, and crossed over to the Oakwood Clock, and then up the path around the playing fields along Old Park Road to Roundhay School gates.

Now, clearly by this point, I was not alone. There were large numbers of boys making their way. Some in groups, chattering like monkeys, and some, like me, alone and overawed. The walk through the gates and along the drive seemed endless, and the building just got bigger and bigger as I got nearer.

Now at this point, things get hazy for me. I am not sure how we were sorted into our classes and then led off to our classrooms. I am not sure if it took place in the lower playground or whether we went to the hall. I suspect it was the playground and anyway, I was in class 1C. Now apparently these were not ability grouped in year one, that came later, but anyway, I and my fellow class members were escorted to the room by our class teacher, Holly Joe Pullen. The form room was in the back corner of the main building, just above the boiler room. What made a big impression on me was that the teachers all wore black academic gowns. I had only seen such things on television and in books such as Just William. We followed quietly along and were ushered into the room. It was the RE room and our teacher was the religious education teacher. The room had big windows on two sides and the teacher's desk was a solid, heavy wooden thing, aged and impressive. It sat upon a dais, as all the teachers' desks in the school did. Behind the desk was a large blackboard, but this one wasn't black, but green. It was a green, ground-glass board and there was some discussion whether this was because the school uniform colour green, or because green was more restful on the eye. I doubt the latter. Each class member took a place behind one of the desks. These were old and very worn, with carved graffiti of rock band names, bored holes, gouged lines and screw holes where hasps had been fitted and removed on an annual basis. Mr Pullen informed us we should purchase hasps and padlocks and we could fit them to the desks so that we could lock our things inside. (This was before lockers became available.) Administrative issues were dealt with, the register taken, and we all listened and looked as each name was called out so we could put faces to names. Dining arrangements were explained and money collected and tickets issued. A timetable was copied onto the board and I think we had to copy it down by hand. Copying from the board became a very common part of a Roundhay School education. They told us the basic rules, such as not running inside, making sure we got to lessons on time, with the correct books, arriving at the dining rooms and lining up, and some of it must have sunk in.

The next course of action was being taken on a tour of the school. We toured the dining rooms, the sports changing rooms, gym, woodwork, metalwork and art rooms, the science labs, the music rooms, the library and then taken on a tour of the Mansion. We were shown the two tarmac playgrounds, the playing fields, and given instructions we were not to cross through the bushes to Roundhay Girls' School, next door. Fraternisation wasn't allowed until the sixth form.

Finally, break came, the bell rang and we quietly and relatively timidly went out. This was when the fun started. We stood around in groups and made our introductions. There were some boys from Harehills. Paul Banks and Dick Rodley, I think, were in my class (Not sure if John Sugden was) and we huddled in a group and chatted to some boys we didn't know. I got talking with Roger Harvey and Chris Mills, and I started to feel a bit better. From out of nowhere, my cap was snatched off my head. An older boy ran off, made it to the corner of the building and proceeded to beat the cap and, in particular, the enamel badge against the brickwork. I was stunned and, before I could do anything, he ran back laughing and handed it back, saying, 'Just christened it!' He charged off chuckling, looking for another victim.

That was the crowning part of my first day and, as I said, I never looked the shiny new boy ever again. If anyone ever took a close look at the Roundhay caps, I am sure that almost every one had been christened in the manner that mine had. Luckily, my mother didn't notice, and I certainly didn't tell her, as her anger would have just added to my suffering.

SETTLING INTO SCHOOL

One of the most striking things about starting Roundhay was how grown up the boys in the Sixth Form were. They weren't boys, they were men. Many had dark stubble on their chins and some were even going bald. Now, looking back, they would probably just seem like ordinary teenagers. Having moved from a small primary school, where I had been one of the top dogs, the most senior group, to suddenly finding myself at the very bottom of the pile, it came as somewhat of a shock. These great hulking near-men were far more scary in the imagination than they were in real life. Unfortunately, I couldn't say the same about some teachers. There were those who could strike terror into a First Form class just by looking in your direction. Mr Lansborough and Mr Hall would be examples. There were, unfortunately, those who were quite unpleasant and cruel, and there were those who failed miserably to control the classes of unruly, intelligent boys whose sole purpose in life was to drive these teachers mad, and we showed them little respect.

I am afraid to say that as I established myself in the school, I was one of those very unpleasant pupils who taunted some teachers, but I learned the skill of picking and choosing the time and the place. Some of my classmates failed to develop the ability to read the situation and suffered as a consequence. I will return with some of the more memorable incidents in another tale.

The first week was mainly an orientation time at the school. We had quite complex timetables, or at least compared to primary school, where the only change of rooms came for PE, singing and games. It was expected that you would be in the room for your lesson, on time and with the correct equipment. Now, in these enlightened times, textbooks were borrowed from the school. You were issued a book, had to add your name to a sheet that was stuck inside the cover, and the teacher made a note of the number of the book you had been allocated. You also had to cover each book in brown paper to help protect it. At the end of the year you had to return it in a decent condition, or you would have to pay a fine. Ridout was the staple English textbook, Whitmarsh for French, but I can't remember the others for maths.

Exercise books were provided for every subject by the school, but you had to produce the old books for replacements. The full books were checked and woe betide you if pages were missing. Any major discrepancies of thickness with the new book would result in you being asked to pay for the replacement.

School meals were provided for most of the boys at 1 shilling a day. The school dining rooms were in what must have originally been the walled garden to the Mansion and I remember two modern single-storey buildings. We had to line up at the set time, and there was more than one sitting. If we were on the second, the first sitting boys would leave through the back and we would enter through the front. We rushed to get a table. Some had a teacher sitting at the head, others had a sixth former and many had whoever was lucky enough to get there.

The risk in being head of the table was that a teacher could rock up and they would turf you off and take your place. The benefit of being head of the table was that you had to share out the food, and this had some real advantages. It was your role to cut it into eight pieces and put it on each member of the table's plate. If it was something you liked, quiche for example (We called it cheese pie) then it was surprising how one eighth could end up being much larger than the others and that piece just happened to be served last onto your plate.

As new boys, we didn't get these roles easily and we were just happy to get a place and eat. Before anyone could start there was always grace and the most common was, "For what we are about to receive, may the Lord make us truly thankful!" There would be a clatter then as every child started eating. Speed was an important skill, for two reasons. Firstly, if you enjoyed whatever was being served that day, then there was a chance of seconds. The teacher supervising the dining room would ask if anyone wanted more and there was a swarm of hands waving from those who did. Of course, you had to have finished and there would be checking and some chastisement and disappointment, but if you were lucky, a second serving was provided. The second reason was that when you had finished and the table was cleared, then you could be let out for what was left of dinner time. Of course, missing out on a second helping was required to get extra play time. This rush did nothing for your appreciation of food, nor your digestive system and my wife still sees this as one of the reasons I wolf down my food and don't really savour it. The other is having two brothers.

Now school dinners were a hot meal that was provided for children after the Second World War and, on the whole, I loved them. The meals varied, but they always had a pudding. What was there not to love about Spotted Dick, Jam Roll, Treacle Pudding, and all served with custard? Sometimes it would be vanilla custard, sometimes chocolate or pink. I can't say I was ever sure what flavour the pink was supposed to be. Another delight was Manchester Tart and I am sure I have missed other culinary delights.

One long-term result of these dinners is probably a high incidence of heart disease amongst the old boys. Later in life we have to look after ourselves, but I don't half miss the puddings and custard. Whilst waiting to go into the dining room, we queued underneath two very large pear trees. When they fruited, the pears would fall from the trees and often they had wasps in them, but many were ripe and whole and they were delicious, if you got them at the right time.

Lunch times were soccer time and games filled the playing fields. Jumpers and jackets were placed on the turf, more often mud, and highly competitive games ensued. I can't say I had any real talent for soccer, but I made up for it with enthusiasm. Break times and some lunches were taken up with a game called 'Wall Ball'. A tennis ball was all that was needed and one boy would kick it against the wall and the next had to return it. This went on with varying angles and further distances until someone missed. It could also be played, like tennis, by hitting the ball with the flat of the hand. All areas of brick or stone wall had boys playing, and one of the best was just above the steps down to the bottom yard. A good angled hit or kick could send the ball down the steps and make it almost unplayable. Mind you, I have seen some brilliant shots from boys leaping down the steps and making an almost impossible return. Because of the need to fit in several lunch sittings, the day at Roundhay was long and so was the dinner break. The school day was 8.40am until 4.00pm and I seem to remember that school detention was on a Saturday morning when I first started.

It was a tumultuous time for us new boys and, I assume, similar for the girls next door, but it was exciting and I really felt quite grown up. Looking back, it seems so old-fashioned, but at the time it was the 1960s and anything was possible as the world was changing at pace.

SMELLS, EXPLOSIONS, MAYHEM AND MADNESS

One of the new challenges of high school at Roundhay School was chemistry. The thought of laboratories for a boy just leaving primary school was one of wonder and excitement. It was in such places that strange concoctions were created and experiments carried out, and I looked forward to my first lesson in the lab.

The chemistry labs were old and were furnished with large, solid benches that filled the room in rows. Each bench had sinks with tall thin taps that arched like upside down umbrella handles, rectangular porcelain sinks and gas taps. The wood appeared to be old dark mahogany and was scarred with evidence of a long history of careless boys' experiments. There was at least one fume cupboard, but I don't remember ever using one during my time studying chemistry. The lab had a distinctive smell: a mixture of gas, other chemicals and solvents. There were tall stools arranged around the benches and we had to wait outside in a line on our first lesson and were then allowed in, and directed to take a seat. The floor had bare boards that were uneven due to a history of wearing by shuffling feet and scraping stool legs.

We took our places and waited to be addressed by the teacher. The first lesson comprised our learning how to use a Bunsen burner, connecting them to the gas, sitting them on the asbestos boards, and positioning the tripods and gauze and then lighting them. We were then shown how to control the flame by turning the collar and the flame changed from a dancing yellow to the noisy blue spear with a cone of blue at the top of the burner. This excitement soon ended, and we spent the rest of the lesson copying notes and drawing a scientific diagram.

Health and safety were very different in those days and the asbestos boards were old and fibres were clearly peeling away, but we all used them. Another practice that is now long banished was the mercury that we had in Petri dishes, spilled onto the bench tops and pushed about in balls of mirror-clear metal. Apparently, the tales of milliners going mad (mad hatters) and lighthouse keepers going insane and throwing themselves off the lighthouses were because of the poisonous vapours of mercury. Both professions came into regular contact with liquid mercury and maybe that explains some antics that I describe below.

Now, the calibre of teacher at Roundhay was quite marked. There were those who had authority, charisma and were, frankly, excellent teachers, and there were those who had none of the above skills. Some made up for their lack of talent in pedagogy with a sadistic nature and no hesitation in using physical punishment, but some were just out of their depth. Student teachers or early career teachers were no match for the clever and moral lacking students who made up the lower classes at Roundhay. I have many tales of student cunning and ingenuity where, without mercy, torture was inflicted upon some teachers whose only crime was lacking in experience. I will recount one now to illustrate the point.

Probably the hardest lessons to teach to an unruly bunch were the sciences, because of their practical nature and use of potentially dangerous materials and equipment.

A new chemistry teacher arrived to take us in our second or possibly third year and his name was Mr H. He arrived at his first lesson like a lamb to the slaughter, wide eyed, bushy-tailed, and we salivated with the knowledge of how we would torment him. Why would we do so, you may well ask? I suppose because we could, and there was something of a pack mentality in the sport of making teachers suffer. I guess it was payback for how some masters victimised us. The point was, he arrived and made the fatal error of showing a sign of weakness. That was all we needed and then it was game on. He tried to be friendly and all he got in return was rudeness and surly and disrespectful responses from the boys in the class. Of course, it was not all the class, but sufficient to make his lessons excruciatingly embarrassing to sit through. He was a typical teacher at the time: tweed jacket, baggy trousers, tie and checked shirt and he would wear a white lab coat. I know he carried a briefcase. The reason to tell you this will be revealed shortly, and to make matters worse, he had a strange voice. It was a little quiet and had either a Yorkshire or possibly Lancashire accent. This was an added bonus and allowed us to quickly mimic his voice and we would use it when we were speaking to him or asking questions.

His lessons were a shambles, and he would often send boys out to stand in the corridor. The problem with this was that other science teachers, such as D.H. might catch you outside and he was merciless. Boys could be returned to the lessons and a stern warning issued to the class about what would happen to the next boy sent out that he caught. It was also a clear reprimand of Mr H and a reminder that sending children out of lessons was not the 'done' thing. This had the desired effect, but only lasted for the rest of the lesson.

Matters got worse as Term One progressed. One lesson, Bunsen burners were on full bore, and smells and gases filled the lab. We were so brazen we dared to smoke at the back. Mr H's nemesis was John S. Now John seemed to take a particular delight in winding the poor teacher up, and he developed a knack of fainting to order during Mr H's lessons.

Picture the scene. The lab was full. Bunsen burners were ablaze. Hot liquids were everywhere and Mr H was trying his best to get the class to follow instructions and to listen to him. Just as the teacher was as stressed as he could be, John would appear to faint. He would be sitting on the stool with his legs through the bars when suddenly he would fall straight backwards and hang upside down, apparently unconscious. Poor Mr H almost lost his mind and shot over to help the boy, asking those seated next to him what had happened. John was pulled upright and miraculously regained consciousness. He was excused from the lesson and sent to get some fresh air. I seem to remember this happening more than once and the effect was always the same.

Poor Mr H began to disintegrate before our eyes as the term progressed. It was like a scene from Conrad's The Heart of Darkness. The man started to unravel as we cruelly picked him apart. The problem was that it was just so easy.

I am telling you this tale with no sense of pride. As a teacher of forty years' experience, I know how hard some classes can be, and how you can literally dread them all week before you have to take them. Having said this, I have seen classes that made ours at Roundhay look like kindergarten in comparison and the outcome more severe for the teacher concerned.

Class 2C 1967/8

The final straw came one morning when Mr H made the fateful mistake of leaving his open briefcase on the teacher's desk in front of the class. He had his back to us all as he wrote notes on the board. For obvious reasons, his lessons had become much less practical and much more chalk and talk. I guess he thought that we could get up to less mischief that way, but how wrong he was!

John S, I believe it was him again, sneaked up to the briefcase and started looking at what was in there. He slipped out a letter and scurried back to his place. He opened the letter and read it surreptitiously. His eyes opened wide, and within a few minutes, he returned it, but then began to quote from the letter, loud enough for Mr H and the rest of the class, to hear. Apparently, it was from Mr H's fiancée, Flo, and they must have gone away for the weekend. She was very effusive about what a lovely romantic time she had enjoyed.

The quotes were just audible and Mr H finally caught wind of them and turned a very bright red. He snatched his briefcase off the desk, checked to see if the letter was missing and then just carried on writing the notes. The rest of the lesson was agony, but somehow the poor man saw it to the end. It must have been a tremendous relief when he could send us all out.

Whatever else I could say about Mr H, he gets full marks for perseverance, as he saw out his first year and others afterwards, and I am sure he became an accomplished, if permanently scarred, teacher.

When I was a new teacher, I also suffered some very difficult classes, but never as bad as some of the newly qualified teachers at Roundhay School did. The worst thing is that Mr H did not suffer the most. That award probably went to Gobbler, but that will have to wait for another time.

HOW DID WE SURVIVE?

When I was a boy at Harehills County Primary School, I bought a book called 365 things to do in Science and Nature. It was a large hard-backed book, and it had a different activity for each day of the year. The book has existed in updated forms for many years and even when I was young, I was amazed to see that there was a section on taxidermy. It explained how to treat a dead pet so that you could preserve it. I can't believe that anyone would have followed the instructions, but I do know that many children learnt how to take eggs from birds' nests and blow them. The book explained how to prick a small hole in the shell, break up the yolk and egg white, and then prick another hole and blow the contents out of the egg. Egg collecting was quite common and because of its widespread popularity, bird species became endangered before it was later banned.

There were many experiments with chemicals that no longer take place, as the substances were poisonous, or when burnt, gave off toxic fumes. Chemistry sets were popular gifts and copper sulphate crystal growing, potassium permanganate and other substances were common features. There was even a chemistry set called the Atomic chemistry set, in the 1950s, that contained uranium. We may be horrified by this nowadays, but how many of us had alarm clocks and watches with luminous numbers and hands? In the 1950s and 60s, radium paint was used, and the workers were susceptible to radiation poisoning as they had a habit of licking the brushes. In the 1950s and 60s they had reduced the amount of radium considerably, but even so, not something you would want today.

It wasn't just the good old chemistry sets, but even in the classroom at Roundhay School, phosphorous lighting and magnesium ribbon burning were carried out with little ventilation and we loved them. It was the bangs, burning and explosions that made science fun.

Roundhay was also the source of other questionable practices, in hindsight. Woodwork was a good example. We used to cut, saw, sand and plane wood regularly and the workshops were thick in dust. I thought it was a lovely smell and never thought much of it until I learned that sawdust was almost as bad as asbestos and that workshops should have dust extraction systems and children should wear masks.

Even the swimming pool was a place of danger. There were the obvious ones of drowning, particularly when good swimmers thought it a wheeze to jump on your back without warning and hold you under water. Most times this wasn't too bad, but if you were caught at the wrong moment, you were just inhaling, then it could become a life-threatening experience. I remember not being amused by such experiences as you inhaled water, and goodness knows what else.

Swimming carnivals also included something called the free dive, where competitors dived in and just drifted as far as they could. This was quite an exciting thing to watch, but it is banned today, as people have died whilst holding their breath too long. The other issue was the lack of chemical balance in the pool. I remember clearly arriving early one morning and the pool being shrouded in a white fog of chlorine that burnt and stung the eyes. Guess it made men of us!

At least I thought I was safe at home, but alas, no. My earliest toys were made of metal and some of lead and I am amazed I didn't suffer poisoning, particularly when the water pipes were also lead and there was also lead in the paint and petrol. They introduced leaded and unleaded petrol, and bit by bit, the leaded petrol disappeared.

If this wasn't bad enough, babies were given Gripe Water to pacify and settle them. Apparently, there was a considerable amount of alcohol in the mixture, which certainly would have helped to calm a restless child and also the fraught mother as many used to swig from the same bottle of Gripe Water. When teething, we were given Bonjela, which used to contain aspirin. Years later, it was discovered that aspirin and children were not a good combination, due to possible liver damage from Reye's syndrome.

At least the sweets were safe! Or were they? I loved Victory V lozenges. They had a very distinct flavour, which was because each sweet contained ether, liquorice, and chloroform. They removed the ether and chloroform ingredients later and they never tasted as good again.

Eating too many sweets could result in a trip to the dentist and Mr Gostling and the others I frequented over the years would never let me escape without at least one filling. They were amalgam fillings, and they were 50% mercury and 22-30% silver, tin and zinc. Mercury again. Shock horror! There was a panic during the 1980s because the fillings contained mercury, but whether this was a problem is still uncertain. I still have some amalgam fillings and they have never caused me any problems, but my family might suggest I am a little crazy. The dentists also used to use gas on us to extract teeth, but I have been told that ether on a cloth was used before gas was introduced. I thought that sounded dangerous, but I have been reliably informed that it was a safe practice.

Even the fruit and vegetables carried a risk. DDT was commonly used as an insecticide and there were clear signs that it was a residual poison and could cause cancer, and its use was banned in the USA in 1972. The other problem was that it killed pests and the beneficial insects. I believed it had been banned worldwide, but when I was living in Papua New Guinea in the mid-eighties, it was used in the tea and coffee plantations.

Fly eradication in our homes often meant using fly papers and later fly sprays. Originally, the fly papers were coated in metallic arsenic. Flies were attracted to the sticky, sweet smelling papers and were killed by the arsenic. It was such a toxic poison that there were cases of murder where the perpetrator soaked fly papers to extract the arsenic to poison their victims.

Probably the biggest risk to our health as children was smoking. Not that many children smoked, but because of the passive smoke we inhaled. My father was a heavy smoker, and he smoked Player's Navy Cut untipped cigarettes. The house was full of smoke and in winter the windows would be shut and there was little ventilation. I remember getting into bed with my parents on a Sunday morning, as a toddler, and my dad would have a cigarette and a cup of tea. I even remember him letting me try a drag on his cigarette. I don't think my mother approved, and he did it probably to put me off smoking.

Socially, cigarettes were totally acceptable and you wouldn't dream of going outside for a cigarette, as people do nowadays. People would smoke at work, in hospital, during meals and you wouldn't have one without offering one to anyone there. Times changed and the damage smoking caused was recognised and restrictions were imposed. When I was little, smoking was only permitted upstairs on the buses, but on single-deckers it was allowed on the back half, but eventually banned altogether. Cinemas introduced a one half smoking division, which never made much sense, as the smoke could cross the aisle easily enough. You could even smoke on airplanes and I remember flying back from Papua New Guinea and the back section of economy was for smokers. Public opinion began to change and smokers were tolerated rather than approved of and nowadays, barely tolerated. I remember going to The Regent pub at Chapel Allerton in the early seventies and the air was thick in smoke. It hurt your eyes and made your clothes smell. The pub was packed tight, and you were in danger of being caught by the lit cigarette end of a careless smoker. I must add that I was a smoker too, so I am not being too judgmental. We knew it wasn't good for us and one of the best decisions my wife and I made was to stop smoking when she became pregnant with our first child.

When I look back, it seems life was very dangerous, and I guess, in truth, it was. We were given much more freedom to roam and take risks, and bit by bit, the environment we experience has become cleaner and safer. Sometimes you hear people almost panic over modern life, chemicals and pollution, but the reality is that we are living longer and healthier lives. I have outlived my dad by nine years and hopefully will continue on for many more, and I am physically active and run every day. When I was young, we were told threescore years and ten was what we could expect and yet now it is four score plus.

It appears that the current generations are less likely to suffer the environmental poisons that we experienced and endured, but they are suffering the issues of affluence: obesity, poor diets and lack of exercise. Added to this is the current pandemic, something I had not experienced in my lifetime.

HE'S JUST A VERY NAUGHTY BOY!

There were several occasions when I got in trouble at school, but luckily for me, they were either not very serious or I just wasn't found out.

I started Harehills the very morning that Mr Harold Wilson, the headmaster, started. He seemed a very kind man to me and I only had to visit his office once after my initial interview. His office was disorganised that first morning and he wasn't sure which class to put me in. Classes at Harehills were streamed, and he asked my mother about my academic ability. She was naturally a modest lady who would downplay her and her children's abilities, but she felt my older brother had missed out because she wasn't pushy enough and so she answered that I was a very capable boy. Now, when I was seven, I had no idea about being bright or not, so I was pleased that she thought so. Mr Wilson was impressed, but wily enough not to take my mother's word for it. He got me to read to him, and the only book he could find in his office mess was his Bible. He passed it to me and asked me to read a passage. I was a good reader and read aloud to him. This and my mother's evaluation convinced him to try me in the top class in the year. As it was, I fitted in and spent the rest of my time until eleven in the top class. I loved primary school and the teachers I had. I was in Mr Kelly's class for two years and I know some found him intimidating, but I loved his teaching and was very happy. I feel the same about all the teachers I had up to high school.

I've just remembered that prior to starting Harehills, I was in trouble at Stainbeck Preparatory School. This was for throwing my pump at Miss Cowling, my teacher. We had to change from indoor to outdoor shoes and she told me I had someone else's pumps on. I said I hadn't and eventually threw one of them at her in temper. I was about five. I was right and had my own pumps, and nothing really came of it. Miss Blackmore was another of my teachers and she now reads my stories. I was telling my older brother, and he commented that she was his favourite teacher as well.

Mr Kelly was strict and did lose his temper, but we always did interesting things and he seemed to like me. Corporal punishment was meted out, but usually it was a slipper in the classroom. Occasionally, we witnessed boys caned on the stage during assemblies. I was only hit once, and that was for being late lining up after lunch. The teacher was young, and was struggling to maintain discipline and overreacted to our not being lined up in class groups on time. There was a long line of miscreants after his duty and we had to bend over in turn and he struck us a hard blow with the blackboard ruler on our bottoms. I seem to remember there were boys and girls. I don't think it was excessively painful, and it didn't scar me for life.

The only other occasion I was in trouble at Harehills was when a friend and I were chasing each other around the cloakroom after school and the caretaker caught us. He was furious and told us to be in school at 8.00am and outside Mr Wilson's office. I was mortified. I had never really been in trouble, and the implication from the caretaker was that he would see us caned for our wickedness. I worried about this all night. I hardly slept, as I was so upset, but in the morning I was there, as was my friend, waiting for our destiny with doom. The caretaker arrived and went in to see Mr Wilson and then he came back out and Mr Wilson said as he left, "Leave it with me. I'll sort it!" We were called in and stood there, heads down and lips trembling. Mr Wilson addressed us with a smile on his face. He said that the caretaker had told him what had happened and that we shouldn't play in the cloakrooms. He had a grin on his face and told us to go and have a good day. I couldn't believe our luck! Life was fair, after all.

At Roundhay, though, there was a wider range of punishments for the breaking of school rules and a wider range of people who could inflict these upon you. There was widespread corporal punishment, slipper and caning, but there were also detentions. These could be school detention, issued by teachers, or prefects' detention, and these were given and supervised by the prefects. School detention was originally on Saturday mornings, but that changed, after my first year, to after school. The other more widely issued punishment was lines, and again, both staff and prefects could give lines. Before I started, I thought that Prefects giving punishments was unfair and I am still of the same mind. There were many students who loved the power over the younger boys and gave lines and detentions with very little rationale, apart from the fact that they could, and they enjoyed it.

One of the main reasons for getting into trouble was the uniform. Not wearing the cap in public, eating in uniform in public, not wearing your tie in public, were all punishable by school detentions. I fell foul to one rule that I am not sure even existed. I was on the Soldiers' Fields after school and was full of energy and was swinging on the branch of a tree. That was a crime most terrible, apparently. I can't remember which teacher saw me, but I was accused of vandalism and bringing the school into disrepute. I professed my innocence, but to no avail. I was to report to 'Finger's' office (the Headmaster), first thing the next morning, for a caning.

Once again, I was incensed by the travesty of justice, but I didn't mention it at home. I would only have been told that I deserved it from my parents and been in even more trouble. Another sleepless night followed. All my life I have preferred to deal with incidents straight away, when I know they will be unpleasant, rather than having to wait. The delay is agony. Even as a headmaster myself, I would rather see the parents straight away if there was a problem, rather than make the appointment a day or two later.

The next morning I was waiting in full view of Mr Glover's Office. Staff and students walked past, knowing that you were in trouble and knowing what the likely punishment would be. The embarrassment was painful enough, and the wait seemed like an eternity. I saw Mr Morris, the Deputy Head, go into the office and a few minutes later, out he came. He spoke to me there and then. Apparently, 'Fingers', Mr Glover, was too busy to deal with me, and Mr Morris had been given the task. He asked what I had done, and I told him honestly. I think his words were, "Not the biggest crime in the book! Don't do it again." He smiled, and with that, I was dismissed. Never had a day seemed better than that one did!

Now there are other more serious examples of misbehaviour that I will tell in the future, but there was one incident that I will finish with.

I had been drinking in pubs from the age of fourteen, so by the time of this story, I was an established pub-goer. I was sixteen, and I had met up with friends at Pete's cellar in Harehills. There were about four of us, Peter, John, Roger and me. They were all a year or so older than me and I was the only one from Roundhay School. We decided to go for a drink in the bar that was underneath the Astoria Ballroom on Roundhay Road. The name of it slips my memory. Anyway, we were kitted out in our trench coats, flared jeans, T-shirts, long hair and whatever else was the fashion of the day. We walked in, stood at the bar and ordered our pints. I had just taken a sip when I turned around to look at the tables for a place to sit when I was struck by horror. The room had about twenty Roundhay staff sitting at the tables. I nearly choked on my drink. It must have been a staff night out. I am not sure who was most surprised, me or the teachers. Les Lees was the first to react. He was always a man in control. He walked over to me and whispered that when I had finished my drink, that would be a wise time to leave. My friends were a bit nonplussed, but I explained the situation and, within a remarkably short time, we finished our pints and headed for the door.

I can only surmise that as Mr Lees had dealt with the issue, then the other teachers felt the matter closed, but nothing more was ever said or done. Of course, my friends thought it was hilarious, and it made their night, but I was horrified.

TWO JACKETS TO ELLAND ROAD AND BACK

I was wondering why football is such a popular game to play and I think it comes down to one thing. To play it, you just need a ball (and it can be any ball of any size) and, as long as you have someone to play with, you can play a game. Apparently, it was invented using an animal bladder, inflated and tied off, from at least the Middle Ages, and probably long before that.

One of the earliest sites for soccer was Bourton-on-the-Water, where it was played in the river Windrush between two bridges. It is a madness of getting the ball through the bridge at either end with few other rules. I mention this, as Bourton was a place I went to when I was visiting my aunt and uncle with my grandma and grandad. We used to go every Easter on the coach and when there in the early 1960s, we went for a day trip to Bourton-on-the-Water. The memory of the visit and the history of the game has stuck with me ever since.

Every young toddler, at least in Leeds, was given a ball and taught how to kick it. I think that in the heart of every father is the hope that they will have produced a talent that will one day play for Leeds United.

For those of us who were around in the 1960s, Leeds was in its heyday. The stars were Billy Bremner, Jack Charlton, Norman Hunter, Peter Lorimer and coach Don Revie, and every kid wanted to play like them. As a student teacher in London, East Bedfont Primary School, one Scottish lady teacher's claim to fame was that she had taught Billy Bremner when he was a lad.

It didn't matter where you were: on the sand, in the road, on a field, your back garden or on a piece of waste ground, you could always set up a game. My father was Scottish, but he still had the same hopes for his three sons. One Christmas, I remember Santa bringing a very small pair of boots for me and a bigger pair for my older brother, Andrew. We also had a football each. The boots and balls were heavy leather and made by hand in India. They had round, hard leather toe caps, leather soles, and they had studs made of many circular leather pieces nailed together and into the sole. The balls were hand-stitched thick leather with a bladder of rubber and the hole was laced closed; mine was a size smaller than my brother's. It didn't matter that it was wet and freezing cold on Christmas morning; we had to get the boots on and go out into the back garden and kick the ball around a bit. The boots were unforgiving, and within a short space of time, I had blisters and found that my technique of kicking a stationary ball was somewhat lacking. I would place the ball and then have to take several paces backwards before running up, kicking the ball, experiencing a shuddering shock as it was so heavy and it would slew off at an angle. Not my finest moment, but it was a start!

Andrew was first cab off the rank in having the chance of actually playing soccer and that was as part of Ladywood Church Scouts. Ladywood was a magnificent old church, very large and grand, set in wonderful grounds. Unfortunately, the old church has since been demolished, a smaller new one built, and the ground used for housing, but at the time it was a thriving Methodist church. We were christened at the church and Andrew joined the cubs when he could. My father was roped in to train the soccer team and he took to it very seriously. Practice was arranged to take place on the Soldiers' Field near Oakwood, on a Saturday morning, and I tagged along to watch. Dad even bought a whistle, and I was impressed with the shiny silver ACME Thunderer. They had a kit to wear, and they looked very smart, which was almost as important as how they played. There was a competition, and they had to play home and away games. Andrew was keen, but no real star and the same could be said about the rest of the team. I don't know if they ever won, but they all seemed to enjoy it.

It was at an away game at Crossgates that Dad left our dog Sabot (my brother says Sabeau) behind. The dog was a toy poodle and my mother was beside herself and, as I have recounted before, blamed my dad and made his life hell. The dog was not found, despite Dad driving around the entire area searching, but miraculously just arrived back home hours later.

After his Cubs' experience, Andrew never really got into football, but we would play on the Soldiers' Field with friends. As I have said, you don't need much for a game, and jackets or jumpers would do for goals. Sometimes we'd start off with just me and my brother, but by osmosis, stray boys would turn up ask to join in the game. The truth is that football is much better when there is a group of you. If you had a small number, then attack and defence was the best. The way we played the goalie was fixed, but whoever possessed the ball, their team was attacking. Later, at Roundhay School, we would have two teams and the attacking team kept attacking until they put the ball out of play.

I remember once, when we must have been about ten, going up to Red Hill and playing on the soccer pitch adjacent to Wetherby Road. There was a large group of us and it teemed down with rain. The ground became a quagmire, and we were soaked, but it was fantastic, as we just threw ourselves around, and got thick in mud. It was one of those times when others just joined in and we created a full game. I know the bus driver wasn't too happy when we piled back onto his bus, wet and thick in mud, but he still let us on. I seem to remember we had to stamp the mud off on the pavement before he would.

At Harehills, soccer was the game of choice during winter, spring, and autumn. The playground sloped down from Roundhay Road and somehow there could be two or three soccer games going on whilst there was skipping, hopscotch and assorted chasing games in progress, all interlacing with each other. We played with tennis balls, but it was a wild affair and there were surprisingly few crashes between the children as they dashed around, intent on their individual games.

It must have been year one of Roundhay that Dad really got into Leeds United and started to go to watch the games and took me and Andrew with him. I must say, it was always a bit of an event. It was hard to get parked anywhere near and then you had to walk through intimidating crowds of soccer fans who were getting quite notorious at the time for aggro. After saying this, they tended to be oblivious to families and their focus was on the other team's fans, who were similarly focused on them. There were lots of police and the mounted officers were quite frightening as the horses were massive and not always fully controlled.

At this time, there was no caging-in of fans and there was a low wall that separated you from the elevated pitch of the finest grass I have ever seen. There were only terraces, at least where we were, and the games were exciting, fast and skilful, but Norman Hunter could 'bite your legs!' We started going regularly and the final time I remember going was, I believe, against Glasgow Rangers in the Inter-Cities Fairs Cup quarter final. They had drawn 0-0 in the first game and Leeds won 2-0 at Elland Road. The Rangers supporters were quite menacing and I think there was some trouble, but they took no notice of us. The only incident, and this must have worried my dad, was that coins were thrown from the back of the crowds and I was hit by a flying old penny. Leeds went on to win the cup final against Ferencvaros, a team from Budapest.

I don't remember ever going to the soccer again until I was about twenty-two and I went to Manchester and to Old Trafford. I think Manchester was against West Ham and it ended a draw. We had a few pints before the match and can't say I was fully focused on the game.

At Roundhay, soccer was the break and lunchtime sport, apart from wall-ball. Games were set up over the whole grounds and hot and sweaty teenagers went in hard and, sometimes, skilfully against the opponents. There were no holds barred and frequent fights would start as testosterone and angst met face to face. I remember hitting a boy who was a friend normally. He started arguing with me, Steve I believe, and I just let go one punch to the temple and he fell to the ground, rolling and holding his eye. Not my finest moment, but not, unfortunately, my only time of being involved in a fight, but certainly the shortest biffo I was ever involved in. Fights and soccer seem to go hand in hand and playground fights always resulted in a stampede of boys, but rather than running away, they ran towards the fight to get the best position to witness the altercation. Eventually, a teacher would arrive and drag the miscreants, often bloodied, away to judgement from a higher source.

There was a period where we played indoor soccer at the Judean Club and we played for Lidgett Methodist youth club. We were actually quite good, and I was in goals. I got the job as no one else wanted it and I was stupid enough to throw myself around and wasn't worried about getting hurt. We won the Leeds district and had to play Spalding. We lost there, as we had to play outdoors and we expected to play indoors. The pitch was muddy grass, and we only had training shoes, which meant we could hardly move without slipping. A bit of a shame but, it was within the rules.

On hot weekends, as teenagers, we would often gather at Roundhay Park and play impromptu games on the arena, or the Soldiers' Field. Wonderful times we had, and some lads were skilled players. The girls just had to wait and they would sit and chat and take very little notice of what was going on. Nowadays, they would probably join in and enjoy the games, but times were different. When I was first married, we would play friendly games at Meanwood Park Hospital grounds as my friend Pete worked there. That was a more organised game for invited players, but even then tempers could flare.

When I first started teaching, I was invited to play against the boys' first team. I had to buy some boots and kit, but I embarrassed myself on my first outing by cutting down this really good player. I tripped him as he ran by and everyone thought I had done it maliciously, but it was just through lack of skill. I believe that was my last soccer outing.

In 1981, I took up a sport that required even less equipment, and that is running. I did my first half-marathon in 1982 and even though I am not very good, I have run almost every day ever since and hope to continue on for the rest of my life. My friend, Peter, has played soccer all his life and was still playing until it became impossible in the UK with the pandemic. I take my hat off to his endurance and fitness.

I almost forgot to mention my brush with Leeds United fame. I won a cake making competition, held at Lidgett Methodist Youth Club. Actually, my girlfriend at the time thought my scones were better than her cake that had sunk in the middle. She insisted we swapped. Someone turned the cake upside down to hide the sunken top and it won first prize, and so I received my prize from the guest of honour who was Peter Lorimer. My girlfriend was not amused, and I had to surrender the prize, a gift token, to her in the end.

WE ARE ALL IN FOR THE HIGH JUMP

I don't know if it is just my memory or whether it is a fact that we seemed to have some lovely summers whilst I was growing up in the late sixties and early seventies. I know we had some hard, grey, icy cold winters, but summer meant the arrival of summer sports, and these made a welcome change from rugby and cross-country. There were only two summer sports, and they were cricket and athletics.

There was something almost magical about the ritual of cricket. It was played wearing whites, which never made sense as grass stains and red off the cricket balls always challenged my mother's washing. Initially, we played wearing shorts which must have looked fairly comical as we struggled in oversized pads, with straps that cut into the legs as we ran, but as we grew older, we were allowed to wear long whites. Cricket involved equipment that other sports didn't require: pads, gloves, bats, and the unmentionable cricket box. The equipment at Roundhay School was old, well-used and threadbare and everything had a particular smell. It was an aged odour that was probably a mixture of sweat, linseed oil and pad whitening. Whatever its origin, I can still smell it today. For those unfamiliar with the box piece of safety equipment, the box was a plastic, avocado-shaped cup that protected a man's 'crown jewels'. Initially, they were not deemed necessary for young boys, but once puberty arrived, they became essential. It only took being struck in the groin by a hard leather cricket ball once to make you ensure you used one in the future.

There is something about the male psyche that finds endless mirth in seeing another struck in the nether regions. Professional cricketers and novices all share the same delight in witnessing the discomfort of even their own team member, writhing in agony, wondering if they will ever be able to have children or stand up straight again. That moment of, 'There but for the grace of God', adds even more sniggering, whilst trying to offer support to the player bent double, hands clasped about their genitalia, seems to bring out the two extremes, sympathy and glee.

The cricket pitch in front of the school had a square in the middle, but we youngsters never got to step on it unless it was to gather the ball that had been hit for a four or six. Our strips were on either side and were less manicured and levelled, but allowed for us to learn and play house matches. Cricket is so unlike the strenuous sports of rugby and cross-country, as so much of the time is spent doing nothing. Either you are observing whilst your side is batting, or you stand around waiting for the ball to come somewhere near you. The best players get to do the most and the others stand around daydreaming until that moment when the reverie is broken and your team are all shouting at you to 'catch it!' Usually the ball has been skyed and you dither underneath it, the weight of everyone's attention focused on you, and the knowledge that if you drop it, you will be lambasted and ridiculed for your lack of skill and attention. You see the ball, remember instructions: watch the ball into your hands, remember to have soft hands and to cup the ball, move smoothly into position still watching the ball at all times. Sweat appears on your brow. You wait what seems an eternity. The ball falls and smacks into your palms, bounces out onto the sward, and there is agony in the hands and, in the heart, sheer embarrassment. The rest of the players are either shouting abuse or rolling about on the grass in hysterics. What is even more humiliating is when you do all the right things, but the ball lands a yard to the side of you. I have experienced both of these and I was a reasonable cricketer. Goodness alone knows what the least able or interested boys experienced! They suffered so many degradations during lunch and playtimes when teams were being chosen and they were always the last picked and sometimes not even wanted by either team at the end. That must have fostered an absolute loathing of sport and organised games. I wonder if they exacted their revenge on sporting Adonises when they held positions in industry and the professions and interviewed candidates? Did they look at the sporty ones and think to themselves, 'I'll choose you last'? You couldn't blame them if they did.

Cricket is one of those few sports when you only get one go. If you are out first ball when batting, that's it for you. Worse is when you don't even get one bat and you are run out from the other end without facing a ball. Again, I have experienced the unfairness of that. I suppose it is a bit of a metaphor for life, which is part of the beauty of the game. The shame is that living in Australia, I see the ugly side of cricket. We played with fairness and good sportsmanship was paramount, unless someone was hit in the groin or dropped a sitter, whereas children in Australian schools are taught to sledge the opposition mercilessly and to win at all costs. That may have made them the best in the world, but tarnished them with a hideous reputation as louts and cheats.

The other sport was athletics, and this had an even more free and easy feel as often we just lolled around the pole vaulting pit, the long jump or high jump pits and lounged away a lovely sunny afternoon. Not so, unfortunately, in the first year. At these times, we were drilled with a new range of activities that were not on the primary school calendar. Who can forget about forty boys in a long line running up to the throw line, lethal aluminium javelins raised above their shoulders and hurling the blessed things and watching them soar through the air like a scene from the film Zulu? We weren't allowed to run and retrieve our javelins until the master in charge gave us the all clear. The difference between the shortest and the longest throws was quite marked and sometimes I wondered if the shorter throws were deliberate, as the boys responsible had a shorter distance to retrieve them. It really was quite a sight and merely carrying them back to start again was quite a challenge to avoid being stabbed in the leg or the eye by a boy carelessly carrying their weapon without full control. Health and safety would surely have a thing to say for such lax attention nowadays. I actually enjoyed javelin throwing and spent quite a few evenings practising for the athletics days. Unfortunately, there were always one or two better than me.

Another event that would have raised the ire of health and safety would have been the discus throwing. We had no nets around the throwing circle and wayward discuses shooting out in any direction was an everyday occurrence. Runners on the track had to keep a sharp eye out for javelins, discuses and shot puts raining down on them. I suppose it was all good training for the battlefront, which my generation mostly missed out on. But at least we were prepared!

For those of us who survived intact, there were other challenges ready to cripple the unwary, and those who did not know of the Darwin Awards. High jump! Sounds safe enough, but not when you were being taught and had to land on a sandpit with the give of a concrete slab. At first stage, we were taught the scissor kick and most managed to land on their feet, but as we progressed, the Fosbury Flop offered the approach of twisting and passing over the bar backwards and head first. There was no other way to land than on your neck and shoulders. How many of us are complaining about bad backs and have no idea why? Well, maybe the answer lies here. I remember landing mats being introduced, and this helped, as the mat meant you only fell a shorter distance and it was cushioned. The drawback was it gave you a false sense of security and accidents were common when you missed the mat and landed on the grass.

As I grew no taller after the age of twelve, this was not to be my sport. However, I found an even more dangerous activity to try my hand at. The pole vault was something that I thought a daredevil ne'er-do-well should have a go at. For some reason, it was not a popular event and was in its infancy. The storeroom was full of poles, mostly bamboo, with a growing number of aluminium ones. The carbon fibre bending poles were certainly not available at Roundhay and most of us put up with the bamboo ones that were left. Now these were fairly serviceable when hurtling along the runway, jabbing it into the receiving hole, suddenly lifting oneself up to a reasonable height, dropping over the bar and landing on a sand mound. Four or five feet seemed quite safe, but as we developed our skill, power and speed, I saw a number of them break. I never saw an injury, but that was more by chance and good luck than anything else. As we progressed, the aluminium ones were much safer, and we reached quite presentable heights. The danger then was falling down onto sand where the wind was driven out of you and, for a split second, you wondered if you would ever walk again. Even that wasn't the real danger, as that was the concrete edging that ran along the runway. If you didn't make the jump and fell back towards the runway or sideways, then there were several hard objects lying in wait to break your fall and possibly your back. We just laughed at each other's misfortune and injuries and carried on challenging each other to jump higher. You may well be asking about the supervision, but often there was none. As we got older, we just collected the equipment after school and set about practising and returning the gear when we had finished. I got pretty good at it and, due to the lack of numbers, and my foolhardiness, I won my only medal at the school athletics day in the pole vault. I still have it somewhere.

These were halcyon days and I guess I was lucky. I know that not everyone enjoyed school and even my experience was mixed but, on balance, I loved it and I think it was my primary schooling at Harehills in particular that led me to become a teacher.

THE MERRION

One of the major differences as shops changed to supermarkets was the creation of shopping centres. Two in particular spring to my mind. The first was the building of the Merrion Centre in the centre of Leeds and the second was the opening of the Seacroft Centre.

The Merrion Centre opened in 1964 and it was a marvel at the time. I remember going to visit with my mother and it had a moving walkway, and it was the first I had ever experienced. The walkway led up the slope from the front doors and was probably only about twenty yards long and, as a child of nine, the joy of riding it was immense. Most department stores had lifts, and a few had escalators, but the walkway was innovative and spoke of the future where science would automate life. To be honest, I am not sure that it served a great purpose, but it attracted shoppers to its exciting range of stores and supermarkets.

The centre was built during the era of concrete. What it did offer was shopping sheltered from the elements and in a modern, clean environment. Shops, pubs, a club and a bowling alley were all available under one roof. The complex housed a piece of artwork by Rowland Emmet – *Featherstone-Kite Openwork Basketweave Mark Two Gentleman's Flying Machine*. It was very Heath Robinson and the moving sculpture used to attract crowds of children watching it in motion.

One of the features was the multi-storey carpark. I think it was the first I had seen, and it was the response to the growth of privately owned cars. The centre allowed you to park and shop out of the rain and to take shopping out to the car using trolleys. How modern we had become!

My mother had got some vouchers for the Bowling Alley that was underneath the carpark, off Merrion Way, and so we were going to visit. This would have been around the same time she got them for the Ice Rink. I believe the vouchers gave you two games for the price of one. We had never bowled before and the nearest was watching my grandad on Chapel Allerton's crown green in the park near his house. However, bowling alleys were on programmes and films from the USA and seemed so special and modern. They showed what life would be like and seemed to fit in with the programmes we watched, such as The Jetsons. The journey to the centre was exciting, and we drove into the carpark. My dad struggled to get the Cortina around the bends and up the ramps as there wasn't much room. Eventually, after a large amount of stress, he manoeuvred to find a place to park, and we walked down the steep staircase to the bowling alley.

The first clue as to what you were to find came from the sound. The thunder of the rolling balls and the lightning strike as the balls scattered the skittles was magic to my ears. If this was what it sounded like, what would the experience hold? To add to the sound of the balls was the deafeningly loud pop music that blared from the loudspeakers. There was also a scent that was unusual, but inviting. It was a heady mixture of oil, ozone, and frying chips, and is a scent that you only find in the alleys. When we reached the foot of the stairs, the sight was overwhelming. In a world that seemed drab and grey, before me was a feast of colour, movement, people, sound and lights. It was a large venue with about twenty-six lanes. My parents had even less idea about what to do than my brother and me, but the man at the desk was helpful. The whole ritual of taking off your shoes and trying on the two-colour bowling shoes was exciting. I realised what another element of the centre's aroma was sweaty feet!

Shoes on our feet, we felt pretty special and slipped about on the carpet. The man told us which lane we were on and we made our way over.

It was just so exciting. We had to get balls and, after a check of the ones on the carousel, we headed off to the racks to find the lightest ones possible. We returned and had trouble setting up the scorer and so help was sought. The assistant sorted us out, and we were ready to start. Dad must have given us basic instructions and I think he probably went first to show us how. He managed to hit the pins and our eyes opened wide as the remainder were lifted, the fallen ones swept into the dark space at the back, the pins replaced and the ball magically returned down the gutter, hopped up and was ready for the next turn.

My brother and I were staggered. How did it all happen? Dad bowled again, but missed the remaining pins. My brother, Andrew, went next, and he did reasonably well; the ball bounced a little, but no one seemed to take notice. Again, I think he managed to hit at least one pin, but he hit some more on his second bowl. Next was my turn. Wearing shorts, I walked to the where the balls were. I picked mine up. I was shown how to place my fingers after drying them on the jet of air. I walked forward, stood still, raised the ball, skipped forward, and let fly. The feeling of being in front of the whole world and everyone watching was marked, and in truth, the thunderous crash of the ball striking the lane from a height did attract attention from those present. There was also a jarring of my two fingers that seemed to grip the ball after I had let it fly. The ball landed and then barely moved forward, its gentle roll taking it into the gutter. Luckily, it had just enough momentum to reach the back of the lane, otherwise an attendant would have had to march down between the lanes like a fairground attendant on the dodgems or waltzer, with swagger and poise, and retrieve it. This would have caused me great embarrassment.

I turned, walked back, red faced. I was offered advice and words of encouragement from my brother and parents and I waited for the ball to return and then I prepared for my second go. This time, I was determined to do better. I stood, ready and balanced, and I got it to glide down the lane without the great thump. That, at least, was an improvement, but I still failed to hit the pins and again it went into the gutter.

My mother was quite good, and she hit a few of her pins. After the first round we began to improve and towards the end, I was hitting pins. I was completely baffled by the scoring and couldn't understand why you had fewer goes if you got a strike. It was even more confusing with the last round.

After the first game, we got some quick drinks and then we were off again. I was getting tired by the end and the last bowls were a struggle. It was a great experience, and I was quite emotionally overloaded by the time we left and drove home. We went a few more times over the years and I have taken my boys on many occasions.

A couple of years later, another shopping centre was opening, and that was the Seacroft Centre. The Queen was arriving to open it and I know for a fact that the building wasn't finished and that most, if not all, the shops were still vacant. Posters and plants were placed in the windows to create the impression that they were occupied, but it wasn't very convincing. The Queen and Prince Philip were coming to open the precinct, and they arrived by train and then drove in a Rolls Royce to the centre.

It was a well-publicised visit, and my brother Andrew and I went to see her drive past. His best friend Christopher Cawkwell lived in one of the tall flats near Wellington Hill and the Queen was to pass by at a certain time. I don't remember how we got these little flags to wave, but we all had one, and so did most of the crowds there. We knew the set time, and we waited in the flat and then went down to a vantage spot on the roadside. Like most of these events, it was running late, and we waited patiently, ready to wave our flags and cheer. Eventually, the time arrived. The crowds were large, and we were poised on the kerb edge as the first car shot past. Suddenly there was cheering and waving further up, and then we joined in as the Rolls shot past. I caught only a quick glimpse, and she was sitting in the back on our side. She had a pale green, maybe turquoise coat and hat and she waved and looked at us all. I have a memory of her eyes meeting mine, but that could be wishful thinking. Anyway, it is my claim to fame and my only contact with the Queen. Brief indeed, but isn't it quality rather than quantity that counts? She visited my eldest son's school in Wakefield shortly before we left for Australia, in celebration of the school's 400th anniversary, Queen Elizabeth Grammar School, named after the queen that bestowed the charter to the school.

I have visited the Merrion Centre since and I can't say that it has really improved, and I believe the Seacroft Centre was demolished, eventually. Both were ugly and the Seacroft Centre was a bleak, dehumanising site that offered little to the local inhabitants.

Thankfully, shopping centres have learnt a great deal and offer much more than they used to. They are now past their heyday and retailers are struggling with online shopping and out-of-city mega-centres.

THE CHANGING HOME

In a surprisingly short period, the homes that we live in have undergone quite major changes. My parents' first house was in Lawrence Avenue and I imagine it was built after the First World War. My dad saw owning a house as an opportunity to change and modernise them and the first alteration that he made to the house was to partition one of the bedrooms to make it a three-bedroom house. Number 36 was originally a two-bedroom semi, and like many similar houses, it still forms part of the major housing stock of the suburban landscape. Like other houses, it has been changed, modernised and altered to meet modern tastes, technological and decorating advances.

My first memories are of a small house with a separate wooden garage. This isn't surprising, as there were few cars, even when I was born in the 1950s, and the garage was more of a shed and never housed a car during our time there. We had the first television in the street and were one of the few families to own a car, an Austin A7 Ruby, followed by a Ford Prefect. Within a brief space of time, the streets were changed forever as cars parked alongside the pavements, filling the streets. Nowadays, it even the houses that do have garages seldom use them to house the cars and the garages are usually used to store garden equipment, bicycles and assorted junk that can no longer fit in the house.

When we started outgrowing the house at Lawrence Avenue, with the birth of my younger brother, we moved to 19 Gipton Wood

Crescent, which was not far, as moves go, just the other side of Easterly Road, but the house was a bigger one and a step up. This was a three bedroom semi-detached, and I didn't realise it, but it was a better spot to grow up in. It had very close access to the Little (Fairy) Woods and just a little further to Gipton Wood. When we moved in the roads were still cobbled and the houses didn't have driveways, just paths that led up to the front and side doors. The design of both houses reflected the social attitudes that were prevalent at the time. The kitchens were tiny, and my Scottish father referred to them as the kitchenettes. There were no fridges, but they had a pantry that fitted into the space under the staircase. This space was shared by a coal store that had an outside door and so the pantry was still quite small. Both of the houses had only one form of heating and that was through fires in the dining and front rooms. There were boilers built into the chimney spaces and the fires used to heat the water.

The fuel for the fire was coal, and this was replaced by smokeless coal during the 1960s in response to London's Great Smog in 1952, with the Clean Air Act of 1956 and finally another Clean Air Act of 1968. I can still taste the sooty swirling smog that blanketed Leeds in autumn and winter. It had a green tinge and made the journey on the bus a nightmare, as you were unsure where you were and I often got off at the wrong stop. Thousands of people died each winter because of the increase in bronchial disease. The thick fog produced an eerie, shrouded city, deadened the sounds and created a horror and alien landscape. All the city buildings were black and, as a child, I assumed they were made of black stone, but in the 1960s buildings were washed and sandblasted and the true colour appeared like magic.

The house in Gipton Wood Crescent was near the crest of the hill, and the pathway up to the house was steep, tree-lined and had flag stones. The front had a wooden fence and a bank up to the front door. Inside the house it was quite dark, and it had rather splendid real leaded windows made with separate pieces of coloured glass, held in a lead framework. Because of this, the windows were a bit wavy and the house interior very dark. All the pipes were lead and the change to copper was only just starting. I am not sure what attracted my parents to the house, apart from my mother liking the extra space and the more upmarket district, or at least as she saw it. My father was probably attracted by the challenge. He was an engineer and Do

It Yourself was becoming a feature of modern life.

There was a real sense of a science-led optimism. This was seen in TV programmes at the time: Supercar (1961) The Jetsons (1962), My Favourite Martian (1963), Fireball XL5 (1962) and many others. Science and technology would improve the lot of the ordinary man and woman, and it was in the home that these changes were more obvious to me.

I don't think that my dad could wait to get started, whilst my mum was too busy looking after all of us, cooking, washing, cleaning and holding down a job. I can't remember the order of the developments, but they started with the removal of the windows. My dad removed the lead windows, a room at a time, and replaced them with large plate-glass ones. The lead was removed and gathered, and he took it to a metal merchant and got a payment. The plate-glass certainly brightened the rooms, and ventilation was provided by a couple of small side lights at the top of the windows. These were left open during summer but shut the rest of the year. Dad worked through the house doing the windows, and shortly afterwards they had gas central heating fitted in downstairs. The boiler was placed in the disused coal store, and it made a major difference from previously having to keep fires going. Most bedrooms also had fireplaces and, now they were obsolete, dad had the chimneys capped and removed the fireplaces and blocked the chimneys off.

Now, in case you think we were spoilt, I must add that there was no heating upstairs, so the bedrooms were icy during winter. I don't remember the heating ever being on at night and many were the nights I completely cocooned myself under the covers and I am surprised I didn't suffocate. I would wake up and the windows would be frozen over and covered in a wonderful filigree of ferns, as the condensation had frozen. My brothers and I would scrape away a small section and look longingly into the garden, hoping that it had snowed. Often we were disappointed, but sometimes the back garden was a wonderful sight.

Another problem with the central heating was the vast amount of water from condensation. Pools filled the window-sills, and going around with a sponge and a jug and soaking the water up was a daily routine.

My dad's next challenge was modernising the doors. The doors were traditional panel ones and modern ones were flush. He fastened panels of hardboard over each side of the door, covering the panels and this gave a smooth profile and when painted Dulux brilliant white, the house began to look modern. The only problem was that the paint took ages to dry and with having three small boys it wasn't long before one of us had placed our hands on it, left a forensic hand print, and required turps before we left traces over the furniture or our clothes.

Picture rails adorned each downstairs room and dad soon had them gone and the walls were stripped of the old floral wallpaper. It was practical and trendy to cover the walls with woodchip paper that could be painted over, when required, and lasted for years. The woodchip was also painted brilliant white and soon it was a dazzling experience entering our house. The next challenge was the ceilings. These were a little cracked, but nothing that a bit of polyfiller couldn't have fixed, but no, the new way was to glue polystyrene tiles onto the ceiling. My dad went into this with gusto. The new tiles added extra insulation, dampened noise and provided a perfect death-trap if there was a fire. The tiles would burn with acrid, deadly black smoke and, to add to this, would drip burning plastic onto anyone found underneath them. These tiles could also be painted over, which probably added to their danger. Over time, woodchip gave way to anaglypta wallpaper which provided an embossed pattern which was then painted. Now we didn't only just have white, at least not at first. There were experiments with green bamboo patterned wallpaper used as a feature, bright orange geometrically patterned paper that was challenging even then, and later experiments with plum flock wallpaper. But in the end, the ease and the simplicity of childproofed white painted woodchip or anaglypta won the day.

Curtain pelmets were removed from the now large, airy windows and small tracks were installed. We even stepped into the realms of science fiction by having fibreglass curtains. As a young lad, I couldn't get over how glass could form a fabric, and to add that modern touch, they were orange.

My dad was really getting into this DIY and he started furniture-making night classes. The first piece he made was a glass-fronted bookcase, and it sat in the front room for the rest of his life. I can still remember the books. He had the self-help series of How to Win Friends and Influence People by Dale Carnegie. There were also My Family and Other Animals by Gerald Durrell and a host of other

Penguin Books. One book I remember vividly was Hurricane because it showed a scantily clad lady as a hurricane raged on a Pacific Island. I guess that was one of my mum's. His second project was a drinks trolley. I remember going with him to collect it and bring it back home. He was very proud of it and it was a very modern style, with a small tray above a larger one. It was on castors and was beautifully crafted. Again, this sat in the front room and came into its own during the Christmas parties.

There was still a lot that he had plans for, to bring the house into the modern world, and technological advances were lining up to change the way that we all lived.

FREEDOM, CINEMAS, COURTING AND SNOGGING

As a youngster, I had gone with my older brother to watch the matinees at the Clock Cinema. The cinema was an impressive building and had an Art Deco feel and look. Entry was through glass panelled doors and the curved ticket booth faced you. Tickets were bought and then there was a climb up the stairs past a waterfall. At the top of the stairs, the tickets would be checked and torn in two. You were given half the ticket back and you could then enter. There was an upper balcony, and it was always special to go in there, particularly if you could get a place at the very front. You were wise not to sit directly below in the stalls as some horrible youths would drop things down onto you, and some even spat onto the heads of those below. I believe the cinema had an organ in front of the stage, but I remember little about it and I never saw it played. I don't know if the cinema was ever used as a theatre, but it looked very much like one. The curtains were full, rich red velvet that matched the seat coverings and there was a complicated arrangement of curtains being drawn back as the lights partially dimmed and the adverts came on. For the trailers, the lights dimmed further, and the screen was revealed and then when the feature film started, the cinema was in complete darkness. The entire process was grand and impressive. The sound was loud, and with the beams from the projector streaking across the heads of the audience, it was a magical experience.

The matinees were crowded, crazy affairs with hordes of children noisily watching, shouting and running around. The films were ancient even to us and they often showed silent movies, Laurel and

Hardy, some cartoons and I even remember Batman in black and white, with old cars and I believe it was silent. The most common staple were the old cowboy films. The ushers were strict, elderly men and women, who marched down the aisles with their torches and woe betide you if you were picked out for noisy misbehaving! If you were fortunate, you were warned, if not thrown out, and suffered the embarrassment of being marched past everyone else. We got quite savvy and money could be saved by one paying for entry and the others standing outside by the fire exit. When the lights went down, the one inside would sneak to the toilet, go to the fire exit, and open the doors. If lucky, the entire group would get in, but sometimes an usher was waiting, wanting to see our ticket stubs. If you couldn't produce one, you were escorted out. The quality of the old film reels meant that there were often breaks and we would watch as the celluloid films melted and then there were loud groans, boos and the stamping of feet as the film stopped and the lights came on. The ushers became quite angry, as there was little they could do to quell the mass anguish of hundreds of children. They made an example of one or two, and the scene of children being escorted out had a limited impact on the rest. After a wait, someone would splice together the film and continue, but not always from the same place in the story.

Apart from the matinees, I had spent many times attending the cinema as a child, usually with my dad, but becoming a teenager meant being able to go without parents. At first, we used to go in groups and our choice of films was not ones that my parents would have wanted to see and, to be honest, I wouldn't have wanted to be seen anywhere with my parents at that age. We did go to a range of cinemas, both in Leeds city and the suburbs, but the Clock Cinema at Harehills was the easiest to get to and our usual haunt. My friends and I could walk there, and it had the added advantage of being fairly cheap. The cinema is still there, but has been put to other uses for many years, but in the 1960s and seventies it was still a thriving cinema. The films it showed were the blockbusters of the time, but maybe a week or two behind the city cinemas. In these times, it was permissible to smoke in the cinemas and the air could be thick with it. Later, the cinema was divided into smoking and non-smoking sections. When I was about thirteen years old, I had become a smoker, and an evening in the cinema meant that you and your clothes stank afterwards. Those of my friends, who were non-smokers, must have suffered quietly as they sat with us. There were ashtrays at the back of the seats in front and the cinema was dotted with light as, like fireflies, someone would strike a match or use a cigarette lighter. The risk of fire must have been high, but I don't ever remember hearing of any. One danger was sitting too close to those on the balcony above as I have, on more than one occasion, seen a cigarette end flicked down into the audience below by some horrible oik of a teenager.

If you were lucky and had a bit of money, then there was the opportunity to buy drinks, Sunkist popcorn, ice-cream tubs or a Split ice lolly. If not, then you just had to make do. When I was a teenager, films had the added interest of having love scenes, but when I was a young lad, these used to spoil films. I remember my favourite up to this point was Zulu as it had no love content, but as an almost teenager I went to see Dr No. I would only have been ten in 1964 so it may have been a re-run a short time later. I thought it was fantastic and Ursula Andress, walking out of the surf in her bikini, had a profound impact. This was followed up in 1965 with She, where the glamorous Ursula impressed again. Cinema-going held a whole new attraction for me and I was even more impressed when One Million Years BC came out in 1966 with Rachel Welch scantily clad. I didn't care that it was historically anachronistic; it had everything I wanted in a film, adventure and beautiful girls.

Needless to say, there was a year or two when the cinema was meeting my growing interests and desires and then came the tour de force, Barbarella, in 1967.

'Barbarella, an astronaut from the 41st century, sets out to find and stop the evil scientist Durand Durand, whose Positronic Ray threatens to bring evil back into the galaxy.'

That may have been the plot, but who cares! It was a movie based on sex and Jane Fonda was delightful. The stripping off of her spacesuit is a scene that is forever burnt into young impressionable minds, to be replayed in the memory over the years.

When I became a little older and we had developed a circle of friends in the youth clubs, larger groups of us would go. We were a group of friends, girls and boys, but none of us had 'girl and boy friends' up to this point. Asking someone out was a real hurdle, and it was safer to attend in groups and hope something would just happen.

We would sit in our line, positioned in a way that meant you were next to your favoured friend and during the film you had to make the agonising decision of whether to put your arm across the back of the chair behind your chosen girl. If you did rustle up that courage, you waited to see if there was any sign of welcome, or rather, one of irritation. The other move was to put your hand on the chair rest and hope that the person of your dreams would put her hand on top of yours, thus sealing a relationship. Such times of innocence.

The next major step was to invite someone out on a date. As money was an issue, a trip to the cinema was just about the only financially viable option. The advantage to the Clock Cinema was that at the end of the rows were double seats with no arm rest separating the couple. These seats had positives and negatives for couples. The disadvantage was that they were at the end of the row and within full view of the usherettes, who would soon put a stop to any hanky-panky. The advantage was that it was wonderfully warm and close to another human and this was something not experienced since being a baby or toddler, and that was with your mother. This was also a good place to practise the art of snogging, but I will leave you to reminisce about this yourself. This period of awkwardness probably only lasted a year or two, and then the object of going to the pictures returned to watching a good film.

In the late 1960s and 70s, there were many great films, and some that were thought provoking as well as being humorous and entertaining. I have tried to recall the major ones for me that I saw at the Clock Cinema. The Graduate, 1967, Midnight Cowboy and Easy Rider, 1969, Kelly's Heroes and Woodstock, 1970, Klute and Straw Dogs, 1971, Deliverance, 1972, Sleeper, 1973, and Blazing Saddles and Young Frankenstein, 1974 make up my list. Within this list are some films I found challenging. Midnight Cowboy with John Voight and Dustin Hoffman, Deliverance with Burt Reynolds and John Voight, and Straw Dogs with Susan George and Dustin Hoffman were far from easy viewing and showed an often unpleasant and frightening side of life. There were some, like Easy Rider and Woodstock, that marked a cultural place in time. The music was wonderful, but the films showed the dangers of a growing drug culture. And others like Blazing Saddles, Sleeper, The Graduate, Young Frankenstein, Kelly's Heroes and Klute that made you laugh, if you were in the right mood, uproariously, or just entertained. I almost forgot that there was a series of films that I also found impactful and these were the original Planet of the Apes films. The original with Charlton Heston in 1968 really started me off with an interest in Science Fiction.

I could relive these times all day as they were a critical part of growing up, a time before responsibility emerged and life became serious.

David M Cameron

NAKED BATHS, AND STRAIGHT-ARM TACKLES

Roundhay School was nothing if not created as a Grammar School clone of the traditional public school. The buildings were imposing and its traditions were overbearing. The masters were still living in a time when it was normal to wander the school like ravens, black and satanic, and they could be cold and merciless. Gown attired, their sleeves flapped like giant birds ready to fall upon any unsuspecting boy who had broken a written, or assumed, rule.

The floors were bare boards, the walls unadorned, and the air thundered with the noise of eight-hundred boys as they beat their way like Attila's Hordes down the staircases and corridors in between lessons. The only force that could stand in their way was the gown draped masters who strode against the tide, parting the flow like Moses. It was a harsh, unyielding environment, which did not cater for the gentle or lacking in confidence. It was a male domain, designed and run to produce men, when men still dominated England and the Western World. It is interesting to note that there were nearly twice as many places for boys in Grammar Schools as for girls. Roundhay Boys had eight hundred and the Roundhay Girls six hundred.

The curriculum varied between the two genders. Boys had a wider choice of science subjects than the girls, and the girls had more of an Arts focus. I believe I had to choose only one subject from History, Biology, Economics, Art, Music, Woodwork and Metalwork, to do at Ordinary Level, whereas I think we had to do three Science subjects. As a Grammar School, sport was seen as essential for creating men who could be leaders, and the only proper sports were Rugby Union, Cricket, Athletics and, of course, Cross Country Running. I think it was probably based on the idea that if we were physically exhausted, then we would not bother too much with the girls on the other side of the boundary bushes between the playing fields. Maybe I am being unjust, as I am sure they felt teamwork, leadership and perseverance could be gained from participation in the above sports.

Under 13 XV 1967/8

I was delighted to arrive at Roundhay and find that we could do proper sports. Roundhay had changing rooms, and it was a thrill to change in a room that was not the classroom. There was a strong smell of sweat and old liniment, mixed with linseed oil, leather, and what I later discovered was testosterone. It was a challenge to get changed with no one seeing you naked, but somehow it was achieved. Blue Kelvin rugby shirt, black shorts, boots, socks and a little nervousness saw us ready for our first house sports. It was a cold afternoon, with an icy breeze that shot up the legs of the shorts and dampened any enthusiasm. Arms wrapped around our bodies, we listen to Joe W show us the basics of how to pass a rugby ball, how to pass it backwards and how to move it along a line as we advanced down the field. The first session was not too thrilling, but it was actually sport. The second skill was tackling, and this was much more exciting. 'Keep your head to one side, take them round the ankles,' was followed by the lie, 'Go in hard and you won't get hurt!' Needless to say, some of the smaller boys were paired with some of the bigger boys and they put paid to such a tale. Some went into the tackle with genuine enthusiasm and came out concussed, but some chickened out and just dived anywhere, apart from at the legs of the advancing player. I am sure that a note was made of these boys' names and they would be made an example of at a later date.

It became very clear, in a very short time, who had the makings of rugby players and who had not. As this is a sport where brawn is as important as skill and I was one of the tallest at this age, I was quite successful and thoroughly enjoyed it. Muddy, bruised and some of us not quite aware of our surroundings, we traipsed off the field and entered the changing rooms. Now, this was the first real challenge of the day. In the mid 1960s, someone still thought it was a good idea for teenage boys to strip naked and sit in a two-foot deep large square bath. The bath was big enough to hold about thirty and the steaming waters were a seething mass of naked flesh, often scraped and bloody, clods of floating earth and lumps of soap. Was it a bonding experience? I can't really say. It was just the way it was. What I remember was one or two of the teachers stripping off and joining the throng. Nowadays, that would be totally a 'No No!' and would result in police charges, but then it was not unusual and from my experience, an innocent, if embarrassing, regular part of sport.

Over the time, we were taught the rudiments of the game and trained in our houses, Kelvin, Nelson, Scott and Gordon, working towards our first house matches. The teachers distributed positions depending on your attributes, or lack of them. I was sometimes a hooker, wing forward and scrum half. I never enjoyed being a hooker. You were in the middle of the scrum and rammed headfirst into the other team's pack. Breathing could be difficult, as was avoiding brain damage. Because of my natural cowardice, or common sense, I worked hard as a wing forward/scrum half, and became half-decent.

For those of us, like me, who have moved to warmer climes, we have probably forgotten just how cold a Leeds winter could be, but believe me, it could be bleak. Winter sports carried on, whatever the weather, and I believe this was part of the ploy to make men of us. Snow, rain, sleet, fog, nothing stopped us. Now if you were good at sport, then it could be bearable, you could maintain some body-heat by running around, but if you were one of the timid ones who avoided the ball at all costs, then the weather must have been torment.

I have only recently discovered that my brothers and I have a condition where the blood leaves our fingers and toes in cold weather, and they turn a whitish yellow, look like they have died, basically. I just thought it was normal to wait about half an hour after being outdoors for you to be able to use your hands to hold a pen and write. Winter sport never helped this. One genuine concern I had, though, was the loose maul. When the ball was loose, then bodies would dive on top of it trying to get possession. Piles of boys would form a pyramid, with some poor soul underneath them all. I know from experience how hard it was to breathe and, without the referee pulling boys off, death was just a few moments away. On a good day, with a thick covering of grass, this was bad enough, but in winter when there was a mass of mud and puddles, then it really was dangerous. You could find yourself face down in the mud or water as others dived on top. Panic really does set in when you have had the wind driven out of you and there is water over your mouth and nose and you need air! Again, I think health and safety would prevent such experiences today.

Even worse than the puddles was when the mud froze and rock hard ruts covered the playing surface and the puddles had a layer of ice on top. Real injuries could, and did, occur when playing on such concrete hard surfaces. By the time sports sessions were over, you were soaking wet, covered in mud and blood and numbed by the cold. The hot baths were manna from heaven, but it was only when you warmed up and feeling returned to your body that you realised how you had been injured. With the thawing came the pain. Fantastic times!

Our team was beginning to shape up and the first house match was quite an event. It was looking a little like rugby and less like a riot, and some boys really shone at the game. These were the ones who could run through the opposition with boys flying off in all directions, like drifts from a snow plough. I remember one boy doing this, and when he was about to run past a friend of mine, the boy shot out his arm. I believe it was a reflex action rather than deliberate, but the straight arm was at head height and the running boy's head hit the arm and he was felled, as if hit with an axe. Whilst he was lying stunned on the ground, the teacher used this as an opportunity to teach us that such tackles were banned. The victim must have survived, but I don't remember any great concern being shown for his wellbeing.

I guess it must have made a man of him and, strangely, many of us grew to love rugby and really looked forward to playing.

CALL THAT RUNNING, BOY?

I was speaking with my younger brother recently and he was telling me he had visited Roundhay School just before they rebuilt it. He went into the paved area below the school where the changing rooms and storerooms were, and he was struck by the spectre of the sound of hosts of boot studs clattering over the paving. As he told me this, I too heard the sound of aluminium studs like a volley of gunfire rattling over the stone and the scrape, as some boys slid along the surface as if they were on ice. The purpose was reputed to be to sharpen the studs or wear the surface off and thus provide a weapon against any opposition. I can't say that it was intentional, but after a few woundings, the checking of studs became commonplace and offenders were forced to remove any dangerous ones.

It is not only the sounds that come back, but I have to pause, as suddenly the pinging sound of the table tennis balls on the tables under the opposite side of the undercover area makes an appearance in my memory. It is also the smell. This area had a number of distinct odours. In summer, it was linseed oil from the cricket bats, in winter the stink of Denco Rub and similar liniments that were supposed to warm up the muscles. Over these were two quite distinct aromas. One was sweat and the other testosterone, and both came as a shock when one started the school as a Year One, but soon just became the norm as we developed and contributed to the spirit of manliness at Roundhay.

It seems to be a feature of the male nature that greater effort will be put into avoiding something, than it would take to carry out the task. As examples, I give you washing your hands after going to the toilet and brushing your teeth. Both take only a minute or two, but somehow they are abhorrent to the male psyche. As a child I would go to the loo and then run the tap for a while, even move the towel on the rail to create the appropriate sound effect, rather than actually do it. Similarly with teeth, the tap would be run, toothpaste would be squeezed out, but rather than on the brush, onto the finger and a minute amount smeared about the lips, so that a cursory check from a mother could be passed. You may well think that this is just my issue, but after teaching for forty years and having four boys of my own, I can assure you that this is common.

In light of this, you can image the nature and depth of stench that emanated from the changing rooms and toilets at Roundhay. In the toilets at the Mansion building, the stench of urine was overpowered by the thick, acrid fog of cigarette smoke. This billowed out whenever the door opened and shadowy figures would appear like zombies out of the graveyard mist. I might add here that there was a similar effect when the staffroom door opened and teachers exited into the corridor, leaving the haze behind.

I digress, but male lack of hygiene was also present in the baths and later in the showers. There was the odd piece of cracked and dirty soap lying around, but it was seldom used and showers were water only affairs and did little but remove clods of mud off the skin, and did nothing for body odour. There was the odd boy, but not many, and we were always a little suspicious of them, who had their own cleaning supplies and they would leave changing after sport with a totally unnatural bouquet of fresh flowers. Of course, the ambience was not assisted by the fact that we didn't have many changes of clothes. Laundry was a weekly affair and some of us didn't possess many school shirts, socks, etc. and so would wear them for much of the week. To add to this, we spent every break and lunchtime playing soccer and would work up quite a sweat, the results of which would remain with us the entire week.

Luckily for us, the male attitude towards cleanliness and godliness was not shared by most of the female species. Even walking past the girls' school, one could detect a completely different atmosphere. It was a pleasant experience and one that didn't almost make you gag. Some, though, took this too far and one such teacher applied so much perfume that she could be followed up and down the corridor.

She left such an impression on me that the villain in my first novel, Wickergate, shared the same attribute. I won't mention her name, but I am sure that there are those who will know who it is I refer to. In one of life's coincidences, my wife was taught by the same teacher in Stoke-on-Trent prior to her arrival at Roundhay.

One of life's amazing puzzles is why the teenage females, who have such good habits, should find teenage boys with their bad habits irresistible. This trait must have been an evolutionary imperative or the human race would have died out long ago. Something must have made girls' brains malfunction for several years, so that spotty, pimply, smelly and uncoordinated teenagers appear like Brad Pit or some other Adonis. Clearly, this stage doesn't last long as when married, females spend the rest of their lives trying, and often failing, to change the entrenched habits of their mates. Unfortunately, some men retain their natural urges and state, to remain true by keeping themselves as far away from godliness as possible.

I've finally got there! Sport! Roundhay was nothing if it wasn't a school where sport was valued, and it was seen as a major part of creating men who could be leaders. Of course, there are relatively few of us who actually become leaders, but why let that stop anyone? Make everyone suffer for the few who would lead. After saying this, I enjoyed sport, on the whole, and was moderately capable, but I have always felt for those who hated it and suffered the cold, the humiliation and the boredom of watching others chase a ball, or bat for more than the one delivery. Those who were always picked last when teams were chosen and faced the ultimate humiliation of being refused at the end and told to play for the other side. I wonder what they learnt about teamwork and compassion?

The one activity where this was most obvious was cross-country. At school, I wasn't a great runner, but not the worst. It could have had a great deal to do with smoking, but be that as it may, cross-country season came in winter. The ground was often frozen and the teachers must have been happy not to get changed and referee rugby. As a result, the year group would be escorted onto the Soldiers' Field and then set off on the run. A hundred or so boys would spring into life, like startled rabbits, and sprint like mad things down to Oakwood, cross the road and then head back up to the top of Hill Sixty. I say sprint like startled rabbits. In truth, this was only some. At the back were the unfortunate sufferers. The doomed ones who were disliked by the sporty types and hounded by the staff, with calls such as, "You call that running, boy? I'll show you running if I catch you!" They plodded on in torment, cold and in abject misery.

The greyhounds at the front were soon learning the error of their ways and the somehow impossible ability to pace themselves. Those with the talent strode out with fluid ease, whilst the others clutched their throats, trying to catch their breath and casting glances back to the stragglers far behind, wondering if theirs wasn't the best choice. The large horde was by now a snaking line and the front runners disappeared into Roundhay Park and within minutes passed the teachers stationed at the steps near The Mansion. The ones at the front knew the route and headed into the gorge and soon were sprinting back towards school before those at the back were reaching Hill Sixty. I was probably about a third of the way back from the front and I took particular note of IRKS in his sheepskin coat, chatting to other teachers, fag and pint of beer in hand as I struggled past. I can really see why the staff smiled so much when it was cross-country season. No checking of names took place, just the odd cursory glance, sarcastic comment, or complete indifference as the boys went past.

On entering the gorge, we were out of view of the teachers and some would make a quick stop, the fags would come out and we would emulate our betters and chat over a smoke. After the break, it was hard to get moving again, but we did. Unless it was the cross-country competition, we headed back towards school, across the Soldiers' Field, through the gates, along the drive back to the changing rooms. Our positions were spasmodically checked to make sure we had returned, but otherwise, usually the stragglers were just left to their own devices. I wonder if there are still any out there, forever cursed to plod the trail and never finishing, a bit like Sisyphus!

Nowadays, duty of care would mean that there were much more stringent checks. I do remember Joe W donning his shorts and striding out with the runners, which is more than can be said for most.

The funny thing about all this is that I have spent most of my adult life as a runner. I started in 1981 and completed my first half marathon the next year. I have never been great at it, but for some reason, I enjoy it and it has probably helped to keep me alive, as I have bad heart genetics and I still run every day.

SCOUTING FOR BOYS

It was my elder brother who was the trailblazer for me as I grew up. He was the first to try everything, being four years older than me, and so it was with the cubs. He attended Ladywood Methodist Church cub pack, and he seemed to have a good time. It was always something that I assumed I would do when I was old enough, but as it turned out, it was not to be. I was quite envious as he wore a green jumper, neckerchief and woggle. I think they also had a cap in those days, but I am not sure.

Whilst the family attended Ladywood, my parents got quite

involved. My mother did keep-fit classes there and somehow my father got roped in to running the soccer team for the cubs. The good news was my brother would always make the team and the bad news, it meant dad had to organise practices and attend matches. As my dad and brother were going, I also had to attend, but couldn't take part in any matches. I don't remember minding, and the practices used to take place on the Soldiers' Field, between Oakwood and Roundhay. Soccer boots in those days were a bit of a joke, and thinking back, it was probably because of the cubs that my brother and I got boots and a soccer ball as a Christmas present. The boots were heavy leather with leather studs nailed into the soles and they had a big round toecap that made it difficult to control the ball. In the late 1950s, even professional soccer players were handicapped by their equipment. Shorts were long, heavy cotton, shirts similarly heavy-duty with long sleeves and collars and their boots big and cumbersome. The soccer balls were terribly heavy leather with laces where the bladder fitted. They hurt when you kicked them and soaked up any water and became impossible to kick more than a few yards. But the worst thing was, if you foolishly headed a wet ball. The consequence of a header, if you remained conscious, was probable concussion and long-term brain damage. It was a truly horrendous experience and a mistake I only ever made once or twice.

At the practices, I could occasionally take part, but I can't say that I was any kind of potential Stanley Matthews. I remember attending a few soccer matches and we would go along and support the team from the sidelines. I think pieces of oranges were provided for the players at half-time. I remember one particular Saturday morning when the match was away at Crossgates. My dad took my brother and me in the car. Our pet poodle, Sabot, came along at the request of my mother. I suppose it gave her some time to herself with my younger brother, without the rest of us being there.

We were living in Gipton Wood Crescent at this time, and Crossgates was quite a distance away. The game was not particularly eventful for me, but my brother may have had a different take on it. I have no idea who won, but at the end, my dad bundled the two of us back in the car and we set off for home. We arrived tired, but happy and it was only after a few minutes that mum asked where Sabot was. Now this was not a good question for my father, as he had let the dog off for a while when the game was going and he had forgotten all about Sabot when organising for the team to be picked up by parents, and getting us into the car. We had left the dog behind! My mum went mad, as only she could, and her ire was directed at my father with passion. I believe that she would have preferred it if he had left one of us behind, rather than the dog.

We were immediately sent back with the mission of finding Sabot and the inference not to return without him. My poor dad was really in the doghouse. His whole demeanour drooped and any support from my brother or me was met with a tirade from my mum. It was with some relief that we got back in the car, no seat belts in these days, and retraced our steps. The park was deserted when we returned and our hearts sank when there was no sight of Sabot. We called and wandered the area, but it was no use. Dad got us back in the car and we drove through the streets of the area with the forlorn hope of finding Sabot. He did have a collar with our address on it and we hoped that if we didn't find him, someone else would and they would contact us.

Eventually, we had to head home sans dog. My mother's mood had, if anything, darkened and you could cut the atmosphere with a knife, and if one had been lying around, I wouldn't have fancied my father's chances. Saturday afternoon passed slowly and my mum took to wandering the streets, searching and calling for the dog. My father tried again and set off to look for it. I don't think he would have dared stay at home. But all to no avail. My mother was forlorn and desperate and her heart was truly broken. I had never seen her so upset. It was her dog and her husband and her sons had let her down.

The evening was just setting in and all hope had been abandoned and probably divorce was on the cards, when there was a scratching on the door. We all leapt to our feet, but mum was the fastest. She opened the door and there was a rather tired and wet looking Sabot. The poodle, though not over-endowed with intelligence, had somehow found its way home. This was truly amazing, as it had been taken in the car and it wouldn't have seen the route through the window as it sat on the back seat, but somehow, and we will never know how, it had found its way back.

My mother was in heaven. The thing was hugged to within an inch of its life. Fresh lamb's heart was boiled on the stove and it was fed tasty morsels to build back its energy. I am sure it gave my father a look as if to say, "That'll teach you to leave me behind! I hope you suffered!" As it was, family life returned to normal. My father got some colour back in his ashen face and he refrained from commenting, content that there was some hope of a future for him. Anything he might have said would not have been well received, after he had left Sabot, mum's most precious possession, behind.

In time things settled down and dad continued to take the cub's soccer for the rest of the season, but we never left Sabot behind again. In fact, I can't remember Sabot attending another match. The miracle of his return became just another legend of the family, fading over time.

I never got to attend cubs as we stopped going to Ladywood before I was old enough, but I did go to Scouts. My older brother was friends with David M who lived on Easterley Road, and we used to play Risk with his younger brother, Richard. There was an even younger brother known as Titch, but like my younger brother, he was too young to be included. Richard attended St. Stephen's Church Scouts on Cramner Road in Moor Allerton and he asked if I would like to join. After discussion with my parents and an understanding that my father didn't want to become involved, I was allowed to go.

Richard and I went by bus and the first time I was a little nervous.

Now, from what I remember about St. Stephen's Church, it was quite modern in those days (mid 1960s). The design was functional and the altar section of the church had a dividing wall that could be closed and the area where the congregation would sit became the hall when the chairs were stacked and moved back. I was introduced to the Scout leaders, and I was allocated a pack and I lined up with them. They were all in uniform, but I was in civvies. There was the usual Scout chant and procedures and then we split up to practise various skills towards badges. I think I was put in the knot tying group and we had diagrams that showed how to tie bowlines, sheep shanks, clover hitches, reef knots and granny knots and various others. The night passed quickly and ended with games and then we helped pack away and I was invited back the next week. We were told we would play 'wide games' so not to come in uniform. I had no idea what that meant, but Richard told me we would be in the woods and to come in clothes that wouldn't get spoiled.

The next week came, and we arrived at St. Stephen's. After the initial rituals, we were led down to the woods and there we were told the rules. There were two teams. One team was defending the base and they would patrol and search for any intruders. If you saw someone and called out their name, they had to surrender and were held captive in the base. The attacking team could free the captives by sneaking into the base and announcing they had done so, and then all the captives could escape. There wasn't really a winner, but if you captured all the attackers, then victory would be yours. I don't think I ever played the game where any team won.

I was on the attacking team, and we had to sneak up on the defenders. They were not allowed to stay near the base, as that would make the attackers' task impossible. Lying in the long grass and bushes was a dirty and scratchy affair. Grass cuts were common and irritating after the game, but you never noticed during it. I was in my element and any concerns I had about joining the Scouts disappeared that evening. I was ecstatic! It was all a boy could want. I went home that night, tired, filthy, and euphoric. Scouting was for me!

CHURCH ARMY CRUSADER TEST

For Scout Groups Affiliated to the Church Army.

THIS IS TO CERTIFY THAT

Scout David Cameron

has passed his SCOUTS' CRUSADER TEST and is permitted to wear the Church Army Badge with the Green Background.

DATE 17th May, 1967.

Scoutmaster.....................

Incumbent.........................

Church Army Commissioner...........

STARTING YOUTH CLUBS

It was when I was about thirteen that my interest in girls and adolescent activities appeared. It was probably that Roundhay Girls' School was so near and yet so far away that actually encouraged thoughts of the 'fair sex'. It was almost cruel to adolescent boys and girls to dangle them tantalisingly on the other side of a few bushes that separated the two schools' playing fields.

At primary school, Harehills County Primary, we were only separated during playtimes and even then I seem to remember that changed as we got older. The division was more about the different activities we had, but of course, nowadays girls can do whatever they want, but then most didn't want to play soccer with us, or maybe they did and we just didn't know. Anyway, the primary years were blissfully ignorant of the differences. Neil S came to school in Mr Kelly's Year 4 class and told us his mother had told him the facts of life and he recounted the basics to us. Most of us were shocked. I told him he was wrong, and that you had babies by kissing. The class had an impromptu vox pole and my side won overwhelmingly. It is a clear sign that I know very little, but I was quite good at arguing a case, even if I was wrong.

By the end of primary school things were changing and birthday parties started to include games such as 'Postman's Knock' and 'Spin the Bottle', when parents weren't supervising too closely, but a quick peck of a kiss was the total limit. At High School, things were changing. Hormones, I guess, were being produced and by the second year, boys were starting to become pimply, smelly, and hair appeared. I really can't understand what nice sensible girls find attractive in the spotty, silly oiks that teenage boys become, but I suppose it is good for the continuation of the species that there is something.

At Roundhay, small groups of girls would loiter on their side of the impenetrable barrier and it was surprising how often a soccer ball would end up in the bushes, thus allowing one lucky boy to be able to go and retrieve it. It often took a little longer than expected to find it and a short conversation might take place and an occasional note or message might be passed. It was all very much in the manner of the Colditz escape committee. Of course, there were also the camp warders, or in this case, teachers, who occasionally would take their lunchtime supervision seriously and pounce on any unfortunate lad or girl who was on the wrong side of the barrier. I am sure they laughed about it when they returned to the dense, smoke filled staffroom and reported to their comrades. Detentions, lines or other forms of torture might result, and if you were truly unlucky, it might be a prefect who caught you.

Prefects seemed to be of two sorts. Some were decent, understanding and had a sense of humour, the others were vicious, power-crazed sadists who delighted in catching anyone, and handed out pages of lines and prefect detentions like it was their birthday. I think it was this illustration of what power can do to the human spirit that made me sure that I would never take any position of authority lightly. As a Head Teacher for many years, (Principal in Australia and Papua New Guinea), I have always liked my students and staff and I hope that I have never abused my position. I suppose that is something for others to judge.

In the 1960s, I can't say that there was a lot of education preparing boys for growing up. Biology was the nearest we ever got to sex education, and that was purely functional and mechanical. I can't imagine it was easy for 'Sweaty Betty' or Mr Hyman to deal with an unruly group of adolescent boys who thought they knew everything, but in reality knew next to nothing. I am not sure if we covered reproduction in the Fifth or the Sixth Form. Someone will know!

The other potential source of information was from your parents. Now it is one thing listening to a teacher, but quite another having a talk about the facts of life with your parents. The nearest I ever got was my mum, saying, 'You've covered sex at school, haven't you?'

and her looking mighty relieved when I mumbled back, whilst turning red, that we had. It was a close call, but I managed to escape that ordeal and I am sure that she felt very much the same. As a result, Neil S was the total source of my knowledge up to that point.

We weren't to be put off and there was an irresistible urge to meet girls, and we didn't seem sure how. My older brother Andrew came to the rescue, but he probably never realised. He had started going to Saint Wilfrid's church at the back of Gipton. He also started attending the youth club there and, for some reason, he invited me to go. I can't ever remember having the urge to take my younger brother with me when I started going. It was held in what was then a new church hall. There was a reasonably large group of youths, boys and girls, a record player, table tennis and soft drinks on sale. I was younger than most there and didn't know anyone, but my brother allowed me to tag along. He was four years older and I can only think that my presence was like having a dog. People will stop and talk to you if you have a dog. I became a bit of a focus and I quite enjoyed myself. Everyone seemed so grown up and yet they were only in their middle teens. Nothing of note really happened, but it was good to watch the girls and see how the boys behaved. There was a lot of preening, but for most of the time, the boys would sit in groups on one side and the girls would dance in circles around their handbags.

After my first experience, I wanted more and even started to attend church, joined the choir and was confirmed. See what you will do for a way to meet girls!

Of course, there were youth clubs around Roundhay School, and I was invited to join a group of boys that was going to St. Edmund's youth club. I seem to remember it was a Tuesday night. This was going to be it. I did not know if I was an attractive youth, but I wanted more than anything to be one. I had few clothes apart from school uniform, but luckily my older brother did. I managed to sneak something a little bit trendier than a school jumper and shirt from his wardrobe, and I think I had about half a crown in cash. I can't remember where we met up, maybe at Roundhay Park gates, near the tennis courts, but a small group of us headed to St Edmund's. The church was familiar to us as we held the school Carol Services there, but the hall was large, dark stone and imposing. The group of us approached, walked past the public telephone box on the corner and followed the one boy who had been before into the hall.

There were small groups standing around outside and lights and noise of music coming from within the hall. The door was manned by leaders and we lined up, paid the fee and entered what, for a few years, was to be the centre of our social world.

David M Cameron

A TRIP TO THE DENTIST

I can't say what age I was when I went to the dentist the first time, but I do remember him well. Mr Gosling had his surgery on Easterly Road in a large house very close to the public toilets next to the Fforde Greene public house and across from the Clock Cinema. My first impression of the dentists was a waiting room that was cold and not particularly inviting for a child. There were some magazines for adults, but nothing for younger clients.

Mr Gosling was an elderly gentleman, or at least he appeared so to me. Anyone above the age of about twenty and all teachers seemed old. The dentist wore half-lens glasses that would have helped him with his near vision. Walking into the surgery was like walking through the gates of hell. It was full of cold, hard metal objects surrounding a leather chair that reclined only a little. So unlike the ones nowadays that recline to the point of being horizontal, with your head in the dentist's lap. In those days, you sat fairly upright and the dentist and assistant gathered around you in an intimidating manner. A bib was placed around your neck and you were instructed to open wide.

Of course, before leaving home, your teeth were given such a hard scrubbing to ensure no food remained and there was no chance of bad breath. Toothpaste in these days came in alloy tubes, not the plastic of today, and fluoride was not in the water and had just started appearing in the toothpaste. Pepsodent and the new super exciting Signal with a miraculous series of red stripes were the ones we had. 'You'll wonder where the yellow went, when you brush your teeth with Pepsodent', the adverts announced. It was only when I was much older that the toothpaste in these times had added sugar to make the flavour more palatable. Face and teeth suitably scrubbed, I opened my mouth with 'a ring of confidence', to be assaulted by a hand with a sharp pointed metal implement. Everything about the experience was alien to me. I had only ever had people show me kindness, and no adult had ever hurt me intentionally, a situation that changed as I entered high school, and so it was with a shock that this point would jab into gums, between teeth and into cavities that suddenly exploded with pain. This was probably my first realisation that life wasn't always good and that we could deteriorate as we got older. This discomfort was not aided by the fact that the dentist, Mr Gosling, had a habit of humming and whistling as he worked. His apparent good humour was not matched by my feelings, particularly when he announced to my mother that I needed a couple of fillings, and must ensure I regularly brushed my teeth.

Fillings! The word didn't mean much the first time, but ever after, it always brought fear. I was helpless, sitting open-mouthed and open-souled, totally unaware of what was about to happen. Strange stainless steel implements were arranged on the tray next to me, and suddenly a glass and steel syringe appeared in the dentist's hand. The word cocaine was mentioned and there was a sharp stab into my gum, and repeated at another point. I was shocked. I was left to stew for a while and my mouth became numb and this spread up to my nose. For some reason, I thought that was it. Oh, how wrong can you be?

He returned, and the pale mint green tower that I had noticed, a bit like a crane, was swung my way. He fiddled with the end and then, I assume with a foot switch, turned on the drill and the noise I can still hear now. The sound of a dentist's drill, particularly those used many years ago, has a special place in the fear section of the brain. The wail of a banshee holds no less terror and I challenge anyone not to share the same response to it, much the same as the scrape of fingernails on a blackboard. Ever since, there is nothing more likely to strike fear into the stoutest heart than sitting in a dentist's waiting room and hearing the sound of someone experiencing the drill. The dentist reached into my mouth whilst the assistant hung a miniature vacuum cleaner into my mouth. It wasn't comfortable and dug into the palate below the tongue, but I had no means or repositioning it and it just added to the misery. The drill whirled, water sprayed into my mouth, and the tooth began to disintegrate. I think he may have muttered, 'This won't hurt a bit!', but if he did. He lied. He whistled and inflicted torture and there was nothing I could do. I was helpless, at his mercy. It seemed like an eternity, but I am sure it was just a few minutes. The assistant was instructed to make up the amalgam filling, and she mixed and scraped off to the side. He stopped the drilling, told me to rinse my mouth out and then she handed him another tool and he squeezed the mixture into the tooth he had removed most of and then repeated it with the other. Sharp tools were then in his hand and there was scraping, the instruction to close my mouth, further scraping and then the final instruction to rinse my mouth out with the glass of water. The bib was suddenly whipped off, and I was told to get up, look after my teeth better, with regular brushing, and my mum and I left and walked home. My forehead was numb at this point and when we arrived at home and I was given some orange juice, I found I couldn't drink it, as it dribbled from between my numb lips. It seemed a very long time before the numbness went and life could return to normal.

We changed dentists, at some point, to another on Easterley Road, halfway up the hill and on the opposite side. Having grown accustomed to fillings, I was no longer quite as terrified. This was also helped by improved treatment techniques, equipment, and painkillers. There was one experience I had not had up to this point, and that was an extraction. I can't remember why I was needing a tooth removed. I was sitting in the chair, tense and afraid, when the dentist said,

'I'm just going to give you a little gas. You'll just be a little woozy. Just try to relax. Nothing to worry about!'

A black rubber facemask was clamped over my nose and mouth. There was the strong smell and taste of what is Nitrous Oxide, laughing gas, and I breathed in and knew no more until suddenly faces appeared, swirling around my consciousness, accompanied by a dull ache, and the taste of blood.

'That's it now, David. All done!'

The words of the dentist and the smile of the assistant, and it was all over.

'Rinse your mouth out.'

I did as I was told and then turned to see the concerned look on my mother's face.

Another Cup of Tea – The Teenage Years

'Now don't eat or drink for a couple of hours and then you should be as right as rain!'

I think I may have had gas another time, but I am not sure why, unless they removed double first teeth, but later when I was at the end of primary school at Harehills I had double teeth removed to allow for overcrowding, but this was not with gas.

When I saw the dentist with the overcrowding, they decided I needed a brace on a plate for three months or so to straighten my teeth. I returned to get the plate fitted on the day I was to attend a birthday party of a girl in my class. The brace was fitted, and it was tight. I was shown how to remove it and it was quite difficult and uncomfortable, but then I headed off to the party. I was very embarrassed, and to make matters worse, I could barely speak with it in. I really didn't enjoy the party and I could only nod and just about managed to say yes or no. I believe we may have played postman's knock, but as you can guess, I don't think I was anyone's first choice.

Older still, we continued our progression up Easterley Road and moved to a dentist at the top of the hill and back on the other side of the road. It was a large corner house, and we went there for many years. One thing I remember was that when I was old enough to go on my own, I was instructed to sign a blank form for the treatment before anything was done. I can only think of one reason for this and that was dentist were paid by the National Health for the work carried out and who knows what work was claimed? This seemed to be the general practice of all the dentists I had, and I also think there was an encouragement for extra work to be undertaken. In my adult life, I don't remember the constant need for fillings to be re-done regularly, but the early ones seemed to require this. Maybe I am just getting cynical in my old age, but the payment for work system seems to encourage unnecessary treatment.

Modern dentistry is painless and not as scary for me now, and I wonder if children share similar experiences to those we did in the 1950s-60s?

PASSION, EXTREMES AND HAIR

My memories of childhood are all good ones, with the odd bit of trouble thrown in, but my teenage years were a much more extreme time in my life. I suppose this was, and is, the same for many teenagers, and I must have been a challenge for my parents. I had the fortune of being the second of three boys, and I think my older brother had worn my parents out so that they were more relaxed when I hit puberty. My brother had, from what I had witnessed, been quite an easy teenager, but I suppose he carried all our mother's hopes. He also wanted to become a vicar and almost did, which suggests he wasn't a really challenging lad.

I, on the other hand, was suddenly overcome with an awakening that was far from subtle. Physical and psychological changes arrived early and my first memories are of noticing hair growing in places it never had before. This became a monumental embarrassment and a variety of techniques were employed to avoid others detecting this during changing for school sport and PE. My voice also started to change, and I left St. Wilfrid's in Harehills choir for two major reasons. The first was that Mr Benton, the choirmaster, weeded out the croakers, and the second was that I discovered something much more interesting than singing in a church choir. Girls! Suddenly I was noticing them and the thought of having a girlfriend dominated my waking moments.

As I have mentioned before, St Edmund's youth club and Lidgett Lane Methodist youth club became my social areas and opportunity to fraternise. I have told of my belief that being dark, brooding and mysterious would somehow attract the interest of pretty girls, but of course no one had told girls that this was the case, and I was just ignored. I was saved eventually by the chance meeting with Peter, John, and a new circle of slightly older boys. For some reason, we hit it off and shared our passion for music, both listening and later, playing. This was the late 1960s and early 1970s and the stars aligned in it being a time of musical and social revolution. The sixties believed that love could save the world and, despite a realisation that this was unlikely, music went through a heyday of creativity and technological advancement.

At high school, I was moving from compliance to a time of questioning. I became far more discerning and realised that some teachers were fantastic, some were not and some were pretty unpleasant and should never have been allowed to enter the profession as they despised children and, in particular, teenage boys. The 'Dark Sarcasm in the Classroom' wasn't the problem, it was the violence that was meted out. Part of the challenging of authority was the bending and ignoring of rules. This was the time of long hair and it was the length of hair that mattered, rather than the style. The school rule was that hair shouldn't reach below the shirt collar and some teachers would inspect and enforce this rigorously, whereas others turned a blind eye. A warning to not return to school without it being cut was commonplace, but so was the avoiding of the teacher and hair being tucked inside the shirt collar, to offer token compliance. If you were lucky, you got away with it. If not, higher authority might issue the same warning not to return without it being cut. In these cases, a very light trim might occur, whilst you hoped their focus would be on other worse offenders.

Looking at the photographs from the time, they did have a point. We were a scruffy, wild-haired lot that I can't imagine why any girl would find us attractive. There was no attempt at style and the hair was just allowed to explode. I was lucky for a few years. I had hair that had a wave and I grew it to the middle of my back, when straightened, but alas, not for long. Within a short time, it was waving bye-bye. I still miss my old friend: the hair blowing in the wind, the warm feeling it gave as it stroked your face. Mine was soft and fly away, and fly away it did in my late teens! It still is a sadness, after all these years. Of course, now, in my dotage, hair sprouts from every conceivable place that you don't want it to. Shaving ears, trimming the nose, back hair removal and two inch long eyebrows. Time offers just one mercy, and that is that our eyesight dims and close-up vision blurs, or is it just a cruel trick of ageing? I still remember a young teacher at the school I was principal at, reaching over, grasping a two-inch eyebrow hair and pulling it out. She stood there with an embarrassingly long hair, saying,

"I've been watching that for two weeks."

"Well, I wish you'd said something two weeks ago," I replied.

But I digress! After being one of the first to develop 'hair', it wasn't long before others caught up and facial hair then became a thing of desire. It was the sign that you had become a man. It didn't matter if it was a mere whisper of 'bum fluff' across the top lip. You were a man! Of course, it was another red rag to a bull for some teachers. "Get that shaved off, boy!" became a common catch-cry. There was real division between the boys with faces like a baby's bottom, those with a bit of peach fluff and those with a thick, bristle-like stubble. One boy, John, had hair so dark and thick he needed to shave twice a day at thirteen and hair spouted over his collar from his chest, but unfortunately his head became the first to don a friar's pate before he left the sixth form.

I remember the first time I had a shave. I just used my dad's razor, a Wilkinson's Sword blade, shaving brush of badger bristles, and his shaving soap. (They used Badger hair as it had good water retention. The bristles were three colours, which I believe is unique in the animal kingdom.) I had watched him use it when I was little and copied the ritual. It was exciting, but little did I realise it was to be an everyday chore for the rest of my life. Nowadays it is disposal blades, electric razors or fancy oils and shaving foam or gel, but it was just soap in those times.

With shaving came the ability to sculpt the facial foliage into patterns to attract the female species: mutton-chop sideboards, rakish moustaches were attempted, but goatee beards were a no-go as one teacher had one and no one wanted to be like him. John, with the dense hair, sported a full moustache in the style of Peter Wyngarde, Jason King, and was quite dapper. To tell the truth, though, I can't ever say I was keen on my moustache. I remember it being a trap for food and drink, and I don't know many girls who found the experience of snogging a toilet brush desirable.

After saying this, two of my friends have maintained their versions for most of their lives and their wives must have found them alluring, or maybe they have tolerated them. Sideboards, I felt, had more going for them and at various times they have been bigger, longer and during the eighties, pointy in the Midge Ure, Ultravox style. I have had various attempts at a beard, and in fact, I had one when I married, but I can't say I have ever found them comfortable and the daily ritual of shaving has been maintained for the vast majority of my days so far.

Roundhay School did not like facial hair and the masters would make examples of certain boys. I am not sure why, but they didn't pick on me very often and I attempted the full gamut of styles over the early years. After the dismal failure of the deep thinker approach to attracting females, the trendy, hairy musician proved more successful. I never remember my parents commenting on my hair or wanting me to have it cut, but I seem to remember that my older brother suffered in this respect. Maybe it was because they thought I was a lost cause. I don't know if my younger brother had any issues with his hair length and I must ask him next time we speak. As I have said, my locks didn't last beyond high school, but some suffered at a younger age. The only positive is it has saved me a lot of time with grooming and haircuts, enabled me to avoid head lice during my teaching career and, of course, bald men are always attractive!

David M Cameron

WHAT FOOLISH THINGS

I suppose that the real awakening of adolescence was the realisation that you could find others attractive and that others could find you so. Up to this point in my life, I don't ever really remember it entering my consciousness. You could be successful in certain activities, sport or otherwise, and that was a nice feeling and, of course, your relatives loved you. If you were lucky, that was a given.

I remember Harehills C.P. School having some sort of talent competition when I was in my last year and I put myself forward to do some magic tricks. I had been bought a box of tricks from a toy shop on the way back from Hornsea and I think the shop was in the town of Beverley. There were a few simple tricks, a magic wand and I practised at home. The problem with performing to a large audience was that it needed to be visible and most tricks were one on one. Anyway, I made coins disappear into a glass of water, was able to predict the card that someone picked and other simple tricks. At the performance we had dancers, singers, possibly Paul and Barry Ryan, people playing instruments and my tricks. It went better than I expected and it probably set me up for a life in entertainment, hence a career in teaching. There was something good in being the centre of attention and, as a teenager, I reckoned it was better to be noticed and disliked than just be ignored.

My arrival at St. Edmund's Youth Club was the real start of attempting to get myself noticed. Youth clubs at these times were fairly basic. There would be a record deck with current hits belting out, table tennis, some dancing, but mainly girls around their bags, and a lot of preening, strutting and nervous introductions. Some people appeared to be naturally cool, and they were the ones we all aspired to emulate. The cool kids just had that something, and whatever it was, we all wanted it, or even just a little bit. As I have mentioned before, I can't see what girls found attractive in teenage boys, but I was certainly interested in this beautiful alien species of girls. Apparently girls from Roundhay School had perused the boys, maybe from a distance through the bushes, or at Oakwood or at the shops outside the girls' school entrance, but I can't say that I knew many, apart from the one or two from primary school. The other disadvantage I had was being from a family of boys. Two brothers were not a great help in understanding, nor conversing with girls, and so I was one of those who stood embarrassed. This being said, I wasn't really a shrinking violet either. I wanted to be cool and that meant acting and looking the part. In these times, my wardrobe, and most other boys' wardrobes, was fairly bare. We had a school uniform, and I had managed to persuade my mother that I needed a pair of jeans. There were only two brands that most of us would be seen in and they were Levi's, the number one choice and then Wranglers. Not quite Levi's, but cheaper and still fashionable. I think my first pair of Levi's cost about five pounds, and that was a not insubstantial amount of money. Other clothing was often ex-army, such as navy trench coats, denim shirt or t-shirts. I was fortunate that I could nick my older brother's gear if he was out, and that helped to make me look less nerdy.

My school friends at the time were Chris M, Stuart S, Roger H and Anthony I, and we were gaining a reputation that was not altogether wholesome. We became regulars at St. Edmund's and then started branching out. Lidgett Lane Methodist was the nearest, and it became our home base. I remember there were two male leaders, and they were fantastic to put up with all they did. For some reason, Lidgett had a wider circle of members and there was the old hall building and the new hall and one or two other rooms and a kitchen. Both Lidgett and St Edmund's became venues for our teenage rock band, where we could practise and perform over the next few years.

I suppose the church youth club was to provide a safe environment for teenagers to meet, and potentially to recruit youngsters into the specific faith. I feel very fortunate that they existed as there don't seem to be the same options for youngsters nowadays, apart from hanging in shopping malls and the streets.

These youth clubs would arrange occasional dances, activities and excursions, and I am very grateful for the leaders who put up with me and my friends and tolerated our chaotic years. I never saw the leaders lose their patience, and they had a lot to contend with. Sometimes rival groups would send a posse looking for trouble and yet, on the whole, serious conflict was avoided.

So I was kitted out the best I could be and there was a 'do' at a church club off the Ring Road at Moortown Corner. I had borrowed one of my late grandfather's pipes and had a pouch of tobacco. I had loved the smell of his pipe and thought it might add something to my maturity and charm. I had never smoked one, but how hard could it be? I had also come up with a theory. Girls would find me far more appealing, mysterious and attractive if I sat by myself looking morose, puffing on a pipe. As you can imagine, with this recipe for success, how could I fail to win fair lady? I can't remember the date exactly, but I Can't Help Myself was played endlessly, so it would have been after April 1965. The Four Tops may not have been able to help themselves, but clearly the girls at the club managed to and by the end of the night, two things happened. One, I was feeling dreadfully sick and vowed never to smoke a pipe again, and two, I left without a female companion.

You are probably thinking 'Silly Fool', and you would be right, but did I learn? No! I tried this same foolproof method to attract girls for a surprisingly long time, before I gave up this strategy. It never worked, but I know I wasn't alone in believing that this approach would be successful. I knew others that used it for years, with a similar rate of success.

So what next did I try, I bet you are wondering, and was it more successful? Well, I guess the answer was, yes, it was more successful, but then it could hardly have been less so. Music and pop stardom, well, a little notoriety. It had worked for the Stones, the Beatles, the Pretty Things. Why shouldn't it work for me?

It was a chance encounter that changed everything for me. One evening at Lidgett Methodist Youth Club, a group of older lads arrived. There was one clear leader of the pack and he had a long black coat and long black floppy hair (and still does). He was tall, lean, and had a presence that was undeniably attractive. Now he was cool! Somehow I got talking with his group and wandered down afterwards to the edge of the Soldiers' Field and sat and stood around a wooden bench. We found that we got on well. They were not from Roundhay, but were Allerton Grange lads. We talked about music, and we seemed to have similar tastes. Within his group was another lad, Roger, and our lives have been mysteriously linked over the years to where we now live, two hundred yards away from each other in Perth, Western Australia. The rest I had no great affinity for and one tried to start a fight with me, which Pete put a quick stop to.

We met up the following week at either St Edmund's or the Methodist's, as we called Lidgett Lane, and we got to know each other quite well. Pete lived in a large terraced house at Harehills, off Harehills Lane, near Potternewton Park, and he had an old cellar with its own entrance to the yard. I was invited round, and we used to sit and listen to his record collection.

Pete also had an acoustic guitar. Stuart S and I were there and Pete played a song that was a current hit. Neanderthal Man, by Hot Legs, later to become half of 10CC. The year was 1970. It really was one chord, a rhythm and a chant. Needless to say, he could play it and we sang it. We must have thought there was something in it, as it was suggested, probably by Pete, that we form a band. I was all for it. The complication of not having an instrument and not being able to play one was not going to hold me back. It was a chance encounter and a decision that has had a profound impact on my life, Pete's and later another friend, John's, lives.

THE CLOCK, THE CELLAR, AND THE PAINT THAT NEVER DRIED

Now, whilst my social life had taken over from any real attempt to learn anything at Roundhay School, there was more to it than just youth clubs. The regular meeting place was often the Oakwood Clock. The clock was built in 1904 by Potts and Sons and was designed by Leeming and Leeming for the Leeds Market, but because of alterations at the market, it ended up at Oakwood. (Strange that I now live in the suburb of Leeming in Perth, Western Australia.) The clock tower originally had the road and tram lines running on either side of it before the road was relocated to its present position and crossroads.

We used to meet there on the benches after school, later in the evening, before heading to the youth clubs or to parties. On some evenings, we gathered and seemed to spend the entire night there. As I have said before, I was a smoker in these days and I thought I looked cool standing against one of the poles, striking a match and a pose. It must have fooled some people, as I was quite popular with the girls.

One incident has stuck with me all my days since. For young readers, you may not know that matches were the most common form of lighting cigarettes and more common than the safety matches, where you had to strike them on the band on the box. This prevented them lighting by mistake. Non-safety matches had a sandpaper strip on the box and they could be lit by friction alone. Swan Vesta was a popular make and the name always intrigued me. To keep the story on task, these could be lit off a variety of surfaces and some were thought to be cool. The zip on your Levis was one such surface and a quick flick, flash and flare would impress anyone, and could also set your trousers alight if you snapped the match. I had tried this, but hadn't really mastered it to the point where it didn't just look weird. I was sitting on the bench below the clock waiting for friends to arrive. I decided to have a cigarette and struck the match on the bench itself. The first time it failed, so I tried it again. You need to know that the bench was old, painted park green, and the wood was uneven and split. Moving your bottom whilst sitting on it often resulted in a nasty splinter through the seat of your pants. You are probably guessing where this story is leading. The match was forcefully struck against the wood. There was a flash, but then the match snapped and my finger came into contact with the wood. It slid in the direction of the strike, which was just right for a very large pointy, splinter of wood to stab my finger just below the nail of my index finger and continue well into the finger just and, in fact, beyond the length of the nail, and held my finger to the bench seat.

If you have ever hurt yourself in public, then there appears to be a hierarchy of responses. The first is that all sound ceases, quickly followed by a warm flush that passes from below the waist to your head. The pain comes last, but is none the less for it. I realised very quickly why bamboo under the fingernails was a popular form of torture, as I was in agony. I seem to remember jumping up in reflex, which was unfortunate, as the splinter snapped off the bench and remained under my fingernail. The other reaction that seems to override all others is wondering whether anyone has seen you hurt yourself. Pride is such an important human quality and embarrassment is almost worse than pain. After trying to impress, the opposite had happened, but luckily for me, it appeared no one had noticed the dancing youth under the clock, grasping his hand with tears in his eyes, stifling a scream.

I sat down and, despite not wanting to, had a look at what I had done. I was sitting there, cigarette on the ground, bench covered in the discarded matchbox and surrounded by unused matches. I looked at my finger. A spike of wood, half a pencil thick at the wide end, protruded from my finger for half an inch. I had to do something, and I knew what it was. The spell had to come out. (Spelk in Scotland and North England from Old Norse Spellker.) I didn't want to do it, but the pain was increasing. I grabbed hold with my left hand and pulled. It didn't want to come, but I knew I could only manage to give it one try, and so I gave it an almighty tug. I could feel it slip out, tugging at the flesh surrounding it as if it wanted to inflict as much pain as possible. I think the agony of it coming out was worse than that of it going in. I sobbed to myself, trying to keep the pain in. Somehow, it went unnoticed. The wood was almost an inch long, and the finger throbbed, but the initial agony began to subside. I thought I had it all out, but I wasn't sure. There was nothing else I could do but gather my matches up, strike a match on the box and light a cigarette and moan to myself.

I clearly hadn't extracted all the wood, as over many years small slivers would work their way from beneath the nail to a point where it allowed me to get tweezers on them and pull the piece out. I think it took twenty years for all the wood to make its way out. You would have thought that I would have learnt from such a lesson, but unfortunately not, and I continued to smoke until the age of 23.

Apart from the Oakwood Clock, the other meeting place was Pete's cellar. Peter lived at Harehills and his house had a cellar with an external entry. The cellar was only used to store coal in one room at the time and so Peter turned it into his lair, den or whatever word best describes it. He had some old furniture in it and it had electricity and we set about decorating it to meet the wants of teenagers in the 1960s. It had bare brick, distempered walls and Pete collected a range of partially used tins of paint. To ensure there was enough, the paint was mixed together. Now, I realise that there was a mixture of gloss paint and emulsion, but I didn't know anything about painting and decorating at the time. Pete's parents didn't seem to mind, as it hadn't ever been used and we were clearing it out. The resulting paint colour was a streaky battleship grey, and we set to with gusto. Eventually, it was completed, and we sat back and admired our handiwork. The fumes were strong, so we quickly evacuated it and went out for the rest of the day. The following night, we gathered to inspect the work. It looked ok, in a wild hippy bohemian way, but some parts had dried and others were still quite tacky. Time would dry it, we thought. How wrong we were! Even after a couple of years, clothes could be ruined if you brushed up against the walls. I can't say we really cared, but eventually Peter's father had the cellar renovated and turned into a flat. I hate to think what the workmen would have said to each other about our decorating.

Now we had Pete's Pad, we had to furnish it. Pete's stereo found a home there and, to add to the ambience, a couple of Harehills black and white cast-iron street signs appeared and then the obligatory flashing yellow roadwork warning lights. It looked fantastic. Some hanging fabric just gave it that little something. I think we even had a couple of Mateus Rose bottles with bulbs in them as lamps. The few of us present sat listening to the Moody Blues, Days of Future Passed, King Crimson and Led Zeppelin II. It was perfect. Peter went upstairs and collected whatever alcohol his parents had. There was some Schnapps, and this was mixed with some wine and assorted spirits in a large bowl. The concoction was christened Rocket Fuel, for obvious reasons, as one mouthful nearly blew your head off. The night was a great success, even if our heads didn't agree the next morning, and our clothes carried the painted stains as a reminder, it was the start of an important era in our lives.

By the way, we learnt to hate the flashing lights as you couldn't turn them off, or at least we couldn't, and I think we returned them. Similar ones always seemed to be present at student parties wherever you went to one.

ILLICIT FAGS, BOOZE, AND THE FINGER INCIDENT

Roundhay School did have a number of organised events for the boys and I know that the Girls' School had many as well. Some were less educational than others and included skiing trips, French exchanges and an educational cruise on SS Uganda. A number of my friends went on these, but unfortunately I never did as they were too expensive for our family. This was never a real disappointment, as I just accepted the reality of the situation. What I did go on, though, were the lower key educational geography field trips. There were two climbing weekends, one in Snowdonia and another in the Lake District, but the first of these was to Cromer in Norfolk.

I think we were about thirteen at the time and the field trip was for two nights. Letters for those interested were issued by the Geography teachers and I took mine home, got my parents to sign it and return it with the modest fee. This was quite exciting, as it was one of my first trips away from home without parents or relatives. I know I was very keyed up when the time came. Most of my friends were attending, and we had plotted how we would have fun. Contraband had been purchased and hidden within our luggage, and we also had a small amount of cash.

As a long-serving teacher, I have been on many school camps and excursions, and I take my hat off to the brave teachers who took a coach full of early teenage boys on a trip to Norfolk. The one thing I can say about the Roundhay field trip was that the agenda was not one that would wind up the boys to a state of frenzied excitement. Dour is the word I would use to describe the programme. The well-meaning teachers intended for us to learn a great deal about the features of this part of the United Kingdom, and I am sure that they planned the trip to meet their own interests and aims. The shame was that they were not the interests and aims of the boys at this stage of their lives. I suppose I can't speak for all the boys and to do so would be unfair, but I can speak for my circle of mates. We were interested in girls, smoking, drinking and music and probably in that order. As Roundhay was a boys' school at that point in time, the first item was not really an option unless there was some local talent just waiting for some spotty oiks from the big city. This item was crossed off our mental list, at least until we saw what Cromer's nightlife might be like, but we were nothing if not hopeful.

The morning of the trip, we arrived at school together with our luggage and I don't think we had to wear our school uniform, which was an added bonus. Mr Templeton and the other teachers were already organising the luggage near the bins under the coach, and we deposited ours, climbed on board, and took seats near the back with our mates. The back row was the prime location and any nerdy child would quickly be shown the error of their ways if they had taken the seat wanted by a more alpha male. A quick slap around the ear would demonstrate the child's folly and they would quickly escape to a seat nearer the front and the teachers. Of course, most were aware of this and had learnt to avoid the punishment, but some were poor learners and some wanted to raise their status by challenging the pecking order. They knew they may not be successful, but they wished to put themselves forward as future stags and a little sparring was part of the game.

Eventually, the seating was sorted and order restored. This process happened on any outing and was even more interesting when new boys had joined the school, or when someone had had an impressive growth spurt. It could be quite brutal, especially on rugby away games, where various year groups were transported together. I remember at least one occasion when a boy's underpants were forcefully removed and thrown out of the window as a lesson for impudence towards older boys. The amazing thing was that this occurred without the teachers at the front being aware of what was happening, or not willing to intervene. Pastoral care of students was not really in the teachers' handbook in the 1960s. 'Toughen up laddie!' was more the attitude, and it was survival of the fittest.

Anyway, on this occasion the order was settled, roll call was taken and off we went. Sweets were stuffed into faces and within a relatively short time, one or two required the sick bucket. No sympathy was shown by staff or fellow students, and an attitude of 'You'll learn!' was prevalent. The journey was long. The coach driver had warned us what would happen to us if we messed up his bus. I can't remember his name, but from my experience, they always seem to be called Barry. He actually seemed a decent sort and when requested, he put on the air conditioning which came through vents above each seat when you pulled down what looked like a thermos flask top. The air did help alleviate the travel sickness, and no one dared not ask for, or miss the bucket, as they knew that to do so meant they would have to clean up the bus later.

The roads in the 1960s were not built for speed and there were always hold-ups at various bottlenecks, but eventually we started driving through quite a different landscape. For a start, it was flat, not a hill in sight. As we entered Norfolk, the teachers began to give us a running commentary on the geographical features we were passing through. They explained how the land was drained and reclaimed, but prone to flooding. I can see that you are impressed that I have retained some of the knowledge. In fact, I loved geography and, in particular, physical geography. It explained why the land looked like it did. We made a stop at a small hill. Hill, you may ask, in Norfolk? And the teachers did ask, and I seem to remember it was the mound of an early Norman Castle. A quick walk up and down and we were flagging. Back on the bus and we were heading for the place we were staying.

We arrived at our accommodation and I remember this quite impressive old building that was a hotel. It must have fallen on harder times for it to take school groups such as ours. We were allocated rooms with our friends and it didn't take us long to check outside the window. Below us was the glass roof of the dining room. It was like an old conservatory with sections of reinforced glass panels. They were the type with chicken wire. We had to sort out our bags and our first concern was to hide the contraband. The most obvious place was the gutters outside the windows and as I looked out to the adjoining rooms, some boys were depositing bottles of cider or beer there. It wasn't a good place for cigarettes, as if it rained they would get soaked. I ducked back in and searched around the room. As I have said, the building was very old, and it didn't take me and my roommates long to see that the old floorboards offered possibilities. We levered one up and stashed our fags, matches, and grog. When replaced, the floorboard looked just as it had. We were savvy enough to leave half a packet of Number 6 cigarettes and matches in the gutter outside the window for any checking teacher to find.

After this, we were instructed to wash and to get down for the evening meal. I remember little washing, but we headed down to eat. I remember the food was good and plentiful. The noise was fairly deafening, but the teachers didn't seem to mind. I noticed that two staff slipped out of the dining room and our warning antennae suspected the rooms were being raided. Within twenty minutes, the teachers returned with assorted contraband. There was a stern telling off, and all material was confiscated. I can only imagine the staff's smokes and drink was supplemented by the boys' supply.

There was a meeting where we were told about the next day's programme. We were also set to work writing up the day's programme and what we had learnt. The work was done and then we checked our rooms. We were lucky and our floorboard stash had not been discovered, but the gutter was clear. At lights out we waited until we thought it was safe and then lifted the floorboard and leaned out of the window smoking and sharing some drink. Other windows were open and someone decided it would be a good idea to go into another room. The light was still on in the dining room below. But that was not going to stop us. I seem to believe it was Steve L who was the first to traverse the glass roof to the adjoining window and room. It seemed to support him alright and someone else tried it, but this time there was a cracking noise. The boy on the glass beat a very hasty retreat, and that was the end of that. Luckily, there were no obvious signs of damage and further inter-room movement was managed by creeping along the corridors. Staff did patrol and the excuse of a bathroom break seemed to convince the, either gullible or not really caring teacher that all was well. I can't remember a lot of sleeping that first night.

After a good breakfast, we were ready for our full day, and it truly was a full day. We went everywhere, learnt about the coast, longshore drift, the purpose of groynes, farming in the area and some of its industrial past. We were excursioned out by the time we got back, and famished.

We had some work to do writing up about the day's events and visits, but we were told that we would be able to take a trip to Cromer for part of the evening, thanks to the kindness of the coach driver. Later in the evening, with spirits high, we all boarded the coach and took our places. Unfortunately, before we could drive off, there was a call from towards the back. A boy, who shall remain nameless but etched in the memory, had his finger stuck in the air vent above his head. Now when I say stuck, I mean stuck. It was lodged firmly and no amount of effort would free it. We were all getting frustrated as our visit to Cromer became delayed. We were ready to get out a penknife and remove the offending finger, but the bus driver was a more kindly man than us. He began to dismantle the vent using a screwdriver. The design has probably been much improved on, but on this occasion the panel was the whole length of the coach and it took almost an hour to remove it and free the lad's finger. There were calls of support from the boys. Of course, I am lying, as we were livid, but eventually he was freed, the panel replaced and we were told we could still go, but the time would be shortened to an hour. This was better than nothing, and off we went.

The bright lights of Cromer were very disappointing, or at least they were then. There was hardly anything to it apart from a bit of a pier and we wandered around aimlessly and saw no local talent that would be interested in a spotty youth. I think we got some chips. Eventually, we got back on the bus and returned. That night, we had some smokes and a bit of a drink, but not much.

The next day saw a morning of visits and more note taking and field drawings, and then the return journey began. Clearly, some of the geographical purpose of the trip was successful, but it was everything else about the trip to Cromer that has stuck with me all these years.

THE LAST BUS HOME

I went on buses from the age of four with my brother, who was four years older than me. We used to go from Arlington Road junction with Easterly Road down to Harehills and there we would catch a bus across from the Yorkshire Penny Bank outside the Building Society. The bus there took us from Harehills along to Stainbeck Lane every day, to and from Stainbeck Preparatory School. Nowadays, my mother would be seen as an awful parent, allowing her young children to take such a trip, but then things were very different, and in her defence, we never had any trouble and always arrived safely back at the end of the day.

The buses in those days were double-deckers with a platform at the back used for getting on and off. There was a silver bar to allow people to hold on to it, but the rest was completely open. Most people got about by bus, as cars were an expensive luxury, but were becoming cheaper and more common. There was a narrow staircase that led to the top deck, and this section was reserved for smokers and those who didn't mind the foul smell of old tobacco and nicotine. The prime seat for us boys was the very front on the top deck; this was near to the sign for a hypnotherapist, who could apparently cure a whole range of conditions: fear of heights and smoking, and the sign that said, 'Spitting is forbidden'. Now, I saw no one spitting, but often heard people clearing their throats. If the bus was full, as they often were, then the upstairs would be filled with a cloud of smoke, which was thick and choking. The movement of the bus was much greater upstairs and there was an optical illusion that you were wider than the base of the bus and this made you feel you were almost falling. The swaying and the smoke often made me feel quite ill before we got to school.

There was a conductor on the bus at these times and they would sell tickets and had a special dispensing machine that I loved. The way they pressed the lever with their thumb, and the ticket or tickets shot out, and then were ripped off with a well-practised flourish, was wonderful. Even more intriguing was the coin dispenser. Coins were slotted into a series of almost like gun magazines on the conductor's belt, and again, they flicked out the change with perfected ease. When they had a down-time, they would spend their time refilling the magazines, or counting coins, rolling them into paper and wrapping them in measured tubes. They would then put them in their black metal briefcases and store them away. I suppose they had to do a daily reckoning to match tickets with money taken, and they could save themselves time at the end of the shift.

I used to envy the conductors, but the drivers in their cabs at the front I never gave a thought to. Some conductors tried to impress the ladies and the young lads with the ease they could move around the bouncing bus, run up and down the steps, hang off the bar at the back, and were lords of their domain. They reminded me of the lads on the dodgems at the fairground or those on the Waltzers. The thing that impressed me the most was the power that they had. They would put an arm out to stop any more passengers getting on when the bus was full, and everyone just followed instructions and, without grumbling, waited for the next bus. Some wouldn't let children go upstairs, and looking back, they were probably right to do so; some were surly and intimidating, and some were warm and fun. I even remember some singing opera or show songs and they had quite good voices.

The thing that I always wanted to do was to ring the bell. The bells were bright red buttons with a white plastic surround that said, 'Press once to stop'. There was something so appealing and I don't know why. Maybe Freud would offer some suggestions about complexes and repressed feelings, but I have no idea.

I caught the bus with my brother until he started high school, but I then had to do the journey on my own until I was eight and started at Harehills County Primary. Again, I had no problems and would sit sensibly and wait to get off. The only issues were when buses were full and then you had to stand and some drivers were fast and the bus used to rock about. If you were an adult, then you could hold on to leather loops that fitted onto a bar running the length of the bus, but kids had to hang onto anything, and that was often the back of the chairs which had a silver rail. In these days, it was drummed into children that you had to give up a seat to ladies or elderly people, particularly the parallel bench seats near the platform. I am not sure that would be approved of nowadays as women are independent and equal to men, but certainly, elderly people would still benefit and appreciate a bit of kindness.

Double-decker buses were used by Harehills to take us to sport on the Soldiers' Field and to swimming, and on these occasions we boys would rush to get on the top deck, but Mr Kelly would often choose who he would allow such a privilege. He knew who would misbehave, and he put a veto on them.

The worst time to be on the bus was after school in winter, when it was dark. It was very difficult to see out through the steamed-up windows and much worse when it was also thick fog. At these times, it was hard to tell where you were and I occasionally got off too early or past my stop and had a long walk.

I have spoken about the joys of hanging off the back bar, waiting for the bus to slow to the exact speed where you could jump off, hit the ground running, and come to a graceful stop and carry on walking. When done well, it was magic, but when you misjudged it, a face full of gravel could be the result, added to by a good dose of shame.

When I was going to youth clubs at Lidgett Lane and St Edmund's, the mode of transport was still the bus. We weren't old enough to drive, and we wouldn't have had access to a car anyway, so a bus or a lift from my dad were the only options, and the bus was by far the most common. Waiting for buses became a regular part of life and when in a group it wasn't too bad and we could chat, play the fool or talk about music, girls, or anything we were interested in. When the weather was good and it was summer, this didn't matter, but it could be dire in winter when it was freezing, raining and blowing a gale. Nothing we wore ever seemed to be waterproof, and that included my shoes. I always had holes in them, or they were splitting and wet feet added to the misery; even the trench coats that became the must-have fashion of the time could only deal with so much, but at least they were warm and long, almost touching the ground.

The other thing was that we were quite happy to walk, and I remember nights trudging back from Alwoodley all the way to Oakwood and then to my house. This was a bit of an exception, as we generally socialised around Moortown Corner, Roundhay, and Harehills.

Other haunts were the Judean Club and friends' houses all around this part of Leeds. We got to know the bus routes and knew when the buses should run, but there was often a long wait. The last bus on whatever route was the thing that we knew most. We would try to ensure we didn't miss it, but a wait at the stop, only to realise the bus had come early and that we had missed it, became a fairly common occurrence. Even worse was when you thought you had missed it and started walking and then saw it drive past a few minutes later. This had such an impact on us that our band had a song, written by Peter, called The Last Bus, and this song resonated with our audiences, as we shared the anguish of knowing that you had a long walk home.

Before we had access to cars, we had to carry instruments and amps on public transport, and I wonder what the conductors thought when we would pile on, carrying guitars and clambering upstairs. On many routes, 10.20pm was a common cut off, which would be very early for young people nowadays. I think there were later buses at the weekend, but even when we went to Leeds Poly for the discos, concerts, or just for drinking and playing snooker, it was fairly imperative that we caught the last bus. There was a great sense of achievement when you took your seat and you knew that some of your friends had missed it, even if it meant you had to leave the concert before the final encore.

The double-decker bus even made it onto films with Cliff Richard in 'Summer Holiday' in 1963, as a group of young people drove in a bus to Europe. I remember seeing the film and it starts in black and white, but changes to colour when they arrive on the continent. Another series linked to the double-decker was the TV series 'On The Buses'. This sitcom ran from 1969 to 1973 and starred Reg Varney. It was very popular at the time, but much of its content would now be frowned upon as inappropriate.

But before long the bus experience changed. Modern buses with folding doors and only a driver took over, and the magic and challenge of our youth disappeared. To add to this, we got access to cars, either by owning them, or by borrowing our parents' cars. This was a sure sign of growing up, becoming independent, and no longer being at the mercy of timetables and drivers that wouldn't stop because they didn't like the look of you. Cars were much more personal and allowed romance to blossom, whereas there was nothing romantic about a snog on the upstairs of a smelly bus.

LET THE MUSIC PLAY

My first memory of listening to music was on our radio. This largish piece of furniture was wooden, had valves that lit up and dials that magically tuned in to radio frequencies, something that is still a mystery to me today. My favourite programme was Children's Favourites, which ran from 1954 until 1984, and it had a range of songs that have stuck with me all my life. These included Nellie the Elephant, They're Changing Guard at Buckingham Palace, The Owl and the Pussycat, The Laughing Policeman, Sparky's Magic Piano and many others. Mum and my brothers got to know the songs by heart and we would all join in.

As we got older, our tastes changed. Having an older brother helped as he became interested in the pop music of the time. Hearing the more up-to-date songs was not easy and often meant trying to tune in to the pirate radio stations, such as Radio Luxembourg and Radio Caroline. We had a friend near our house in Gipton Wood Crescent who had a crystal set and he could sometimes pick up such stations, but my brother used to listen on the home radio. Then there was an offer to buy a transistor radio for 50 pence. He sent his money off and waited for the day when the parcel arrived and it was a red plastic, quite modern and light radio. I think it worked on batteries and was portable, which was high tech in its day. The reception was better, and we started to get an insight into what young people were listening to.

We had the Dansette record player and my brother started buying singles. The first I can remember was House of the Rising Sun, by the Animals, released in June 1964. I went with him to Varley's at

Harehills and he returned with the record, turned the player to 45 rpm and listened to the song. I was captured. This was what grownups did, and it was different to Lonnie Donegan, the Shadows and similar artists that were popular. My brother was just 14, and I was almost ten. He started going to the youth club at St Wilfrid's, and there he heard even more. He kept up to date and even my mother started listening to and singing hits from the radio. By 1967, pop music became accepted and Radio 1 started. Tony Blackburn moved from the pirate stations and hosted the first show. From then on, pop was heard on radios and trannies and cars were equipped with radios, so that car travel meant listening to and joining in the popular hits.

Even TV got into the act. Top of the Pops (1964), Juke Box Jury (1959) and Ready, Steady Go (1963) were compulsory listening for the young, or young at heart. My brother's taste was maturing and in 1967, he bought The Piper at the Gates of Dawn by Pink Floyd. I loved it and I still feel that it is a great album. I had really liked See Emily Play, which was their first real hit. I was given a small portable reel-to-reel tape recorder the next Christmas, and I recorded Son of a Preacher Man by Dusty Springfield (1968). The song was quite raunchy at the time and I loved it. Being thirteen, I started borrowing my older brother's clothes and his music. Piper at the Gates of Dawn followed me to youth clubs and was terribly manhandled. The same fate happened to a number of his records when he went to university and I still have a copy of his Easy Rider Soundtrack, but the best tracks won't play and the needle just jumps. Sometimes he would come home and wonder what had happened to his things, and a few altercations took place. His clothes were quite trendy and I remember wearing his black, shiny PVC coat on many occasions.

As I had part-time jobs, I started to buy records. Singles were cheap, particularly if you bought ex-jukebox ones. I was quite into the Small Faces and got most of their singles. I am afraid to say the first single I ever bought was Young Girl by Gary Puckett and the Union Gap. Nowadays, such a song wouldn't be allowed. One of my first albums was Ummagumma. Andrew had bought a Saucerful of Secrets and I had helped wear that out the previous year, and it was with great anticipation that I placed the pristine first record on the mono Dansette record player with compatible cartridge. The needle arm was so heavy that I am sure it almost cut a new groove in the plastic. It makes me laugh when people are buying LPs again because they have a better sound. I just remember the clicks and scratches that marred even a new record after a couple of plays. Ummagumma was quite heavy going, and I liked some, but not all of it. Granchester Meadows is my favourite track still. I had previously purchased The Who Sell Out and I loved it.

My brother had bought most of the Beatle albums, and Bob Dylan's Highway 61 Revisited and The Freewheelin Bob Dylan and Al Stewart's Love Chronicles. I had given them my usual carefree handling. Occasionally, one would be used as a Frisbee, but I hoped he wouldn't notice. I believe even more disagreements and skirmishes resulted and sometimes he would try to stop me from leaving the house wearing some of his trendy gear. As time went on, I did have some of my own. Who could forget Loon Pants, tie-dye shirts, Budgie Jackets and clogs from Boodle Am when the shop was upstairs in one of the arcades in Leeds. I believe there was also one near Leeds Uni. I know it became posher and moved to a flash store on Victoria Street. Oh, those were the days!

There were others who also influenced my musical taste. One from Roundhay School, Douglas (Duggie) was really into the Blues and he had an excellent collection of stuff like Dr John, Captain Beefheart, and Blodwyn Pig, which I wasn't particularly interested in, but he played me an album that changed my taste and that was from a band called Led Zeppelin. He said they were a bit like the Who. Communication Breakdown and the other tracks on their first album opened my eyes to heavy metal.

Another friend was a couple of years older than me and we met at one of the two youth clubs we regularly attended, St Edmund's at Roundhay and the Methodist Club, just a little further up the road. He lived at Harehills, and his house had a cellar that he used as his trendy pad. I loved it. Dark, damp, but an almost adult free zone. He also loved music, and he set up the cellar with a sofa, chairs, and a sound system. Some of the first albums I heard played were Led Zeppelin 2, Crosby Stills and Nash, Threshold of a Dream and the best of all, In the Court of the Crimson King. My life was changed for ever. Music was something I would spend the rest of my life loving, needing and feeling. My enthusiasm for music came from my experience in these formative years. I guess I was just lucky to have been a teenager when rock took over the world.

Bands were masters at their instruments and they saw themselves as artists that could change the world. They did, in a way, for those of us around at this time, but the heady days of belief have greyed and disappeared, like my hair. Records were fantastic, but even better was seeing our gods play live. Venues opened up and Leeds Poly, the Town Hall, Leeds Uni., Queens Hall and many others provided inexpensive opportunities and I, like my friends, took advantage of them. 50 pence for tickets in 1969, but I have paid over 200 pounds in recent times.

SINGLES, LPS, AND THE CASSETTE TAPE

For young people, it may be difficult to grasp how, in the 1960s and 70s, music was such a major part of a teenager's life. I am not sure it has the same value today, where music is freely available to listen to on streaming services rather than collected.

Our grandparents had no means of listening to music apart from the wireless, live music at dances or concerts, at the cinema or by playing instruments such as a piano at home. Family social events often involved sing-a-longs around the piano. Many, if not most, homes would house an upright piano and it was only when recorded music and radio became commonplace that these disappeared. Upright pianos became almost worthless overnight. Of course there were those who persevered, but pianos were often scrapped and thrown out. Their status became so low that I can remember games on TV where teams would have to smash pianos into small enough pieces using sledgehammers and race other teams to pass all the pieces through a small square opening. Looking back, it seems such a waste, but such was the move to modernity and there was an optimism in what the future would hold that has been lost.

At Stainbeck Preparatory School, I remember one of the teachers playing hard 78 records on an old gramophone that had replaceable steel needles and a large trumpet. It wasn't powered by electricity and had a handle that you wound up to get the record to revolve. The quality of the sound was poor and there was a lot of crackle and hiss that would be horrifying nowadays. My memory of these times is in black and white and similar to Cliff Richard's Summer Holiday, where colour appeared in the film when the bus crossed the Channel to Europe. In my memory, there was a sudden change in the 1960s and the world became colourful. As I have discussed before, radios were the major replacement for piano playing and within a few years, these were replaced by television and transistor radios, or trannies, as they were called. It was television and music that seemed to be the catalyst for the world becoming colourful. The radios played serious music that belonged to adults, but then something changed that and music became the possession of youth and their symbol of rebellion. Music on television tended to be variety show music. Perry Como, Matt Monro, Russ Conway, Frank Sinatra and the myriad of others played adult music that soothed mums and dads, but did nothing for teenagers. The last thing that you wanted to be, as a teenager, was anything like your mother or father. In fact, I swore I would never be like them. How little did I know? How many times have I heard myself utter their very words when speaking to my growing children? Ah well!

There was a change afoot, but at first it was pretty tame. Lonnie Donegan and skiffle had a little more life about it, but really was nothing to get excited about. Then something happened in America. Bill Haley and the Comets had two singles: Rock Around the Clock and See You Later Alligator. These became big hits and were the opening for what had previously been black music to burst upon the mainstream. Chuck Berry, Little Richard, and others started the riot, but it was Elvis Presley with his censored hips that started the opening of the floodgates. Heartbreak Hotel, Hound Dog, Jailhouse Rock and a string of worldwide hits spoke to the disaffected youth around the world. This was matched and encouraged by the sale of single records on vinyl. Cheap and readily available, singles were what every teenager wanted to be seen carrying. Coffee bars and other meeting places for teens had jukeboxes and here, the current hits could be played and listened to.

For those of us with little money, it was possible to buy ex-jukebox singles, and these had the centres missing and you needed an adaptor to play them. Singles played on record players at 45 rpm and were often known as 45s. There were vinyl albums on sale and these played at 33 rpm and allowed up to 20 minutes of music on each side. The vinyl records produced a much improved sound quality to either 78s or the medium or shortwave radio, but the first records were all in mono. We had a Dansette record player in the 1960s and it was a fairly basic player with a very heavy arm on the deck. It had a replaceable centre spindle so that a pile of singles could be stacked on top of each other and it would automatically lift the needle, retract the arm, allow the next single to drop on top of the last one played, replace the needle and play each of the singles in turn. This seemed very clever, but the higher records often slipped on the ones underneath.

I remember going down to Varleys at Harehills with my brother to buy the House of the Rising Sun by the Animals in 1964. It was a major event for him. It was the first music that he had bought and the first single in our household. The bunch of young men from Newcastle spearheaded the British movement into the teen revolution. They looked hard, weren't pretty and the song spoke of the USA, which was the Mecca for UK youth. Of course, like most revolutions, the powers that be saw this as an opportunity. Pop music became taken over by the establishment. Radio One started playing pop. The companies that recorded and distributed the classical and adult music cashed in and started hiring, recording, and selling anything they could. They saw the new audience of youth, with their own money to spend as a cash cow, and new British bands were signed up to compete with those from the USA. Cliff Richard was the English Elvis, Adam Faith and the like became stars. Some, like Tommy Steele, started as pop stars but became more mainstream and then general entertainers.

It looked as if the youth revolution would fizzle out until the sharper edged bands like the Animals came along and the revolution in Britain took off with the Beatles and the Rolling Stones. The Beatles were more acceptable to parents and my mother loved their music, but the Stones came from the US blues roots and had a harder edge.

Teenage haunts such as the Texas Grill and the Del Rio would find us spending our spare coins on songs that would be magically selected, and the record picked up by the amazing mechanics, dropped vibrating onto the turntable and then have the needle arm fall heavily onto our selection. The knack was to pick a song that your friends would like, but hopefully hadn't heard before. To introduce them to a masterpiece could enhance your kudos. I remember well Spirit in the Sky by Norman Greenbaum (1969), In the Year 2525 Zager and Evans (1968-69) playing on the jukebox incessantly.

1969 was the major year for my musical tastes and that was where albums became important to me. The Beatles had produced the most influential album, Sgt Pepper's Lonely Hearts Club Band, in 1967, and split after Abbey Road and the Rooftop concert in Jan 1969. They set the scene for all other bands and a cluster of wonderful albums were produced from a wide range of bands and styles. New genres were being created and the psychedelic Pink Floyd and Soft Machine matched the Rolling Stones with some of their best albums: Let It Bleed, Beggars Banquet and, later, Sticky Fingers. Groups such as the Moody Blues, Crosby Stills and Nash, Caravan, The Doors, Cream, Fleetwood Mac, Family, Jefferson Airplane, Bob Dylan, Led Zeppelin, Yes, Deep Purple, The Who, Frank Zappa and The Mothers Of Invention and The Small Faces came on to the scene.

What every self-respecting teenager wanted was to be seen carrying an armful of high status albums. They were so heavy, but they were possessions to be proud of. They were fragile and suffered sound quality loss from the moment you slipped them out of the sleeve, statically charged. I still have many, some which belonged to my older brother and my friends, but they don't often get an airing.

It was shortly after this time when we used to gather in Pete's cellar and listen intently to any new albums on his stereo system. Pete was lucky. We still had the mono Dansette at home and I would play stereo records with a compatible cartridge. It was in this environment that my musical tastes were honed, lying back listening to In the Court of the Crimson King and discussing the meaning of lyrics, the virtuosity of the band members and listening to the stereo effects of A Whole Lotta Love, as the guitar swirled in a figure of eight.

The next major step in music reproduction was a giant backward step. We were round at another friend, John L's house, when Pete arrived without his usual wide ranging new collection of albums. He carried what looked like a small suitcase. My interest was more than piqued as he opened it up to reveal a small deck and two speakers connected by cable. He set it up, plugged it in, and produced something we had never seen from his pocket. It was a cassette tape. It was so small, lightweight and he opened the front door of the player and slipped it in. It was a pre-recorded cassette and I can't remember the album. He shut the door and pressed play. There were two initial reactions: the first was 'Wow!' and this was followed by,

'What is that hissing!'

The deck was amazing, but the tape had a dreadful hiss. Of course, the cassette didn't have Dolby Noise-reduction at that first time. That came later, as did high-quality tapes, Chrome tapes and finally metal tapes, which improved quality, but were soon replaced by the compact disc.

The human mind has an amazing ability to focus and the quality of television and sound recording that we first experienced was dreadful compared to even the most basic televisions and sound systems, but we didn't care. We experienced the music when it was in its halcyon days. Real artists, musicians who could play, took risks, were self-indulgent sometimes, often under the influence (as were the listeners), were popping up everywhere. Concert tickets were fifty pence. There could be five bands on a set list and people would sit and listen without the need to whistle or scream out. Music had something to say and even though it wasn't the revolution we had hoped, the world changed and in some ways for the better.

Unfortunately, music no longer has a value and streaming means people aren't prepared to buy it. Vinyl has come back, but it is only a boutique trend and will fade away again. My biggest worry is that because of the pandemic, bands can no longer play live or tour. This was their only means of making a living, as sales are almost non-existent and it may be years before it can start off again. If the art goes, we may find ourselves subjected to the charts dominated by three or four writers whose material sounds identical, but has been researched and formulised to appeal to the maximum audience. What we need now is a new revolution! Come back Punk! Come back Folk! Come back Progressive Music! Come back Rock! Come back Motown! Come back Soul! The world needs real music more than ever. Maybe Video didn't Kill the Radio Star, but image has seen the music die.

LET THE MUSIC PLAY LIVE

Whilst still attending Roundhay School, I started going to Leeds Poly at weekends. I managed to get in originally by looking older than I was, a skill that is only beneficial when one is under age, and by having my older brother's Student Union Card. The union at the Poly had a couple of snooker tables, cheap beer and, best of all, regular concerts, all at a cheap price.

I wasn't aware, but the University circuit for bands was only just starting and we enjoyed fantastic bands, at fantastic prices and in venues that were small enough to have great views and be up close and personal with the acts. I was trying to think what the very first band was, and I think it was Jon Hiseman's Colosseum. Their album was Those Who Are About To Die We Salute You and they were a jazz, rock, blues band. I have checked and can't see it mentioned, but I believe there was a xylophone player and one of my friends who had too much to drink kept pushing the xylophone around as he could reach it from where he sat at the front of the stage. I think a roadie intervened to stop his antics, much to the relief of the musician. Being an audience member at these times was quite serious and most of the concerts were full of earnest sorts with long hair, sitting quietly on the floor and appreciating the musicians and their music. I wasn't completely taken by Colosseum, but I was captured by live music.

From then on I was a regular at the Poly and saw Yes when they were doing their version of Paul Simon's America and they had the Poly packed. They were brilliant. I had never seen such musicianship, and I loved Chris Squire's bass playing, Bill Bruford's drumming and Jon Anderson's vocals (my wife hates his voice). America was only released on a sampler album, but was released on a compilation cd years later.

Cat Stevens performed there when Tea For the Tillerman was a major hit in 1970. I did learn to hate the record, as I took part in a 24 hour table tennis hit out, whilst attending the Methodist youth club at Roundhay, near St Edmund's. I can't remember what we were raising money for, but a small group of us had to play continuously. I think there were six of us and we took turns playing whilst the others rested. We played singles and doubles and we slept in the same room, camping on the floor. There was a record player and someone had just bought the album. It was played constantly over the twenty-four hours and by the end it drove me mad, when added to the constant noise of the table tennis ball being hit or bouncing on the table. Anyway, we managed it, but it put me off table tennis and the record. Cat Stevens' performance was fantastic, and he had a beautiful voice, calm manner and a great band. I saw him about a couple of years ago and he still sings magnificently and he doesn't look all that different, hair just shorter.

The cost of tickets was around the 10 shillings, fifty pence mark, but even that was quite a lot when I was young. As a result, my friends and I would attempt to gain entry through the back of the Poly building to avoid paying. This worked well, but security became wised up and for a while there was a bit of a cat-and-mouse game, before finally it was a mission impossible and we paid like everyone else.

Unfortunately, alcohol was also a new experience at around this time. I am ashamed to say that I was only fourteen when I started, and this is something that, if there are any children reading, I would not recommend. I got away with it as I looked older than my years, and this is an attribute that has long since lost its appeal. I suppose we are only young once and being foolish is something that all youths have excelled at over the generations.

The end of the concert meant a long walk home as most of the buses had stopped running, or were so infrequent as to make it not worth waiting. Many nights I wove a meandering path down towards the Spencer Place part of Roundhay Road, through Harehills and then up past the Clock Cinema to Gipton Wood Crescent. It was probably quite a risky walk, late at night, but I never gave it much of a thought and I never had any problems. To be honest, I had nothing that would have been worth stealing.

Another band that left an impression was Fleetwood Mac. They performed after Peter Green had left and Christine McVie (Christine Perfect as she was) had joined them. She had been in the band Chicken Shack and joined Mac for Kiln House in 1970. I can't remember a great deal about the performance and listening back to the album, it lacked the spark of Peter Green's Mac and Lindsey Buckingham's Mac years later. One thing I clearly remember is that another friend, I think it was Chris, was sitting under the PA stack that was set on tables. We took little notice of him as he was well oiled and the band was tight, if not a patch on the previous version. Suddenly, mid number, the sound of the guitars and keyboard stopped, and it left just drums and the bass. I must admit I wasn't sure if it was supposed to happen that way, but Mick Fleetwood and John McVie just carried on as if it was planned.

The instigator of the power cut crawled from beneath the stack of speakers with a sly grin. He was lucky, as a pair of rough and big roadies suddenly appeared with confused and not happy faces. They searched around to find the cause of the power outage and one climbed under the speakers. He reappeared with an even angrier expression. He gave the other roadie a short explanation. A signal was sent up to the band whilst the first re-plugged the power cord into the socket and the number continued with a full complement of musicians. The band was relieved, but the looks on the roadies' faces were set to kill. Luckily, my friend had made his escape, and he never learned the error of his ways. The way that John and Mick just carried on showed what a talented pair they were and still are. Fantastic!

Quiver, later to join the Sutherland Brothers and enjoy some success on the singles charts, played at the Poly. Mike Cooper, who was a folksy rocker, impressed me enough for me to buy The Machine Gun Company with Mike Cooper. The album was ok, but not as good as he was live.

The Poly also had the benefit of a large common room and they would play some great music there and hold discos. Hot Snot were the DJs. A few years later, I was playing in a band with friends and we used to practise there on Sunday afternoons. Good times!

Across the road from the Poly was Thomas Danby College. I

think it was a further education college, and there I went to see Manfred Mann's Chapter Three and Stackridge. Chapter Three was formed in 1969 after Manfred Mann broke up, and I think they were newly formed when I saw them. They were clearly more experimental than the previous pop band and I didn't know the material. I wasn't over-impressed. However, I saw Manfred Mann's Earth Band twice at Imperial College in the 1970s, and they were fantastic. I had bought Nightingales and Bombers on cassette in 1975 and they did a few songs by Bruce Springsteen, who I hadn't heard of.

With Stackridge, I didn't know what to expect, as I hadn't heard their music. Another friend loved them and I went along, not sure what it would be like. What I did experienced was a strange and wonderful evening's entertainment, full of humour, and it was unlike anything I had ever seen or heard. They were relatively short-lived as a band, breaking up in 1977.

Of course, there were many other venues in Leeds. These were fantastic times for live music and, being a teenager who loved music, this was heaven!

PIPERS, CHABLIS, PETE'S CELLAR AND THE POLY

As I have said before, there were certain advantages of having an older brother, one of which was that he went away to university.

My brother was at Durham University at the time and, from what I gather, had a pretty good time. I know that one of his highlights was helping with the light show for an up-and-coming band called Pink Floyd. This was when their first album was being released and they had a couple of hits. The first, Arnold Lane, was only a minor one, but the second, See Emily Play, was massive. Neither was really typical of much of their astral-travelling psychedelic improvisations that made up their shows, but I loved See Emily Play. Anyway, my brother bought the album, Piper at the Gates of Dawn, and left it at home whilst he returned to Uni. This was wonderful for me and I gained great kudos by taking it to the youth clubs and parties that I attended. Needless to say, it became very scratched and unplayable, but luckily for me, I suppose my brother became interested in other music and things at university and I still have the album now.

The other thing he left behind was his student union card, and that was my passport to a range of venues that required student ID At this point, our band was still in its infancy and we used to practise every moment we could, electronically amplified at the Lidgett Lane youth club, as they allowed us to blast out our raw numbers, or else at someone's house. The usual house venue was Pete's cellar. I have previously told the tale of how we decorated it and added road signs and flashing street repair warning signs, but I hadn't mentioned that

Pete had a fairly loud stereo system in place and he had a great taste in new music. The end of the 1960s and early seventies saw an explosion of youth culture and music. At Roundhay School there were those into Blues albums and it was through a classmate, Duggie, that I heard Led Zeppelin I. He said it was like the Who, whom he knew I liked. I can't say that I saw much of a similarity, but I loved it anyway. The first two albums that I ever bought were The Who Sell Out, which was great and Ummagumma by Pink Floyd, which was a bit of a disappointment.

What I didn't realise at the time was that the University circuit for rock bands was just opening up. Prior to this, bands played at venues such as pubs, and the Mecca ballrooms, but the new experimental music was more warmly received by university and polytechnic students and their unions used to book rising acts to fill their halls at the weekends. Leeds University became quite a famous venue and Leeds Poly was not far behind.

To gain entry to such hallowed halls, when tickets weren't just on public sale, you required a student union card. Peter, John and other friends had access as they were older and attending one of the Leeds colleges, but as a schoolboy I couldn't get one. Hence the joy I felt with my brother leaving his Student Union Card at home. It had a photograph on it, but I don't think anyone ever really checked and we looked fairly similar. There were students manning the doors and as long as you looked the part you were in.

Most nights there was the bar, the snooker tables and the common room where loud music blared away and the room was almost dark. Several years later, our band was allowed to practise in the common room on Sunday afternoons, and it was a fairly shabby room in the full light of day. The place used to hum most nights with large numbers of students, clearly not studying. The air was smoke filled, and the beer was cheap and quite drinkable. Some weekends, there were discos on the lower level and, occasionally, less popular bands played. I once saw Jail Bait, an American band, on the lower level. At this point I was a student in London, but the thing that stuck with me was their asking mid-act if there were any girls who fancied a good time after the show. I had seen nothing as blatant before.

The bigger concerts were in the main hall and I saw some outstanding performances and fabulous acts. I have mentioned before that the first was John Hiseman's Colosseum, and then Fleetwood Mac when Christine Perfect joined, but others were Cat Stevens, and Yes, just before they really took off. The Yes concert was completely packed out, and they were impressive, both in their sartorial style and their musical ability. Bill Bruford was still on drums, and Peter Banks was the guitarist. They played Paul Simon's America in a way that completely blew me over. Twenty minutes of bliss. I loved Chris Squire's bass playing in particular and, despite my wife's horror, I have enjoyed every version of the band ever since and I have seen most of the lineups.

I didn't realise at the time just how lucky I was to be immersed in what I believe was the most important period of popular music. There was a coming together of musical ability, creativity and technology that produced some of the greatest music in the rock era. New albums were coming out seemingly daily and every time we went to Pete's or another friend's place, someone would have something new: Days of Future Passed, the Moody Blues, The Court of the Crimson King, King Crimson, Led Zeppelin II, Atom Heart Mother, Meddle, The Dark Side of the Moon, Pink Floyd, The Land of Grey and Pink, Caravan, Free, Deep Purple, David Bowie, Family, the list of music and bands just went on and on.

We used to gather as a crowd at Pete's, John's, John L's or Paul's, maybe sixteen of us. We would buy a bottle of whatever we wanted to drink. For me it was cheap white wine, Chablis, from the off licence on the corner (six shillings, I believe). Some lads liked a few bottles of beer, maybe Newcastle Brown, some Strongbow and for the girls, Woodpecker cider or Martini and lemonade. We would sit in a thick haze of smoke and chat and drink, but mainly become lost in the music.

Wild Nights? Well, not really. We did little harm. We certainly didn't go out looking for trouble. We were more interested in our band, music and girls. What we did, though, was stand out from the crowd. We dressed flamboyantly, often from Boodle Am when it was in the arcade or near the uni, or from jumble sales. Tie-dye shirts, Loon pants, Budgie Jackets, Oxford Bags, clogs, Afghan Coats, Levi jeans with patches and flair inserts, trench coats, rucksacks, white brogues, Ben Sherman shirts, Levi shirts and jackets, I've had them all. I bought a lovely felt trilby from a St Edmund's jumble sale and it looked very dapper. The problem was that some thug at the

Roundhay Rugby Club took a shine to my hat and threatened to beat me up if I didn't give him it. Luckily, Pete just walked up and explained the error of his ways and my hat was saved. We did some stupid things that must have caused alarm to the older generation. I remember we would pretend to be fighting at the traffic lights at Moortown Corner whilst the cars were stopped, and we would occasionally roll over someone's bonnet to make it look impressive, but we did no actual harm. It was just a lark. We used to drink and underage drinking was common. The roles were different from the way they are today. It was the boys who tended to get drunk, and the girls looked after them. Nowadays, the roles seem reversed.

Long-haired, wild and reckless, I would imagine I was any parent of a daughter's worst nightmare, but the mothers I knew seemed to like me. I can't see why, but maybe they could just see through me!

PUBERTY BLUES

From the age of about thirteen, I entered the most turbulent period of my life to the present date. Mid 1960s was a time of upheaval, anyway. 1966 had just seen England win the World Cup, and I managed to get some stamps with England Winners on them, which I still have. I was just finishing the first year at Roundhay School and in September 1967 was in the second year. The change from primary to secondary was quite marked, and it took most of that first year to settle in.

I had heard terrible tales of bullying that happened to new boys, but apart from the first day christening of my cap, (the removal by an older boy and the smashing of the enamel badge on the ground,) I can't say I ever really experienced any personally. I am sure that it took place, but being quite tall, fairly sturdy and, because of growing testosterone levels, quite feisty, I was left alone. One thing that was very true was that I, and probably most boys, received no preparation for the physical and emotional upheaval that was about to hit us. We weren't totally stupid and had noticed that older Sixth Formers looked very different. To First Years they appeared like men: facial hair, deep voices, long hair and arrogant. The teachers dealt with them in a totally different way and physically, at least, they were young men. I was unaware how child-like they still were mentally.

I had thought it very unjust that prefects could put you in detention and set lines or similar punishments. I had railed about this injustice to my mum, but she just said that everything would be fine, and in most instances it was. I think school detention was still on

Saturday mornings in that first year, but they changed it to Wednesday afternoons by the time I ever got one.

There were many rituals and organisational procedures, so it took time to settle into Roundhay. One of the first was that we were allocated a desk in 'Holy Joe' Pullen's classroom over the boiler house. He informed us that we could purchase a padlock hasp latch from the workshops and we could fit it to the desk, buy a padlock and keep our books and belongings in them. These were wooden desks, and they were quite old. They had a hinged wooden lid and, as this was long before lockers, it was the only way of avoiding carrying a hundredweight of books and equipment backwards and forwards to school. The desks were well-worn, and it appeared the history of every boy who had sat at mine was carved into its solid surface.

The previous owners had removed their hasp and padlock when they changed classrooms. After getting some money from home, I went to buy the hardware and, with the help of a trusty screwdriver, managed to fit it. Luckily, there were plenty of old screw holes to utilise amongst the initials, band names and girlfriends carved deeply into the wood. It felt quite grown up having your own locked desk and within a couple of days, everyone had secured their own.

They issued text books on a loan basis and there was the threat of being charged if the book was damaged, which was a bit of a laugh as most were old, well-used and defiled, copies. They were stamped with their date of issue and our names recorded, along with the book number of each text.

I have not considered it before, but there appears to be something in at least masculine nature that wants to mark their territory, and so we carved our initials into almost everything: desks, cliff surfaces, tree trunks, plaster. Now it is spray cans and marker pens, but then it was carving. There were some accomplished carvers and their names were left for posterity in fine Roman script. I was never that good, but it helped to pass a boring lesson to pull out the compass and get to work, adding or improving an earlier piece I had started. When we ran out of desk space, we would start on wooden pencil cases, mathematical drawing instrument cases or our rulers. As we became more interested in music, band names would appear and the ex-military rucksacks that were the fashion at the time were emblazoned with band names of the time. The more obscure the band, or avant-garde, the greater the kudos. I still remember someone having The

Doors emblazoned on their bag and I was impressed, even though I hadn't heard of them.

The teachers didn't seem to notice the desks, or if they did, didn't care. They would sit perched on their dais, resplendent like black crows in the academic gown, ready to hurl the blackboard rubber at any unfortunate boy who drew their attention. On a number of occasions, I saw the intended target missed, but some poor neighbour take the full force of the wooden eraser as it struck them an almost lethal blow to the skull.

Most rooms were devoid of any decoration. Few had any posters, and I never saw school work displayed. Most rooms were a pale green or blue and the corridor was faded green. Even the blackboards were green. They were green ground-glass and the theory we were told was that they were more restful on the eye. The exception was in the science labs where there were moveable roller boards. Notes were written in science and when the teacher got towards the bottom, they would slide the board up, hiding their notes from any student slouches who had not kept up. We spent many lessons just copying notes or, even worse, just copying homework instructions. Many teachers took great delight in rubbing out the top of the board when they got to the bottom, and protests were met with a snide comment and a smirk.

Some teachers thought they were funny, and we learnt those we had to laugh with when they told what they thought was a joke. "Please sir? Can I go to the toilet?" "Of course you can!" was the reply and when the boy stood to leave the room, "Where are you going, boy? I said that you could, not that you may!"

By the end of the first year, we had got used to the routines. We knew how to get new exercise books when they were full, without being charged for removing pages, knew our way around the school campus, got used to what days we needed which equipment such as woodwork aprons, sports gear, and so on. As a result, we started the second year with confidence and looked forward to welcoming the new First Year boys. We were the ones christening the new boys' caps. We were no longer the little fish, and we moved around the school with a growing swagger.

To add to this was the fact that many of us had changed over the summer holidays. The changes came in various ways and they were hair, voice, muscle and height. These could arrive together, or individually, in any order, and as we were so ill-prepared, we were not sure if it was normal or not. Certainly, my parents had relied on the school to deal with such issues and it was an area of education that Roundhay School certainly failed at, but within the hidden curriculum there was a lot of information and misinformation passed around by the boys.

I would rather have died than had to have a face-to-face discussion about the birds and the bees with my parents, but I know one or two boys who experienced such a talk.

My first recollection of any changes came from going to the pictures with my dad. For some inexplicable reason, I found myself getting quite uncomfortable when there were scenes with attractive actresses in the James Bond, or other films. The feelings would go, and I never gave it much thought. The second change I was forewarned about, as I was part of the choir at St Wilfrid's Church. I knew voices would 'break' at about the age of twelve and you had to leave the choir when it happened. Breaking meant that your voice would go deeper and then suddenly higher as your vocal chords began to thicken. This meant you could no longer control your voice, and you had to leave until your voice settled down. Some boys suffered badly, but I don't think I did. After a short time, mine just settled down to the timbre it has now. After saying this, voices still change over time and mine is probably a little deeper than it was.

I did have a growth spurt, and I was one of the tallest boys in the Under 13s Rugby team, but alas, that was the end and I have remained 5 foot 7 and a half inches ever after and that half inch is very important. My cap size was 6 and seven-eighths, but I don't really know what that meant. I would have loved to have been a couple of inches taller, but that was not to be. Of course, each of my four sons is considerably taller than me.

These changes I took in my stride, but hair was the one that was a killer. Despite knowing it would come, the arrival of bodily hair was something that you didn't want to be the first to have, nor the last. Sport was the problem area, as we had to have a bath, naked, after rugby, or a shower when they became available. These were times when you were vulnerable to the gaze of your peers. This was bad enough when you looked just like them, but when you were different, that was a problem. Comments would be made, and egos bruised after taunting and ribbing. Luckily, I was not the first, but not long after, and no attempts to hide evidence would succeed for long.

During that second year, the balance changed, and it was those not yet sporting this new sign of manhood that suffered the jibes and the flicking of the wet towels. Luckily we all grow out of this, but there was considerable eyeing other boys' development to compare how we had been placed in the pecking order.

With the changes came the question of hygiene and teenage boys have a powerful aroma that any teacher entering a warm classroom towards the end of the day can testify is choking. Teenage girls don't seem to notice and I can only assume they lose their sense of smell for a few years. Mothers often let their sons know they have body odour, and deodorant is introduced.

Never doing things by halves, boys take to it with gusto. This is aided and abetted by advertisers who know how to win boys over. The right deodorant copiously applied can attract beautiful ladies, make them uncontrollable with desire, and throw themselves at the spottiest, least attractive young man. Teenage boys believe this with a passion and Brut was more than liberally added to the natural bodily smells. Boys don't quite understand that changing clothes, bathing and showering would have far more beneficial effects, so they drown in the pungent deodorant and sprays.

To add insult to injury, becoming self-aware is assailed by the eruption of pimples. I don't think anyone really avoids the dreaded teenage spots, but some suffer more severely than others. I remember knowing each one as a mark of horror, but I am not sure that other people really noticed.

For many of us, this was a difficult time, but an unavoidable one. No matter how hard it was for us, it was much harder for our parents as they had to suffer us, our moods, irrational behaviour and thoughtlessness towards them. I think most boys, or at least I did, spend the rest of their lives regretting what they said and did to their mothers, but I can't speak for girls.

FAIR CRACK OF THE WHIP, FOR THE GURUTS

Time seemed to pass really slowly in my early teens, but now it disappears in a flash. I think I am still waiting for that day when I will become grown up and I know some would say that is because I am a man and they never do. What I do remember about my early teens was the intensity. Life was a matter of extreme ups and downs, with very little in between. Two things seemed to dominate my life, and unfortunately, studying and my education at Roundhay School weren't either of them. The band and girls dominated my life. One was out of my control and was due to raging hormones, and the other was something that I just loved. Music was enjoying its halcyon days. It had passed beyond simple songs and real musicians were becoming gods. It was the age of the rock guitar and musical virtuosity, and I wanted to be part of it.

Now, several things were standing in my way. One was lack of equipment and the second was my lack of ability to play. Others may have been daunted by such obstacles, but not me. I was always a realist, and whereas I could play a few chords on the guitar, I wasn't as good as Pete and therefore I chose to play bass. I started on the acoustic guitar, but clearly we were going to have to move on. Pete, being a couple of years older, had jobs as well as studying, and so he had access to more money than I did. I can't remember the exact time, but at some point he became the owner of a red semi-acoustic electric guitar (I think this was his first one) and amp and speaker system. This became established in his cellar and we were in business. I say we, but I was still to have an instrument. Another of Pete's friends, John, was also part of our group, but he didn't have an instrument apart from playing piano if one was around, so it was clear we would have to invest if we were to progress. I think I heard of someone selling a bass guitar for about five pounds and I managed to get the money somehow and I became the owner of a fairly basic and battered bass. I loved it. It was heavy, the strings were thick and the tuning machine heads enormous. Oh, what joy! I was almost set up. Now the origin of John's electric piano purchase is shrouded in mystery. My memory tells me that I heard from someone at Roundhay that it was for sale in an electrical music shop at the top of one of the arcades in Leeds. I can't remember the name of the shop, but it sold amps and speakers that were manufactured in Leeds. Anyway, I remember passing the rumour over to Pete, who let John know, and he went in and bought it for a stunning six pounds. I remember, clearly, arriving to view the wonderful keyboard. Now, John has a completely different memory of how he came to buy the electric piano but, regardless, he did invest in it and we were beginning to assemble the basic gear that a band needed.

John's electric piano was not quite in tune and he opened it up to discover that it worked more like a harpsichord. Short metal plates of varying length and thickness were mechanically plucked when the key was depressed. John realised that tuning could be achieved by undoing the locking nut and minutely adjusting the length of the metal plate. He was always very thorough and the next time I saw him and his electric piano, it was now in tune.

John and I both eventually equipped ourselves with amps and speakers, all secondhand and of limited quality, but they were ours and they could produce very loud volumes of sound. I became really interested in playing the bass and started going to the music shop in the centre of Leeds that sold wonderfully expensive instruments, sheet music, strings, plectrums and 'How to' books. Who could forget Bert Weedon's - Play In a Day book? Would that it were true! The shop was a magical emporium with bright, shiny, chrome and coloured instruments that called to me like the sirens, but alas, without the necessary money, they were always going to be beyond my reach.

Rather than be disappointed by my equipment, I took pride in its battered appearance. If you could play good music with this equipment, then you really could play. If only!

In Pete's cellar we set to. As we really didn't have any idea how to play other people's songs, we started writing our own material. New material such as Going and Last Bus became the backbone of our growing set and what we lacked in musical prowess we made up for with arrogance, attitude and somewhere a kernel of originality. One thing was missing, and that was a drummer. We got a friend from Roundhay school, Dave B, and he was a fine musician. He started on drums, but changed to play guitar in his own band.

After our first gig, he was replaced by another friend of Pete's. Bryan appeared one day with a new drum kit he had got on hire purchase. The kit looked the business and so did Bryan. There was just one problem. Bryan seemed totally devoid of any sense of timing or rhythm, which was a bit of a downer for any rhythm section, but not for us.

The talent we were short of, we compensated for with style, or at least that's what we thought. Pete's dad worked for Leeds transport with the buses and his mum ran an old people's home in their house. I often wondered what the old folk thought of us belting out rock from the cellar beneath their lounge. Pete's dad contributed to our style with a couple of khaki bus jackets that were modified, and Pete's mother added triangular patches into his Levis to make them even more bell-bottomed than before. His original ones were smallish triangles, but they became bigger over time. Long hair (I think Pete might have had a moustache at the time) and we were ready to take on the world. Now we had a music set of about fifteen minutes and, with growing confidence, if that was possible, we decided to take our place on the world stage. Where else would a budding group of superstars start, if not in a talent competition, and not just any talent competition but the one held at the Leeds Transport Club?

I have just listened to a documentary on the Beatles, and Paul McCartney said that they had entered talent quests and that they had never won any, so I don't feel in bad company. The night came. My dad and others helped transport the gear, and we turned up ready for the big time. The club was the typical working men's club and the talent show was in between rounds of Bingo and rounds of drinks. It was quite a large club, and it had that smell of stale beer-soaked carpet and old tobacco. The club was filling, and the MC gave us a few minutes to set up and I think we were on fourth of fifth out of six. The MC spoke to Peter whilst John and I were setting our gear up and apparently he had asked the name of the band. This was a bit of a shock as we hadn't thought of one, but Peter told him we were the Gurus. The night started, we had a pint. I think I was probably fourteen. The turns were the usual: a comedian, an organist, a male cabaret singer, us and a little girl singer. Our turn came, and the MC got on the mike.

"Now ladies and gentlemen, a new band of young lads! Fair crack of the whip for the Guruts!"

This was said with all the confidence and aplomb of a seasoned MC, in a broad Yorkshire accent and clearly with no understanding of what we were called or its implication. Very taken aback, we took to the stage. John was on vocals and we did three songs, Atlantis, Going and Last Bus. The audience had that shell-shocked look of stunned mullets and at the end there was a courteous ripple of applause, and they quickly ordered another round of drinks to steady their nerves. I think the little girl came next and clearly she was the darling of the ageing clientele and following us, she couldn't have failed. She restored their faith in human nature and they rewarded her with winning the event and the prize.

We were not easily defeated. Of course, the audience wouldn't like us. They were old, over twenty-five at least. What did they know about music or talent? We packed up, a little wiser, determined to carry on, but knowing that this was not our kind of venue. One thing was sure, we could only move on up from here!

THE GLEDHOW LANE SHOOTOUT

After our initial foray into music, there were only two things I needed to do to realise my dream, and that was to get a guitar and learn how to play.

Now my history of great musical successes entailed recorder at Harehills, choir and a fleeting dabble with learning the violin. The violin career was a very short-lived experience. My mother had bought the violin from a second hand/antique store on Roundhay Road at Harehills. It was three-quarter size and was shared between my older brother and myself. It was a wonderful, strange looking instrument and hopefully had been played during its life by others with more talent than I had. The violin teacher was an elderly lady who lived off Harehills Lane and I know she had a small iron railing outside her house. After my first lesson, I refused to attend, much to the horror of my older brother and my mother. I remember vividly refusing to let go of the railing and screaming whilst my mother tried to drag me in. I was still a youngster at primary school, I must add, and I don't think that my older brother continued much after my performance. Maybe it was a good grounding for my rock/punk days that came later. The violin then spent the rest of its days in the coal store that later housed the central heating boiler. A rather sad end for something that would have had an interesting tale to tell.

Anyway, I digress. A guitar was what I needed and I must be honest that I can't remember where I got my first acoustic, Spanish guitar from. I probably bought it from a mate, or stole it off my older and long suffering brother. Resplendent with a rather old, new guitar, I got Pete to show me some basic chords. Tuning was challenging in those days and sore fingers from practising for hours resulted from my new obsession.

Social time would find us at one of the Youth Clubs, mainly Lidgett Park Youth Club, or St. Edmund's, but we were widening our horizons and Alwoodley Youth Club also became a venue. There were several things happening in my life. Up to this point, Roundhay School had occupied me with homework and Rugby. I was never a natural at soccer, but I was quite good at rugby and, being one of the tallest at thirteen years old, I found I had an aptitude and a love of the game. I took an active part in House rugby, and Kelvin did quite well. I was picked for the Under Fourteens and there was training during the week and matches on a Saturday morning. What I lacked in skill I made up for in enthusiasm, and I even got an honourable mention in the Roundhegian Magazine that year.

My school friends were particularly Anthony I, Roger and Chris M but Roger left when we were about thirteen, as his family moved away. We all played rugby and Roger was particularly good. He lived not far from the girls' school entrance on Gledhow Lane. Roger had an air rifle and there was an element of wildness about us. I regret to say that sometimes, when his parents were out, he would shoot at the birds in the garden from his bedroom window. He was a good aim and unfortunately, several birds fell victim to his skill. He even got me to have a go once, but as I was a novice, the birds were safe from me. His father must have been into shooting, as I was once invited to go with Roger to their rifle club on the way into Leeds in Sheepscar. I was allowed to have one go on the range that was below ground and fired .22 shells from a rifle. I can't say that I was particularly impressed with shooting and I have never had any desire to shoot again, apart from the odd go at the fair with air rifles.

One incident that I do remember, and I am sure that Chris does too, was one day during the school holidays. I was at Roger's with Chris and we had been listening to music and just hanging out when Chris had to leave and go home. Chris, I remember, was wearing Levis and a T-shirt. He left, and Roger and I were in the upstairs front bedroom. Roger's rifle was there and you can probably guess what's coming. Roger picked up his air rifle, opened the window and, just as Chris was running across the verge, took aim and fired. It was just like in the movies. Poor Chris shot forward and fell prone on the grass, clasping his derrière. Roger and I laughed nervously and watched as Chris climbed to his feet and staggered back into the house. This was probably a good time to mention that Chris' father was a policeman, but I don't think Roger had given this a thought.

Chris was furious. He clutched his buttock and then pulled his jeans down. The slug had not penetrated through the jeans, but it had certainly pierced his skin. There was quite a hole where the force had struck, but not a lot of blood. He was absolutely furious and would have attacked Roger if we hadn't placated him. First aid was administered, and soon he regained his composure. Luckily for Roger, and probably me as the accomplice, these were times when boys did not tell their parents anything, for fear of repercussions. Chris was probably worried that his parents would stop him from seeing Roger or me, so his parents never found out.

Whilst all these things were occurring, I was continuing my basic guitar playing, and Pete and I would get together. A friend of Pete's, John, was introduced and he could play the piano. Now this was something! Pete could bash out a tune on the guitar and the odd melody on the piano, but John had received lessons and could play. Pete's house at Harehills had an old upright piano in the living room and, despite not being the most accurately tuned, Pete and sometimes John would create their own songs. The three of us formed the core of what was to become a band. We started to write simple songs, probably as we didn't have enough skill to do good enough versions of other people's material.

One day, Pete and John came with a song they had written. I learned afterwards that they had nicked a theme off the Moody Blues. It was a simple song, but it had something about it. It was called Atlantis, and it had a lilting melody that John sang well and I produced a simple bass line on the acoustic guitar. It was the first song that we did as a band. I remember taking the guitars on a warm, sunny afternoon into Potternewton Park and we sat under a tree and played. It must have had something, or maybe it was back to the mysterious allure of teenage boys, but a couple of girls came over, sat down and listened. They seemed quite impressed. Now this was much more successful than being the pipe smoking misfit and I was sharp enough to pick up on that.

THE WHO MOMENT AND ADVENTURES ON ILKLEY MOOR

Youth clubs became the centre of my social scene, and they were places to go during the week. Weekends tended to be the pictures or hanging around friends' houses and, of course, there was the band. I am not sure how it came about, but we were given permission to practise at Lidgett Methodist Youth Club on a regular basis. It was possible on the promise that we would play a concert for them, but anyway, it provided a venue where we wouldn't annoy parents or neighbours, just other youth clubbers and leaders. We used to set up in the new hall and started thrashing out music at an unbelievably loud volume. They shut the doors on us and, apart from our group of friends and fans, they left us on our own.

Someone asked us to play at their birthday party/bash and we had Pete on guitar, John on keyboards and vocals, myself on bass and Bryan on drums. Bryan had no sense of timing, which was a disadvantage for a drummer, but he was the owner of a snazzy drum kit. The party was an afternoon do in a hall. It was only a small venue and I can't remember where it was exactly. It could have been Alwoodley, as we had started hanging out at the youth club there and had a group of local friends.

Food was set up at the back. Someone was the DJ for the afternoon, and we played a set in the middle of the proceedings. Our repertoire had expanded and John had written a song that was called, 'Let the Children into your Heart' or something similar, but anyway, he was to start the set on his own. There were two reasons for this:

one, we hadn't learnt the song and secondly it certainly wouldn't have been assisted with our ear-shattering thrashing. It gave me the opportunity to mingle with the audience. They were all dutifully sitting on the floor, as was the mode for the times. Music was something to be appreciated, taken seriously and not as just a dance accompaniment. The hall was fairly full and when John started, there was a rapt young audience, entranced by his music and confidence. Some 'smarty' had blown up a condom and the metre long zeppelin was bounced into the audience. The age of the people at the party meant that many, if not most, did not know what it was. I clearly remember one young girl patting it up into the air and saying, "Look! They have balloons!"

I stand in awe of John's courage and confidence in starting the set in such a way. He did this for several shows, and the style was not what people expected from a school band. Bryan, Pete and I took to the stage to accompany John, and we set into Going, Last Bus, I'm Leaving and others. At this point I am sure that the mother who was overseeing the do was regretting having a live band.

Things were going well, as far as we were concerned, and the audience was dully appreciative, but this was the calm before the storm. Peter was playing a red semi-acoustic electric guitar. It was hollow bodied and Peter had restrung the guitar with a new set of strings. This resulted in tuning being a problem. Between each number, Peter had to re-tune, and he was becoming more and more frustrated. It must have been bad, as John and I noticed, and it meant we had to cope with tuning and a drummer who had no sense of timing. About six numbers in, Pete realised what was the problem. The body of the guitar was coming apart at the edges and the neck was no longer stable. In true The Who fashion, Peter proceeded to smash his guitar, whilst the rest of the band tried to finish the number in some sort of form. The audience was a mixture of shocked, amazed and impressed. There was quite a lot of applause and it was the end of our part in the party, as there was no replacement guitar.

Bryan was furious! He smashed his drums sticks down at the end of the number. "I've never been so embarrassed before in my life!" he claimed, which came as a bit of a surprise. True to his word, though, that was the last time Bryan played drums for us. The rest of us stalwarts were not easily thwarted, and we returned to our regular practice sessions at Lidgett Lane Youth Club the following week.

One of our friends, David B, had some acquaintance that played drums. He was a nice lad, and he brought his drum kit to have a tryout. He was not quite like us. We were wild and into 'progressive music', and he liked T-Rex and David Bowie. He had a well groomed, almost mod hair cut, whereas we were long-haired and unkempt. He was OK as a drummer, certainly an improvement, and we played together a short while before it was clear that our musical styles were incompatible.

Dave B appeared with a drum kit shortly afterwards and, as in most things, David showed he was musically talented. He played drums for us and our music began to improve. However, he left after a while as I think he was more interested in playing guitar than drums. David carried on being a part of our circle and he had several repeat entries into the band's history and in the end he has been involved in the music industry for the whole of his life and made it a career.

Whilst all this was going on, I was taking part in several club organised activities. The first of interest was an orienteering competition on Ilkley Moor. This was a multi-club event and groups of four, two girls and two boys, were given a map with checkpoints marked where hidden clues could be found. I think these were letters. We had about eight hours to collect as many of the letters as possible and write them down on our check sheet. You had to plot your own course around the moors and navigate the entire way with only a compass as aid. We had a packed lunch, some sweets and a drink. There were safety bases dotted in one or two places if you needed help or got lost. Large numbers of inexperienced teenagers wandering Ilkley Moor in bad weather in summer had the potential for disaster, but it was well organised.

I think it was Chris that was the other boy with me and the two girls we didn't really know, but they were young and attractive, so we didn't care. I suppose Cedric R and the other leaders must have organised the teams. Maybe we should have got to know the girls better beforehand, as it may have avoided what was coming. I had no idea what orienteering was, and it differed greatly from the athletic map reading, long-distance run it is nowadays. This was a hike, and we wore hiking boots, anoraks, etc. It may have been summer, but the weather changes quickly on the moors. The peat bog land is difficult hiking, but the glorious heather was in full bloom, and there was the problem.

We got up onto the moors, and we were making good progress. Our feet were soaked from traipsing through the bog, and clouds came in a heavy drizzle and chilled us to the bone. It was at this point that one of the girls looked thoroughly miserable. I think she might have a been a year or two younger and she was quite small. Her cheeks looked flushed, and she said she didn't feel well. Where we were, there was little we could do about it. Her friend chirped in to tell us that her friend was allergic to heather.

Now, common sense would have suggested that sending your daughter on a hike through the heather of Ilkley Moor when it is in full bloom was probably not a good idea when she was allergic to heather. Clearly parental supervision was lacking, or maybe they didn't know what she was doing for the day. Anyway, we carried on until she was unable to walk and then we had to carry her the rest of the way until we could find one of the safety posts.

We found one and deposited her and her friend there to be taken by ambulance back to civilisation. We carried on, not willing to be beaten by the cold, wet, blisters, exhaustion and loss of half of our team. We made it to the end and, I can say, we were pleased to do so. It was a real adventure, and we loved it. I learned that the two girls were fine and so, all in all, it was quite a good day.

As it happens, it was much better than the experience of one other team who apparently came across the body of a man, high on the moors. That was kept a bit hush-hush at the time so as not to alarm parents.

The event can't have caused too much of a stir as there was another one the following year I took part in, which was much less exciting and had sunny weather.

COVENTRY CAPERS

As I have mentioned before, I attended St Edmund's Youth Club for several years. Roundhay School also had a strong link to St Edmund's and I remember attending carol services there annually. The church itself was quite old and intriguing. Each year we would gather in our classes and march up the streets, in what the locals must have felt was an invasion of unruly, long-haired youth. It was always interesting what new and novel words boys created for the traditional carols. The three kings sold a range of items and another carol involved Durex, which created high mirth amongst the testosterone overdosed boys.

Anyway, I will return to my tale and leave Christmas for the correct season. St Edmund's had arranged a visit to Coventry Cathedral for the club members and it meant a couple of nights at the centre attached to the modern cathedral. This was 1968 and I know it was so because my older brother had recently bought the Beatles White double album. This was the first release, and the album had its own individual number stamped on it. These albums are now worth quite a lot of money, which is a shame for my brother, as I didn't really take great care of it.

I put my name down to attend the excursion and, on the day, a coach arrived at St Edmund's and so did those who were going. I can only hazard a guess that there were about fifty teenagers, with leaders and one or two volunteer parents. One volunteer was Mr Smith (name changed), a local businessman. Many of those attending were pupils of Roundhay Boys' and Girls' Schools, but others were from Allerton Grange and maybe other schools. The group was known to each other, but there were cliques amongst them and seating tended to follow these groupings.

It was quite a long drive down to Coventry and there was a lot of excited chatter and I think one or two of the leaders, but mainly Mr Smith, told us in no uncertain terms, to 'Shut up!'. Now, in fairness to him, he was middle-aged, owned a thriving business, was used to being in control, and was probably totally unprepared for the din we produced. I would have been thirteen, as were most of those present, and I can't say that I was a likeable teenager, at least not in the eyes of the adults present. Long hair, spots, attitude, rock band member, outspoken, aggressive (sometimes) and willing to try anything, were not the attributes that middle-aged parents wanted their daughters associating with. However, these attributes were attractive to several teenage daughters of such parents. As a result, the said Mr Smith took an instant dislike to me, particularly as his daughter seemed to want to hang around with me and my friends. He wandered down the coach and seemed to keep a keen eye on his daughter. I was sitting next to her, and his expression made it very clear that he would brook no trouble from me. The sad thing was that I took this as something of a challenge. He didn't like me, therefore I didn't like him and now I had a purpose for the weekend that was other than just enjoying my time.

(As a parent and a grandparent myself, I now fully understand how he felt. Luckily I have only had sons, and I am not sure how I would have handled a 'boyfriend from hell', and I was certainly his worst nightmare.)

The journey down the M1 was uneventful and eventually we arrived at the hostel attached to the Cathedral. A very approachable and modern member of the clergy who handled the centre welcomed us. We carried our bags in and were allocated dorms with bunk beds. The girls had a couple, and I believe the boys did too. There was a door between the dorms, but that was locked and kept the genders apart.

We soon discovered who was on the other side and there was calling through the door and some rather inappropriate suggestions and a lot of laughter. We chose our bunks, left our bags, and went down for an evening meal. My group of friends included Chris M, David B, Stuart S, Nigel C and more of my mates from Roundhay. As it was late, there wasn't anything to do after we had eaten and cleared up before going to our dorms to settle down for the night. I had a bottom bunk and, whilst we were getting ready, one boy appeared with an evil gleam in his eye. He had gone downstairs to get something he had left and at reception saw the keys for the doors hanging there. I will not name that boy, but he is forever to be recognised for this act, as he held in his hand the key for the adjoining door. It was a high-risk endeavour, but offered even greater reward. He advanced to the door, inserted the key, and opened Pandora's Box. There was a click, the handle was turned, and we were met by a strange smell. Whilst our dorm was filled with body odour, and Brut, the odour that hit us, was perfumed and pleasant. What a contrast!

Voices became hushed. There were giggles, and some boys wandered into the female realm and one or two brave souls crossed over to the dark side of our dorm. There were some whispered voices, some fumbling, and who knows what. I only know that none of the adults would have slept if they had even an inkling of what was taking place. I chatted with Mr Smith's daughter and we got along quite well, certainly better than I did with her father. Nothing happened that should have upset him, but I still don't think he would have appreciated his daughter talking to me whilst she wore her nightdress.

After the initial excitement, the dorms returned to their appropriate order. The joy was the breaking of the rules, rather than anything else. The door was locked, and the key returned, and no adult was aware of what had happened. Breakfast was good and then we were escorted to the cathedral for a tour. I had visited several times, as my aunt used to live in Coventry before moving to Kenilworth, and I used to visit each Easter for several years. The old cathedral had been bombed during WWII and Coventry was the second most devastated city after London. The remains of the original 11th century cathedral still stand next to the modern one and the altar cross in the new cathedral was made from burnt rafters from the old.

The new cathedral is a very modern building, and there is an enormous sculpture by Jacob Epstein showing St Michael's Victory over the Devil. Inside is an enormous modern tapestry of Christ and the floor has coins set into it. The building was ultra-modern for its day and not to everyone's taste, and it must have cost a fortune to build.

That evening we were weary and after the meal we were addressed by the clergyman who ran the centre. He asked if we had questions and there was a twenty-minute question-and-answer session. At one point, I asked him about the cost of the cathedral. I asked how the church justified spending so much money on a building whilst there was so much poverty in the world. The priest smiled and said that it was a good question that he and the church struggled with. At that point, Mr. Smith interrupted and said, 'Don't listen to him, he's just anti-establishment!' He was clearly not impressed with my question, but the official of the cathedral smiled and continued to answer me. If there had been any doubt about how I was thought of by Mr. Smith, it was crystal clear how he felt now. His eyes burned into me for the rest of the trip.

The evening was spent playing table tennis or listening to music. There was a record player and, seeing as I had my brother's Beatles White Album with me, it had a good workout. I am sure it was not treated with care and it was probably scratched and damaged. When we retired later, the dividing door may well have been opened, but the excitement was probably less. We left after breakfast the next day and, if looks could kill, I would have never survived the coach trip back to St Edmund's, particularly as Mr. Smith's daughter sat next to me on the way back.

24 MILE MIDNIGHT HIKE AND THE FIRST REAL CONCERT

The youth club scene in the 1960s and 1970s was really excellent, from my experience, and I think we probably enjoyed it at its best. There was always something going on and I have nothing but affection and respect for the young men and women who acted as the leaders of a group of unruly teenagers. Britain was changing financially, socially and culturally, and teenagers were enjoying freedoms that their parents couldn't have imagined. The establishment of the time was seeing their control diminish. Television, pirate radio stations, youth culture, the pill, female liberation and fun, were all challenges for the generation who had experienced the deprivations of war. Unions were shaking the status quo and working people were enjoying a higher standard of living.

As school students, we were lucky to be given educational opportunities that our parents had never had. University, Polytechnics, Colleges and training were usually free of cost and grants were provided. Education was seen as a means of broadening the mind rather than a way to a job, but we didn't know. It was just how it was. I can't say that I appreciated these opportunities, but I certainly enjoyed myself as much as possible. Youth clubs were the churches' response to keep the youth on track. In the case of my friends and me, they achieved only limited success. That being said, I was not all bad.

I remember taking part in two walks to raise money for some good cause, and sponsored walks and other similar events were only just getting going. Prior to this, there had just been the flag days.

Poppy Day and other charity fund raising days relied on the selling of flags with sharp pins. People with tins would stand around and get donations from passersby and pin a small flag on their chests to show they had donated. These tended to be on Saturdays and they weren't that common then, so most people were happy to donate. I remember giving up a Saturday morning when at Harehills County Primary to sell flags in Leeds.

Whilst attending Lidgett Methodist Youth Club, we were asked if we would take part in a 24 mile midnight hike. It was a whole of Leeds event and started off and finished near the Town Hall. There were hundreds of young people and in a similar way to the orienteering, it was well organised with first aid for mainly blister repair, check points and drink stations. Quite a few of us from the club took part, and it seemed a great idea. I think we headed out of Leeds towards Guiseley, past Menston, the Silver Cross factory and Harry Ramsden's fish restaurant, and then back into Leeds. It took place on a Saturday and the police were involved in controlling traffic, etc. It would have been much the same as the organisation of the fun runs, half-marathons and marathon events that came later in the decade.

We all started out with great excitement and little idea of what 24 miles meant. We strode out in a mass of kids stretching for miles and we chatted and laughed. God knows what the residents thought as the throng passed their houses in the early hours of the morning. After a while, the chatter became less, the feet more sore, the temperature fell and tiredness kicked in. I can't remember what time of the year it was, but it still was very cold at four in the morning.

Reaching the halfway point was something, but it brought home the realisation that we had the same to do again. I seem to remember that Fire Brigade by The Move was a big hit, so it would have been 1968. I recall being in some sort of exhausted trance with the song going around and around in my head. A lifetime later, the dawn cast a grey light over the pavement as we trudged along. The lines of hikers had thinned out over the miles and now there were only scattered groups who kept going, marking the time with step following step. It was necessary to keep a check on the other groups ahead to ensure we didn't get lost. I suppose some children must have given in because of exhaustion or injury, and been taken back in cars, but the majority persevered. I think I arrived at the Town Hall early Sunday morning at about 8.30am. Tea and cake were provided for hikers and youth groups met back up with others from their clubs. Conversations were few and eyes looked downcast and in need of sleep and when all the group were accounted for, the leaders drove us home and dropped us off at our respective houses. I can't say it was a great fun, but it was an experience. It can't have been too bad as I went back for another go a year later. The week after the hike, we had to collect our sponsors' money, the hardest part, and then deliver it back at the club to send off to the charity.

Another great feature of Lidgett Lane Methodist Youth Club was that it let our band practice there on youth club nights. There were two halls, and we were allowed to use the smaller, newer hall. There was an agreement that, in return, we would play a gig for them for free. We were building up our repertoire and most of our songs were originals. I think I have said that the band did not play covers as we didn't have the skill. Well, that wasn't quite the truth. One of the tracks we played early on was a song called 'What's Going On?' by an Irish band, Taste. It had the guitarist, Rory Gallagher. It was a rather adventurous choice for us as Taste was quite a musically accomplished band. I am not sure our version did it justice, but we gave it a go. We were extending our set a little and playing better by this time. We still didn't have a great song list, but it was growing. There were the rock numbers, I'm Leaving, Going, Last Bus etc, slower numbers like I Think and Atlantis, and then the odd parody such as Get It Up (Based on T-Rex's Get It On).

We were asked to play for a Saturday concert/disco. We did this for free as payment for being allowed to practise there every week. We were to play on the stage in the old hall and on the day we set up in the afternoon and did a sound check. A boy called Paul had created a lighting rig with the help of another boy, Danny. It was very basic and had highly questionable wiring, but there was a row of coloured bulbs and he could turn the lights off and on individually by playing what looked like a little keyboard. We weren't going to complain, as it was the only lighting we had and better than any other local band had at the time. I think Paul and Danny regularly got electric shocks from it, but they were fit, young and expendable, so we didn't care. I must add that we also weren't immune to electric shocks. Because we played as loud as we could, we often blew the fuses in the amps. The method of fixing this was to wrap silver paper from cigarette packets around the fuse and push it back in, 'Do not try this at home folks!', but it worked.

We were set up for our first gig after the Busmen's Club talent evening and nerves were jangling. (I believe this was before the guitar breaking do, so Bryan would still have been the drummer.

> LEEDS 628364
>
> # ATLANTIS
>
> PETE   JOHN   Lighting and Electriceries
> DAVE BRYAN   PAUL and DANNY

The original band card produced for the concert

We had been to the off licence and had a small bottle of whiskey hidden in our kit. There was a trap door on the stage and this led down to the storage room. The band and lighting crew disappeared down in the hole for a half an hour before we were to start. We passed around the whisky, but we had to keep it secret. Alcoholic drinks were definitely banned from the Methodist youth club.

The set was to start with John playing, 'Let the Children into Your Heart', on his own on the stage above us. He climbed up, and the curtains opened. We listened from below, continuing to pass the drink around. We had little, but sufficient to take away nerves and sense. We heard John finish the number and there was a reasonable round of applause. Someone suggested it would be funny not to appear at the arranged time, and much to John's horror, we left him standing and waiting. It was mean! Eventually we climbed out, took our instruments and launched into our first number. We went through our set and it was not great. The drumming was wild, the guitar playing loose, and we learnt a very great lesson: alcohol and playing are not a great combo! The audience were not totally thrilled, but we managed. I think there was a general sigh when the DJ returned.

THE UNKEMPT YEARS

You would have thought that after our group experience at Chapel Allerton's Methodist Hall, we would have realised that maybe we weren't going to make it, but we soldiered on with optimism and arrogance. It is true that we practised constantly and, as with most things, practice leads to improvement in skill. There were better bands around at the time, as far as musical virtuosity, but as we primarily wrote our own songs, there was no one who sounded quite like us.

We were always hampered by lack of equipment and, in particular, a PA system. The microphones were just fed through an amp into a basic speaker, and there was little room to add effects. In reality, the amp was always on full volume in a vain attempt for the vocals to be heard over the drums, guitar, and bass. John was on keyboards and did most of the singing, with me adding additional vocals. All bands suffer from tensions between the members and ours was no different. Peter and John were in many ways opposites. Peter wanted a rawer, rock sound and John was into melody and maybe more subtlety. That is a basic explanation of the complexity that has remained to this day. The tension between the two added dynamism to our writing and playing and we probably benefitted from it, even though it led to many arguments and personnel changes. The funny thing is that they have continued playing together for most of their lives and are still good friends.

As our early performances had shown, there was no lack of excitement at our gigs. We had stuck with the name Atlantis for the band, after the title of one of our most enduring numbers, and we were starting to get a following. We had our regulars who were the girlfriends and friends of the band. These came from Roundhay and Alwoodley mostly, and like us, they were a motley crew. I am not sure what our image was, probably a poor man's hippy in the late sixties: trench coats, tie-dyed T-shirts, loon pants or jeans and, at one time, leather and wooden clogs. Hair was long and unkempt and there was the occasional moustache, sideburns, beard or other teenage signs of manhood.

Peter and John were no longer at school. John was working in printing and was the most affluent of us all. This even manifested itself in his purchasing a new Ford Capri, bronze colour and with a vinyl roof. You could see why that would impress the girls! Peter was a little directionless, but this was soon to change when he found his vocation. I was still at Roundhay School and so my hair and facial accoutrements had to pass the rigours of teacher inspection. Long hair had to be hidden down the back of the shirt collar when there was a check. Luckily, I had wavy hair and so the actual length was not so obvious. Alas! My luscious locks and waves were about to wave bye-bye as my genes were set to make me follicly-challenged for my adult life. I would have done anything to retain my hair and anyone who has lost theirs knows the stake that is driven into one's ego and confidence. It must be many times worse for women, but in the sixties baldness was stereotyped by the 'Up and Over' hair of the Hamlet advert, the Bobby Charlton, or the orange toupee that gave the appearance of a dead hamster on the head. I have a lot more I could tell about this, but I will save it for another tale.

Back to the band! We had a gig booked at St Edmund's church hall, and we were feeling quietly confident. We had built up our repertoire and enjoyed some success, in the first half acclaim of the Chapel Allerton riot night, and now we were ready to sock it to them. I believe we played twice at St Edmund's. On one of the gigs we had a support band, and that was Trident and comprised three Roundhay lads. They used some old piece of shortwave radio to produce quite an eerie sound as they tuned it, a bit like the Theremin that was used on the Beach Boys' Good Vibrations. They were the support act, so they set up in front of the stage and, as the headline act, we were on the stage.

I think that must have been the second gig, as our first concert there comprised two sets, the same as at the Chapel Allerton riot gig, but without the aggro. We set up during the afternoon and did a run through, sound check, and we were feeling chilled and confident. The stage curtains were drawn, and the doors opened and the crowds of teenagers poured in. Now, maybe it was just a quiet weekend in Leeds, but the place was packed with a swarm of teenagers who seemed in a good mood and were ready to enjoy themselves. I am not sure if they were quite prepared for the assault on their eardrums and eyeballs, but they appeared up for it!

There must have been a disco running, to fill in the spaces between our sets, and the throng were soon taking up their gender roles, the girls dancing in circles and the boys standing around, attempting to look cool, but really looking like spare parts. Socials such as this were an opportunity for pairings and whispers of who liked who led to couples forming and breaking up.

I am sure that social occasions over the generations have seen a similar pattern of coupling with just changes to the situation, location, and time. In the sixties, these were the more colourful but unkempt years. Looking back at some of the photographs, I cringe at the fashions, but I am sure that the current trends will be equally cringe-worthy in the future. The youth club organisers must have been very pleased with the attendance and soft drinks etc. were doing a roaring trade.

It was our turn to play. We were plugged in, turned on and tugging at the lead to start. Paul M was still doing the lighting, so we were all in danger of electrocution, but that just added to the buzz, or was that just a shorting guitar lead? The curtains opened, and we headed off at breakneck pace. We had decided not to start with John's solo slow number and hit them with a rocker. I think it was 'Going'! Reg was drumming and having a great beat helped enormously. For some reason, everything seemed to gel and at the end of the first number, there was more applause than we had ever had before. The rest of the set also was warmly received and, at the end, they were clamouring for more. I think we had planned about two half hour sets and we had some decent material saved for the second. The curtains closed, and the DJ took over again.

We looked at each other and smiled. It was the best reception and start that we had experienced, which boded well for the second half. We joined our crew out in the audience and there was a lot of positive chatter. After a while, we returned to the stage to prepare for the second half. There was a growing nervousness. Would the second set be as well-received? We had seen what could happen at the Chapel Allerton gig, but as the curtains opened to the cacophony of the first number, we lost our apprehension and just got on with the performance. The lights were quite effective and there were no casualties. At the end of the first number, we were again greeted with good applause. This was unfamiliar territory! A successful gig! We bashed on and finished our numbers. The audience wanted more, but we had nothing left unplayed. We hadn't considered an encore! Not to be put off, Pete suggested we do 'Get it Up!' a parody of the T-Rex 'Get it On!' with lyrics that put into question Marc Bolan's personal habits. I think he thought the audience wouldn't remember we had already played it and he was probably right, or at least they didn't care. It was fortuitous that the vocals were almost inaudible, as the lyrics might have raised concern from the youth club organisers, who were still smiling at the success of the event.

This number went well, and they still wanted more. We gave them an impromptu blues number, with John singing anything that came into his head, and we finished with that. The curtains closed, and we basked in our glory. A successful gig! We'd done it and therefore we could continue doing it and building on the material. It should have been so simple. Creative differences have a way of spoiling a mood and the euphoria was short-lived. There were two sides: those of us, including me, who wanted to build gradually on what we had achieved, and those who wanted to make major changes and throw out old material. Peter wanted to make some changes. He felt we needed an additional guitarist, and in hindsight, he was probably right. He also wanted to take the band beyond just rock-and-roll and delve into more challenging genres. Was he right? Probably! But the truth is, it shook the tree and more people created more challenging dynamics.

Still, it was a good night and good enough for the youth club to book us for another gig a few weeks later.

CHAPEL ALLERTON HALL RIOT

Our band was becoming more accomplished, and we had settled on the name 'Atlantis'. Somehow we were building a reputation and I am not sure whether it was for our music or our outrageous overconfidence. The answer lies somewhere in between. One big difference from most of the local groups was that we wrote and performed our own songs. We did do a couple of parody songs based on hits from the time. Who can forget "Get It Up!" based on T-Rex's 'Get it On'? Well, probably almost everyone who ever heard it, but we liked it. I cannot really remember how we ever got booked in those days, but we did. It was usually youth clubs or parties.

Somehow we got a gig at the Methodist Hall at Chapel Allerton, which is just behind Harrogate Road and the main shopping street. The hall is a large imposing stone building, and I knew it from when I had visited my Grandma's house on Regent Terrace, as a child. I had never been in it and we felt that because we were booked for a concert, then we ought to do a recce and see what the facilities, size and acoustics were like. A week or two before the concert, the band and accompanying friends visited the youth club that was held there for a sneak peek.

It was a dark night when we arrived at about eight in the evening and the club was not really bustling. There were chairs along each side of the hall and a stage at the far end. Music was being played from a record deck and it was the usual fare of recent and perennial hits. The lights were dim, but I can't remember any coloured lights. We had gained a new drummer by this time, a lad called Reg, and he was quite an accomplished musician. This was so much so that our friend Roger, still a friend and neighbour, told me that he was far too good for us. Reg brought something that the band had missed and that was a regular beat and timing. It made my job as the bass player much easier and more enjoyable. The girls that were with us were mainly from Alwoodley and the band, Pete, John, Reg and me, were accompanied by John L, David G, Roger C and others. I point this out, as what happened during our visit concerned them rather than me.

The hall is about a hundred yards from the then police station, and you would have thought that the locality would have modified teenage behaviour. We stood around. Some of the girls danced around their handbags in a circle and we just chilled and tried our best to look cool. At one point in the evening, a large group of teenagers arrived and the calm atmosphere changed a little. An atmosphere descended on the place, but we were capable of handling ourselves and weren't too intimidated. We definitely weren't looking for trouble, but our dress and persona made us stand out. Pete was probably the centre of this. He had a manner that made him the focus of attention, and he was a couple of years older than me and considerably taller.

What happened next I was oblivious to until after it had happened. John L had gone to the toilet and was in the cubicle, and Dave G was at the urinal. Some lads came into the toilet and, without warning, Dave turned around to see a chair descending onto his head. This was totally unprovoked and Dave was not an aggressive lad normally. He blocked the blow and at the same time, Peter must have been made aware of what was happening as he rushed in and a fight ensued. Peter and David proved successful and got the better of the altercation. John in the toilet heard all that was going on and ended up climbing out of the window to escape. This was clearly a shrewd move. Dave and Peter returned to the main hall and Dave had blood dripping from a cut above his nose. Luckily, his glasses hadn't broken. Common sense prevailed amongst the group, and we made a tactical retreat from the club as quickly as possible to avoid further aggression. We managed to disappear into the side streets of Chapel Allerton and nothing else happened.

Now, anyone sensible would have taken this as an omen, but not us. We were booked to play, and we were not going to miss out on our, I believe, six pounds performance fee. The afternoon of the gig we arrived at the hall. The equipment was transported in a couple of cars that we had. I think Pete and John had cars at this time, as they were older. Somehow we got our equipment there and somehow we got it home afterwards. We set up on the stage and we did our sound check. As usual, we were far too loud, but that was the norm at the time. It was decided that we would do two forty minute sets and there was a DJ before us and then during the interval. The DJ's gear was set up on the hall floor to the left at the back as you entered. This was a mistake, but no one knew it. He had a decent rig, lights, and a good range of music. After everything was checked, we had a break and I think we went to the Nag's Head. The Nag's Head was my Grandad's local, but he had long since passed away.

I must have been around fifteen, but I had a face that always looked older and I don't think I had ever been asked about my age or refused service. John and Pete were older and so they weren't ever asked, either. Some of our friends did not look as old and a few of the girls were a year or two younger still. On another occasion, at a different venue, two of them were charged with underage drinking in a pub in Leeds City Centre, but that was a very rare occurrence. There were no problems getting a drink there and at about seven-thirty, we returned to the hall.

The venue was full and everyone seemed to be having a good time. The DJ was playing the music that the crowd liked and we went onto the stage, behind the curtains, and prepared to play our first set. A quick tune-up and a nod from the organiser and the music stopped, the curtains opened, and we started our first number. It was probably the song 'Going', which was always popular. We finished it and, much to our surprise and delight, there was quite an appreciative round of applause. Stunned from this reception, we headed off into 'Last Bus' and again it was well received. The whole of the set went well, which came as a unique experience. The curtains were closed, and the DJ continued.

We were behind the curtains and congratulating one another when we heard the record jump. We didn't really take much notice, and we were discussing the second set when the records started jumping regularly and there were cries of annoyance. I remember peering through the curtains and seeing a group of lads, some skin-heads and they had discovered that if they jumped up and down, the wooden floor moved, causing the records to jump. They thought this was a great wheeze, but others did not.

The poor DJ was looking panic-stricken. Within minutes, altercations were starting. Chests were being pushed into other chests in an aggressive manner, and things were not looking good. Not only was the DJ in panic mode, the organiser was, too. He rushed over to us to ask us to start our second set to help defuse the situation. We agreed. Amps were turned on and the first chord was struck. The blast of sound was quite majestic as the curtains opened, but whereas before there was adulation from the crowd, this time there was mayhem before us. It was like something out of a John Wayne barroom brawl. Fists were flying, there was panic, screaming, and records tossed about.

We tried our best, but even we recognised things were already out of control. We may have got part way into the second number when we decided it wasn't going to calm the hordes, and enough was enough. The anger was not directed towards us and, in fact, we were totally ignored, but things could change in an instant, so we pulled the curtains shut and started packing up quickly. It is funny how only a curtain separating you from a riot makes you feel safe, but it did.

We packed up quickly and took our gear out through the back door. The night was frosty and there was a growing mist. With relief we got packed up, sent the gear off and the rest of the band and hangers-on disappeared out into the quiet streets, leaving hell behind us. I must add that we had collected our payment prior to playing, so that wasn't a concern. I couldn't believe how long it was taking for someone to contact the police, but they certainly hadn't turned up whilst we were anywhere near.

Once we were all in the clear, we reflected positively on the evening's performance, but I think the DJ would have had a very different view. The joys of being a teenager!

YOUR MOTHER WARNED YOU ABOUT BOYS LIKE US

I guess it was just the times, but there was an alignment of the stars and the swinging sixties met with adolescence and a society that didn't know what to think about teenagers. Looking at us now, we don't seem very wild and revolutionary, but in the late sixties, early seventies, we were unsure about what we wanted to be or do. Then again, we certainly knew that we didn't want to be like our parents. And by golly, did we make that clear!

The word bandied around was freedom, and as 'almost adults', we wanted more than our fair share of it. For me, music was revolutionary and inspirational. My wife doesn't see it the same, but I saw the world change from black and white to Technicolor. Clothes became wild, colourful, and a statement of individuality and, despite a general lack of money, we did our best to make ourselves stand out. My mother started wearing short dresses with Mary Quant patterns and colours. Artificial fabrics were all the rage and prices were low. I believe she bought a dress for ten shillings, 50 pence nowadays.

As a teenager we didn't have much money, but I managed to buy a pair of Levis and they were basically my only trousers that were not school ones and, in fact, the only ones that weren't shorts. My father had built wardrobes into our bedrooms. There wasn't a lot of space, but that didn't matter as there wasn't much in them apart from school uniforms. Having an older brother was handy, as I could raid all the trendy clothes that he had. I must say that he was very patient with me, but occasionally we came to blows. My younger brother likes to remind me how my older brother and I fought over the tomato sauce bottle, which ended up splattering over the ceiling. Brotherly love!

As I have said previously, my first social experiences were youth clubs, but by the age of fourteen, we were moving further afield. My experience of parties had started when I was much younger with the usual children's birthday parties. By the end of Harehills County Primary School, we were becoming very interested in the opposite gender and games such as pass the parcel were being replaced by postman's knock. In our teens, this moved on a notch. I am not sure what parents, particularly parents of girls, were thinking when they agreed to host parties. To make matters worse, they had obviously been persuaded not to be present, which was a recipe for disaster.

I can't remember where the first party I attended was, but it would have been either around the Roundhay School area or Alwoodley. We had, for a long while, gathered in Pete's cellar at Harehills but, as we knew who was attending, somehow I don't count those. Times were different, and it was quite easy for teenagers to buy alcohol, and cigarettes were on sale from street cigarette vending machines. Although, as I have said, we didn't have much money. A bottle of cheap sherry, QC or the like, or preferably a bottle of Chablis, could be bought for about six shillings (30 pence). Cider was another favourite and was stronger in alcohol than the current offerings. Newcastle Brown was not a good choice as it was sweet and sickly and gave young drinkers a dreadful hangover and a determination never to drink again. We tried everything in those days. Martini and lemonade, lager and lime or blackcurrant were often the choice of the girls, but avoided by the lads.

There was a very different attitude in the 1960s-70s. The girls tended to drink moderately, and it was the boys who had no sense and drank until they needed help. This was usually provided by a girlfriend, who ensured you got home safely.

Word got around about upcoming parties and it was just accepted that if one of our crowd was invited, then we all were, which probably meant about twenty of us. They were usually planned for a Friday or Saturday evening. The front doors would often be open and you could hear loud music long before you arrived at the host's lovely home. Usually, by the time we arrived, it would already be crowded, and we just arrived and drink, if you brought any, was deposited in the kitchen. Boys would gather in the kitchen and the hallway and the two rooms, front and back, would see teenagers standing chatting, smoking and drinking. I don't remember any dancing. People would bring their latest records to play and I sometimes did, but usually regretted it as people would drag the needle over them, stand on them and they were never the same afterwards.

The air would be thick with smoke and even if you were a non-smoker you would have inhaled half a packet by the time you left and your clothes would reek of tobacco. Some civilised and kindly parents would provide nibbles, but they clearly didn't expect the numbers that were attending. Mid-evening, the pantry would be raided for any food and anything desirable would be liberated and greedily enjoyed. Good carpets had drink spilt on them, cigarettes trodden into them and food and vomit added to the mix.

Parents would have made arrangements to return by elevenish and the host of the party would start frantically cleaning up shortly after ten-thirty. The girl would probably be quite upset by the careless attitude of the guests and her friends would rally around to put things to rights. The boys, including me, saw this as the signal that it was time to leave. We would gather up our records, search for missing friends, often lying ill in the back or front gardens, and head as far away as possible from the repercussions. Physically supporting any incapacitated members of our circle, we made our way along the dark, and now quiet, streets. Our ears were ringing, our vision slightly blurred as the frost and mist settled over the city suburbs. I don't know why, but in my memory, the parties were held during autumn and winter, but maybe that is just my imagination.

I can only guess what the parents must have thought. Carpet cleaning, or replacing, tears and a very firm declaration that this was the first and the very last time a party would ever be allowed in their house. I don't remember many people re-hosting parties until we got older, except for Peter's cellar and at John L's, house where his home became social central for quite a while.

I must add, for educational purposes, some parties that I attended convinced me to never allow my own children to host parties. Apparently, this didn't always work out as they took their chances when we went on holiday without them. They were considerably older at this point than I was in my party days. As parents, we got away fairly unscathed, so I can't grumble too much.

Our dreadful behaviour included: cooking a Heinz Steam pudding in a kettle in one house, hanging the host mother's very large corset over the shade of a standard lamp for all the world to see and marvel at, red wine spilt on a white carpet, and my surprise when opening a pantry door to find a partly clad couple. Of course, there were many others, but I guess you see the trend of bad behaviour.

I can't say that our group was the worst behaved and often we were observers rather than players in the shenanigans, but I guess we were the types that parents dreaded and warned their children about.

The following Monday after a party, without fail, the host girl claimed it was a fantastic party. Their parents hadn't complained and that they would host one again in the near future. I guess this was a way of saving face and, as I have said, few had an encore.

For all our turbulent times and experiences, somehow we all grew up and, in almost every case, became pillars of society in a wide range of professions and occupations. I guess we were lucky that mobile phone cameras were not on hand to record the highlights, and this is a luxury that the younger generation doesn't have. Mind you, people like me are now retelling some of the wild times that grandparents got up to. We may be old, but we knew how to have a riotous time in our youth!

LET THE MUSIC PLAY LIVE AGAIN

There were, of course, other music venues in Leeds and I went to concerts at a number of them. One of these was Leeds Town Hall. Here I saw many acts, but two in particular stood out as special.

One was King Crimson and this would have been early 1970. This was after the release of their first album, In the Court of the Crimson King, but was when the band was starting to break apart, with the departure of Ian McDonald and Michael Giles. Boz Burrell had been with the band for six weeks and he was playing bass, an instrument he had only played since joining the group. He had replaced Greg Lake on vocals, who had left to join Keith Emerson and formed Emerson, Lake and Palmer. Mel Collins was also new on sax and flute. He was brilliant! It was an amazing concert. The sound of mellotrons filled the hall and Epitaph, 21st Century Schizoid Man, were amazing and unlike anything I had ever seen or heard before. The drama of the sounds and the musicianship was spectacular, and it was the experience that took me along the path of progressive music. There was humour and a drum solo that ended with the drummer falling over onto his back. One song played was Ladies of the Road, which now would be politically incorrect and potential evidence in a misbehaviour trial. I left that concert wanting more than anything to be like them and to play in a band.

The second major concert was Deep Purple. It was also in 1970 and the band were at the height of their fame with Ian Gillan, Ritchie Blackmore, Roger Glover, Ian Paice and Jon Lord, as the line-up. Black Night had been a major hit and the album Deep Purple in

Rock had charted at number 2 in the UK. They were a great band, but maybe lacked the uniqueness of King Crimson. They had songs such as Child in Time and Speed King that could tear the place apart, and their musicianship was great. The most memorable thing about the concert for me, apart from the Blackmore's guitar playing and Gillan's vocals, was the drum solo. Now I am not keen on drum solos usually and they seem to be an opportunity for the rest of the band to have a rest and probably a drink and a smoke, or whatever they are into. The band started the introduction to the solo and then they exited the stage, leaving Ian Paice alone on drums. He started the solo in a traditional manner and he was clearly a fantastic drummer. He then moved onto electric drums. Now these were in their infancy and few, if any, of the audience had heard them before. This added an extra dimension and prevented boredom, which was good, as I think he had been playing about twenty minutes at this point. On it went, and the audience had just about lost their patience and their minds when the band returned after what seemed like a lifetime. They finished the track and during the chat to the audience, we were informed that the rest of the band had had a curry across from the town hall, whilst the solo went on. Those were the days! If I had known, I think I would have joined them and returned after the solo. Anyway, the band finished their set, and it was really quite impressive.

Another venue was Leeds University, and I know I missed out on some great concerts. I could have seen very early Led Zeppelin, but didn't go. I did see the band, Family, twice. They had had hits with No Mule's Fool and The Weaver's Answer and they had the magnificent voice of Roger Chapman. They were a big act in their day and their concerts provided me with one of the best live experiences and one of the worst. They were a combination of folk, jazz and rock music and the first time I saw them, they were brilliant. Charlie Whitney was on guitar, Poli Palmer was on keyboards, vibes and flute, John Wetton on bass and Rob Townsend on drums. They were tight, well balanced and the audience, packed in and sitting on the floor, loved them. The second time I saw them, a year or so later, they were awful. They seemed to no longer care. Certainly there were signs of intoxication, or something else. The sound was messy and not at all balanced. I had enjoyed them so much the first time that this was such a disappointment.

One concert I missed at the University was The Who Live at Leeds. It was recorded on the 14th February 1970 and is still held in great esteem and recognised as one of the best live albums of all times. I could have gone, but I think I spent the money on something else. Such a shame.

The Queen's Hall in Leeds was originally a tram and then a bus depot, but became a music venue in 1961. It was a vast building with poor acoustics, and I saw The Jack Bruce Band there in 1971. They were supported by Fuzzy Duck and East of Eden, who had just had a hit record with Jig-a-Jig. I don't know whether it was because it was a vast empty hall with a stage and the audience were sitting on dirty concrete whilst trucks moved equipment at the sides of the stage, or that the acoustics were beyond anyone's help, or whether the bands were just not that good, but I was glad to leave at the end of the show. I never returned for another concert there and I can't say that I missed it.

The Fforde Grene was more than just a Harehills' pub and, for many years, it promoted live music. In the 1970s and 80s, it was alive with great bands. Some went on to become famous, some already were and some were great, but vanished into oblivion. One band that struck a chord with me was called Limelight. I had never heard of them and I expected very little, but they were brilliant. They played mostly Led Zeppelin covers, but were as good, almost as the real thing. I had a brilliant night and often wondered what had happened to them. I have done a bit of research and they did produce one self-titled album of heavy metal in 1980. Other bands at the Fforde Grene were The Sex Pistols, Dire Straits, U2, Simple Minds, Def Leppard and The Rolling Stones. I can only assume the Stones were doing a small-venue warm up prior to a tour. Unfortunately, I missed these acts, but I am sure that many remember them.

Live music really got to me in the late 1960s and my friends and I formed our first band. Just like many music devotees, I would read album covers many times and used to buy the New Musical Express and Sounds to discover what was happening with the acts I loved and the musicians I idolised. Over the years, I have been delighted with the musical skill and originality of the acts I have seen and only rarely disappointed.

BEAUTY AND UGLINESS

I was thinking back to my time attending youth clubs at the end of the 1960s and I was torn between some wonderful memories and some that were not as good as they should have been. Apparently, I was on the St Edmund's Youth Club Committee in 1967-8 and, like Lidgett Methodist Youth Club, they organised several social and educational events for members.

One of these I have very fond memories of, and that was a hike along the River Wharfe that ended with a BBQ at a farm. It was one of those days when everything comes together to make it so memorable. Maybe it wasn't for others, but it was for me. It was midsummer, the weather was beautiful, hot and sunny. The walk started at Collingham and followed the River Wharfe past Netherby to just past the A61, where it ended at a farm. I don't remember it as a big event, just St Edmund's members and I believe we started at about midday and walked along the bank of the river. This part of the Wharfe is slow moving and apparently a good fishing area, but, as you will know, if you have read about my angling adventures, I never caught anything there. We ambled along, a group of maybe twenty to thirty teenagers and three or four leaders, listening to the sound of the river and the birds. Spirits were high and boys' shirts were removed to catch a tan from the strong sunlight. There was chatter, laughter, and good humour. We didn't go in the river, but we lay on the banks taking in the sun, the sounds and the smells. I now know that part of the smell was the Himalayan Balsam plant. These are an introduced and very invasive weeds, but as a youngster I loved them because of their seed pods. The pods are pendulous, almost lantern shaped and when ripe if touched, they burst open and fire seeds out in all directions. Unfortunately, that makes them very addictive, and we spent a lot of time touching the pods to get them to burst open and thus helping spread the weed. Nothing particularly happened apart from good fellowship, laughter and a sense of joy of being young and the world being in front of us.

As the day wore on, we flagged a little under the heat, but at the right time, we arrived at our destination. We were greeted with the smell of a BBQ and quickly devoured the food on offer as only hungry teenagers can. Eventually, we were ferried home in a variety of cars and it has stayed with me as one of those halcyon experiences that is etched into my memory.

Unfortunately, my second experience was nothing like as pleasant. A day's excursion was planned by the Lidgett one and it was another whole of Leeds event. A train was privately hired to take hordes of teenagers to Blackpool for the day and bring them back at night. A disco was to be provided on the train in an empty carriage on the way back and Peter and John from the band were to run it. I am not sure if we had to meet at the club or at the station, but I know that several double-decker buses took us back late at night. We arrived on the train, excited, and our group all sat together. There were quite a few of us. I know Peter, the guitarist, was there, as were several girls we hung around with from Alwoodley and boys and girls from the Roundhay Schools. Our group had about twelve people in it and we were really looking forward to the day. The train was fairly packed, and it differed greatly from the ones that you get nowadays. There was a refreshment bar, but it was very basic and served only chocolate bars and soft drinks. The carriage for the disco was even more basic. They obviously used it for cargo and it was rough and ready and wouldn't accommodate all the kids on the train. The journey to Blackpool was fairly uneventful, and when we arrived, we split up into our groups and wandered off to explore the town. The age range was from about twelve years up to seventeen and duty of care was very different to how it would be today. I seem to remember our group saying goodbye to the leaders, times to meet up at the end being confirmed, and then we were on our own.

Our first destination was the Pleasure Beach. Blackpool was famous for it, and we wanted to make the most of our time. The park was extensive, and we headed for the rollercoaster. The one we went on was called the Wild Mouse. It was a straightforward twisting, turning, speeding and slowing ride, unlike some of the modern ones that take you through tunnels, turn upside down and then do it all again backwards. It was the usual thrill and left you feeling a little queasy at the end. There was another called the Grand National, but I didn't go on that one as it looked too high and fast for me. The next stop was the Haunted House. It was the only time I have been in one and it wasn't scary, but a bit disorientating. I think it might have been a Pirate Ship rather than a typical haunted house. You walked on floors made of rollers, there were rooms of mirrors, some that made you appear tall and thin, and others short and fat. It was quite tame, but fun.

We walked, talked and probably smoked our way around, and then we headed to the beach. Candy floss and ice creams filled a need, and the day passed enjoyably, but a little aimlessly towards the end. Money was always an issue, and it limited the things we could do. I remember fish and chips and a walk on the pier ended the visit, and it was getting dark when we arrived back at the station for the return trip.

These were the times of Skin Heads, Rockers and general teenage angst and anger, and there was a definite change to the atmosphere as we all got back on the train. I suspect alcohol had a part to play and, before we had travelled far, the disco started. It was basically a record deck set in the corner of an empty carriage with a few coloured lights. I wandered down to see what it was like to find that all hell had broken out. Groups of boys were fighting and Peter and John trying to play the records were starting to panic. Tribal rivalry between clubs grew and as I walked back to where the rest of our group was, I passed fights spilling into other carriages. The leaders were heavily outnumbered and were struggling to maintain control, as were the train guards. After a while, things settled, and we hadn't too long to go. At one point, someone pulled the communication chord, and the train came to a halt in the middle of nowhere. It was dark, and we were all tired. We had managed to keep out of trouble and just sat in our places and groups of angry boys moved up and down through the carriages, searching for specific people to settle scores with, or just someone looking at them the wrong way. The train got going again and everyone was told to take their seats and stay in them. This worked for a while and eventually we arrived in Leeds Station. With great relief we poured out, but still the trouble continued with melees as large numbers tried to find the correct buses that were taking us back to the clubs.

We found our double-decker, and we sat as a group downstairs. There was a collective sigh of relief as the train had been a very frightening place. The bus had to go on a round trip to three or four clubs, so it would take quite a while to get back. Suddenly, there were cries and the sound of heavy footfalls from the deck above. The fighting had started again. The leaders went up to try and sort things out, and I think they were very brave to do so. Things calmed down with their intervention and then we arrived at one of the clubs, their members came down the stairs like wild animals, still carrying on their arguments. With their departure, there was a complete change. A calm descended, and we headed over to Alwoodley and dropped off their members and the bus, then just had the Roundhay kids and at about midnight we were able to get off. Some of us alighted at Oakwood, as that saved us a long walk. I can honestly say that I have never been so grateful to have got back from a trip. It was frightening what large numbers of young boys in those days could get up to. I never heard of another such excursion and I can't say that I was surprised.

THE JUDEAN, SPALDING AND FIVE-A-SIDE TRAUMA

Pete and other friends were quite keen on soccer. In fact, Peter still plays, and he is a few years older than me. I had played rugby at school and can't say I have any talent for soccer, but I am willing to have a go at most sports. Lidgett Methodist Youth Club had details for a five-a-side competition and Peter and some others organised a team. I know Chris M, Stuart S, Peter, one other and I formed a team. I was to be the goalie, mainly because I was stupid enough to throw myself around onto the hard gym floors, particularly at the feet of opponents who were going to score. I think it was the shock of the idiot diving towards them that put them off and allowed me to save the goals, rather than my skill, but as no one else wanted the job, I had it. The others were quite talented and together we put together a half decent team.

My memory is a little hazy, but I believe that there was a competition that took place at the Judean Club on Street Lane where they had a great indoor soccer facility. It was a good size, and the rules allowed the ball to be played off the walls. As keeper, I was the only one allowed to handle the ball and there was a small D zone where no attacking players could enter. The goals were much smaller than standard goals, but it was quite possible to score if the keeper stayed on the line. As a result, I developed my famous charge at the player who had the ball, making myself as wide as possible with the hope of either blocking the shot, grabbing the ball or at least putting the attacker off. When I had the ball, I had to roll it out to a free player as quickly as I could, to enable them to score. Speed was the essence of this game and even though we had games of about seven minutes a half, it was frenetic and stamina played a major part. I was permitted to come out of the area as long as I didn't use my hands and I could intercept any free balls.

We played the first competition and did quite well. The next time, we did better than well and won the local round. As winners, we had to continue in another knockout competition to decide who would represent the City of Leeds. This one took place in one of Allerton Grange's gymnasiums on a Saturday afternoon. There was more than one court used at a time and the format was the same as we were used to. We had quite a crowd of supporters and they could observe the games, if they wanted, from the balcony. At the start there were a lot of spectators, but as the day developed, the interest waned. It was definitely more exciting playing than watching, and we were proving to be a force to be reckoned with. In the end, it was between us and another team and we played the game with a large audience, but I noticed that my girlfriend at the time was missing.

The game was played with real passion, a few frayed tempers at some of the physical tackling. I threw myself about with total abandon as we had to win or else that was it for the competition. For some reason, it all seemed to work that day and we ended up winning. The Youth leaders were particularly pleased as we had to go on and represent the City as part of the national competition. There was to be a disco back at the club that evening and the mood was high, as we were victorious. I discovered my girlfriend had been messing about with another of our friends, Paul, which didn't please me. That evening at the disco, I explained the error of his ways in the Basil Fawlty/Manuel method by thumping him once.

As winners, we had to play away against the Lincolnshire winners at Spalding a few weeks after our success. The club hired a coach and a day trip was booked. Up to this point, we didn't have a team strip and Chris felt we should have one, so a set of Liverpool soccer shirts was ordered. They were yellow with a red stripe. Why, you might well ask, would we wear a Liverpool shirt? The answer was that Chris thought the LFC could stand for Lidgett Football Club. This question was asked by supporters in Spalding. I would have thought a Leeds United shirt would have been far more appropriate.

The day came and an excited group of teenagers and club leaders boarded the coach for Spalding. We felt we had a good chance. We were fast, played a mean game, and had beaten all the teams we had come across. We looked fairly smart, if not a bit quixotic, in the yellow and red striped shirts, shorts, training shoes and socks. The journey was long, on winding country roads and some were feeling a little sick by the time we arrived. Lincolnshire was flat as a pancake, rural, and we could see no sports centre when we pulled up. What we saw was a grass soccer pitch, reduced in size, but with much larger than we were used to goals. We were flabbergasted. This couldn't be right.

The local side had a huge fan base, and we were welcomed, not at all. There were jeers, comments on our Liverpool strip, and our footwear. Cedric and the other leader went in to discuss what was going on. They came out to tell us we had to play under these conditions. It was apparently all under the rules. I can tell you we were far from pleased and that if we were back in Leeds, we wouldn't have played. We would never have taken to the pitch. We stood no chance. They wore boots with studs and the pitch was wet and muddy. In our trainers, we couldn't get any traction. There was no rebounding the ball off the walls and basically it was a totally different game. It was very upsetting and I know the leaders were disappointed. We were humiliated! Five strapping rural lads, with shin pads, boots and familiarity with the ground and rules, thrashed us. The goals were much bigger and they could just pick a spot and blast it past me. I threw myself around, but this time it was of no use as I couldn't narrow any angles and the goals just sat open. In fairness to my friends, they didn't blame me. None of us could keep our feet in the mud. Running was impossible, and all the skills we had honed were useless. I think the score was over ten nil and they showed no mercy whatsoever. At least the refreshments they provided were good. Afterwards, it was a very subdued team and coach of supporters that returned to Leeds. What had promised so much was snatched away from us in unfair circumstances, much like a lot in life.

We started playing soccer at weekends on the Soldiers' Field and even in the Arena at Roundhay Park. These were friendly games, and that summer was a long hot one. Afterwards, we would go for refreshments at The Lakeside Cafe. It was a wooden building with a kiosk near the entrance and a more formal cafe inside. I had always thought it was an old tram shed, but apparently not. It was on the site of the children's playground near the car park and the current Boat House Cafe, which at that time was just a boat house. At weekends, The Lakeside Cafe would be the gathering place for teenagers with lots of scooters parked outside, their chrome fairings and mirrors gleaming in the sun.

We carried on playing five-a-side the following year, at the Judean. We never enjoyed the same success, but were always competitive. We went there socially as several friends were members and we sometimes saw bands there.

TEXAS GRILL, PINBALL AND THE JUKEBOX

One of the first signs of growing up as a teenager was going into Leeds City with your friends, and the place where you wanted to hang out would be either music shops or coffee bars. Saturday mornings would see us gather at the coffee bar under the Texas Grill on Vicar Lane in Leeds, run by a lady called Lulu. For some reason, the most attractive bars were subterranean, and this one was particularly handy, as it was almost at the Harehills bus stop. In the late sixties, scooters parked outside would indicate how popular a place it was and, at least for my friends, this was THE place in the city. It was only small and there was a side room that had the pinball machines and the main room that had a few tables and some bench seating. The benches had that orange/red vinyl covering and the whole place had the smell of coffee and smoke. Us oldies will remember when it was normal for eating places, cinemas, pubs and even aircraft to be full of people smoking. I can't say that I miss it, even though I was a smoker at these times. The bar sold Cokes, Pepsis, milkshakes and for the trendy, 'Frothy Coffee'. Sophisticated times, eh? There was a range of cakes, but most were Turkish and very sweet and not to my taste.

We would gather and chat, plan the weekend, and generally hang out. There wasn't a lot of money to spare and I don't think the owner ever got rich off us, but we were at least regular customers. The pinball machines were a real draw. They had everything that you wanted as a teenager. They were from the USA, were loud, flashed lights and those who could master them had real street credibility. The skill was to hit the bumpers with force, flick the flippers at the right time and give the whole machine the right force of push to achieve success without causing a tilt. I played a few times, but never was a master, as you needed copious money or skill to get replays, and I had neither. It was almost as much fun to watch as it was to play and our crowd would gather around anyone playing, particularly those getting high scores.

A group of Roundhay School girls used to meet there as well, and they had a culture quite different from us lads. Their conversations were often one-on-one and used whispered voices. I was always intrigued as to what they were saying, or who they were talking about. They even had their own coded language that sounded like complete gobbledygook to me. I am not sure if it was called Pigeon Latin. It was explained to me and apparently you took the first letter of the syllable and then added a 'urrugh' before finishing the syllable. The word dog became 'durrughog'. Multi-syllabic words were more complex, as each syllable had the same treatment, but, with practice, became quite easy. What was very difficult was listening to the girls speak so quickly to each other in what sounded like nonsense, but they clearly understood and there was much laughter. This was particularly intimidating if they kept looking at you amidst the laughter. I still can speak it in a slow form, but it is a skill without a lot of applications nowadays. I wonder if the girls can remember it, or still use it?

My crowd of the band and associates were not Mods, Rockers or Teddies, and we had friends and acquaintances from all groups. I guess we were a bit more hippy. We loved progressive music and rock, had long hair, despite Roundhay School's best efforts to keep us as proper boys/gentlemen. I remember how we would be inspected by some of the form teachers and told to get our hair cut, which somehow we forgot to do. I clearly recall tucking my hair down inside my collar to escape detection during an inspection. I loved my hair in these days. The feel of it is something that I miss, having lost most of it by my mid-twenties. I also grew sideburns, which were the rage these days. Again, this was a fashion that Roundhay School teachers didn't approve of, or at least the more traditional ones.

The tiny 'Number Six' cigarettes were the most common smoke as they were so cheap and the coffee bar would be full of the stench of tobacco, chatter, and the bells and crashes of the pinball and the accompanying sounds of the jukebox. Jukeboxes were again part of the American attraction of the coffee bars. They were lit like the pinball machines and they were mesmerising as the record would be selected after feeding in the coin. Racks of singles would turn, and a record would be grabbed by a mechanical arm. The disk used to fall onto the turntable and the heavy needle arm come down onto the record you had selected. Your choice of music would play and, hopefully, it was met with approval from those sitting around. I have seen teenagers trying to win favour fail miserably by selecting the wrong record, one that was not seen as worthy. A boy could lose the attention of a girl if they had a naff taste in music.

I can't remember how long we went to coffee bars, maybe a year or two, before we moved on to other venues. There was one at Harehills that we would walk to from Pete's house. Again it was below ground and it was owned by Jack Charlton, the Leeds United footballer, and was called The Trophy Room. I believe he also owned a clothes shop above. It was very similar to the one at the Texas Grill, but maybe a little smaller. We would sit, talk about music, plan a new song, and often walk along to Project Records. This shop was a godsend for us. They sold secondhand as well as new records and soon to be cassettes. Because prices were low, you could experiment a bit. I would look for covers that were intriguing or artists that I had never heard, but I knew had played on other albums I liked. I still have a copy of an album by Keith Tippet, a jazz pianist, who played on a couple of Crimson's early albums. Some great discoveries were made this way, and some dud purchases made. The other advantage of the shop was that if you were desperate for money, you could sell your albums, but you never got a lot for them.

Harehills was an interesting place in the late 1960s. It was quite a melting pot of people and cultures, but I never had any problem there and always, with one exception, felt safe. The Clock Cinema was a great place to see new films and I remember as a teenager watching the films Woodstock, Easy Rider, Blazing Saddles, Mash, Kelly's Heroes and many, many more. Of course, going as a teenager was a very different experience from going with your parents or grandparents. I know that they even had double seats for couples. I remember my first visit with a girl and the vast, imaginary gap that separated us as I tried to work my arm around her shoulders. I can't remember the film at all.

The bus was the means of transport, apart from walking, and we didn't mind spending vast amounts of time waiting for them to arrive. Upstairs was the place to go, but it stank of tobacco and was filled with smoke. The rocking motion was more exaggerated than downstairs and you would often disembark feeling sick. Who could forget the 'Spitting is Forbidden' sign at the front?

We often missed the last bus at the end of the evening and this would mean a long walk home, sometimes in a group, but many times on your own. Peter gave the experience a lasting tribute in the song Last Bus, that the band used to play. Rain, fog, frost, snow, the walk home to Oakwood and then through Gipton Wood in the dead of night holds both fantastic and frightening memories. I got to know the trail through the woods, each and every root that waited to trip you in the dark, so that if necessary, I could run through it without any hesitation. Some nights I just strode through without a thought, others I was quite terrified and listened to every noise, my heart almost drowning the sounds out. What we do when we are young!

A BIT OF BIFFO!

Being from a family of three sons and having four sons of my own, I can't give any insight into the female mind, but I feel qualified to explain some of the behaviours that boys and men face. One element of male behaviour is aggression, and certainly in my experience at primary and secondary school, I came across ways this was displayed by boys and staff.

At Harehills County Primary, there were occasional playground fights. I don't remember many of these, but there were certainly some. They usually erupted over some form of competition or perceived foul play. Soccer was a regular source of argument and sometimes a fight. The major catalyst was tripping. As Harehills C P playground was tarmac, any trip was painful. Most times it was accidental and both players would end up scuffing their knees, elbows, hands and occasionally, faces. Skin would be removed and a small amount of blood let, but usually this was seen as a mark of intense play and a bit of a badge of honour. Going in hard to the tackle was fully expected and respected, but just hooking the feet from under someone wasn't viewed the same way. When the victim got back up, a fist might fly and then there would be a flurry of arms, little contact, but a great deal of excitement. The cry of 'Fight!' would move through the playground like a wave, and in answer, everyone would rush to witness a bit of biffo. I don't remember anyone or anything but pride being hurt, but maybe it did. Teachers would arrive to sort it out and depending on the teacher and their interpretation of the event, punishment dished out, or the two miscreants sent to Mr Wilson, Mr Woods or worse, Mr Kelly. It appeared to only be a male phenomenon, but I suspect those times have changed.

When we moved into high school, again things were different. For a start, Roundhay School was single-sex, the girls' school being next door. The staff was predominantly male, apart from two teachers, Sweaty Betty and the young, new, and very popular music teacher, and as such, the school was built on male values. Issues were usually resolved through physical means. Corporal punishment was casually handed out by some staff in a way that was abusive, but some never used it. Some teachers were respected and their disappointment in your action would have far more impact than being slippered, or worse, caned. In fairness, though, whatever the punishment, as soon as the beating was over, the incident was over and there didn't appear to be any long-lived animosity. There was a, face your punishment and then move on, attitude.

The same attitude wasn't always shown by prefects and some really were bullies, who picked on some children mercilessly. I don't think that I was a bully, but I was involved in several fights. The bullying that took place was just considered friendly banter, but looking back, it was not something we should be proud of. Nicknames were often cruel and someone's physical problems gave intelligent boys an excuse to come up with suitable names. Of course, teachers were fair game, as was Fingers (Glover) the headmaster. He used to march around in his leather trench coat like some member of the Gestapo. I don't think that he ever spoke one word to me in all the years I was there.

Soccer was the source of much of the aggro, as it was at primary school, but this time the tackles were much harder, even if we fell onto turf. The other contributing factor was that we were going through puberty and testosterone was pulsing though our bodies, making our moods swing and our fight-or-flight reflexes were close to the surface. I remember having fights, some quite brutal, with some of my friends, and after a day of cooling off, or maybe just ten minutes, we were back as best buddies. Up to about Year Four, it was fairly tame stuff, but when you are suddenly taller and stronger, punches become a much more serious thing. Boys developed reputations and somehow the entire school was aware of them. The older boys that you looked up to, maybe idolised, were the ones that were good at sport, had armfuls of young girlfriends, were in bands, were good at acting, and very smart, but probably most importantly, were tough. They were the ones with real kudos. Why wouldn't you want to be one of these alpha males? Maybe it was only those of us who aspired to be an alpha male who took notice or cared, but I knew I wanted to be known and respected, if not liked. I don't ever remember the older boys fighting. Why would they? The pecking order was well and truly established by then.

It was in Years Four and Five that the quest for 'Cock of the School' was the goal. As we were all still changing, this order was not fixed, but dynamic, and as a new year started, the jostling for the new positions started again.

The arrival of new boys to the school added to the mix. I remember John P joining the class and I was asked to help him settle in. It was clear after a few minutes he was another alpha wannabe. He was good looking, sporty and amiable, and a threat to some of us in the class. He was a great lad and joined in the class A-list very quickly and with no tension.

I had a reputation as a bit of a tough nut in the early years, due to my size, physical approach to rugby and occasional red moment, but by Year Four and Five, I was playing in a band and was less interested in toughness. This was the late 1960s and a new age of compassion, peace and love was still around. I was told that one boy in the year, Andy, felt he was top-dog and wanted to fight me to settle who 'Cock of the School' was.

Rumour had it that Andy carried a knife. Now this was quite different to me, as my involvement in fights had been heat of the moment conflicts, not planned fights, in the form of a duel. As I wasn't sure I would be victorious, I avoided Andy for a day or two until we bumped into each other. He looked almost as stressed as me. Wisely, I said I didn't want to challenge him and that I was happy to admit he was tougher than me. He just smiled, put his arm around me, and we forgot all about it. His mates had been arguing about who was tougher and wanted us to settle it for them. Anyway, it was over and we both forgot about it. In fact, we played a few times together in the band. He bought a Hammond organ, and he brought it along to a practice at a girlfriend's house, but he didn't stay in the band.

When I was in the Fifth Form, we used to go into the mansion toilet at school to have a fag at breaks. There was the undercover walkway between the mansion and the woodwork, art and biology block and whenever the door opened, a thick cloud of smoke billowed out like some sort of horror movie. The teachers were fully aware of this, but chose not to notice and did nothing. You didn't need to be a smoker, just walking into the densely crowded facility was enough to knock years off your life. On this specific occasion, a few of us walked in and, for some reason that I can't remember, an older boy decided to have a fight with me. There was no room, but it was entertainment for those who were there. He was much taller than me, but by that time, most boys were. I don't think any blows were struck and because of the lack of space and overcrowding, it was more of a sweaty wrestle. I remember my head being rammed into the heavy wooden toilet cubicle frame. I think there were about three or four heavy blows, but luckily I am of Scottish descent and I had a good thick skull. As it happened, Les Lees was walking past, recognised the commotion being more than just the smokers' melee and he ventured in, gown flapping like a raven.

He had an impact that few staff ever achieved. He had respect! He looked at the throng.

"Is it all sorted, boys?"

Somebody mumbled something, probably me and my partner in crime.

"Probably, sir."

"No! It is all over!"

"Yes, sir!"

And that was it. There was a certain readjusting of shirt, tie and tucking into trouser, a sweaty body, numbed head and then I was on my way to the next lesson.

In a previous blog, I discussed some fights that took place on a youth club day trip to Blackpool, and it was at youth clubs that more aggro happened. The reason for the fights was territorial. Rivalry between Roundhay and Allerton Grange was a real thing and one evening at Lidgett Methodist Church Youth Club, a large group of boys from Allerton Grange turned up and they were clearly looking for a fight of some sort. I just happened to walk outside when they arrived, and a tall boy shouted to me,

"Do you wanna fight?"

Now this seemed a rather strange request, but I replied,

"If you insist!"

Looking back, I think he was trying to impress, and I was trying not to lose any status amongst my friends. Like gentlemen duellers, I started to take off my jacket, but he stopped removing his coat and launched an attack. Rather unsporting, I thought, and only had time to dodge a blow and grab him around the waist. Now, there was method in my madness, as he had a much longer reach, and kick, than me, and so it was the only chance. I had first to avoid humiliation and second, a sound beating. I just held on and we wrestled a bit. He couldn't put any power into the blows, but they were coming, so I did what any self-respecting street-fighter would do and I grabbed hold of something soft.

I had the theory at the time that I might not win a fight, but I could make sure the opponent knew they had been in one. I held on, and squeezed! I didn't seem to get any response from the other lad, but the fight was in a stalemate. I wasn't letting go, and he couldn't break away.

This went on for quite a long time and I increased the pressure just to see what would happen, but the experiment was cut short when three or four youth club members who wore leather and owned motor bikes arrived. They had no idea what was going on. The group that my assailant was part of hated greasers more than Roundhay boys. The cry, "Rockers!" went up, and they charged after the new arrivals. Even without their motorbikes, they knew how to accelerate and the rockers vanished, running down the road, pursued by the group of thugs.

My assailant let go of me. "Call it quits?" he said. He didn't wait for a reply and charged after his mates. I was none the worse for wear and just dusted myself down and went back inside the club.

After writing these accounts, I don't want you to believe that I am condoning my behaviour or the behaviour of others, but it was, and probably still is, a part of teenage boys' lives. Violence never solves anything, but in the adolescent psyche it has a high importance. This may be a genetic or a social programming, but it is there. Of course, in adult life most people move beyond this, but how many of our TV programmes, films, books and plays involve violence, not to mention computer games? Teenage years are difficult and in our days, we were rather rudderless. Few teachers tried to guide us and parents were often embarrassed or ill-equipped to do much, apart from trying to model appropriate behaviour. It was a time when emotions were extreme and changed in an instant. There were some wonderful things and also some horrible ones, but most of us grew up to be decent people.

DRUGS, SEX AND ROCK-AND-ROLL

Being born in the decade after the end of the Second World War put me in a position to witness a period of great social, technological, environmental, and cultural change. The start of the 1960s saw a change from a black and white, monochrome world to one of colour. Most of my time at primary school, the world appeared both physically and emotionally grey. The major buildings in Leeds were black from the atmospheric soot and television, when it arrived, was again in black and white, and even the cinema used to show black and white films at the Saturday Matinee.

After the war, the returning Soldiers were not going to fit easily back into society as they had experienced too much and they wanted to improve their lots in life. They wanted to live in decent houses, wear decent clothes and have all the mod cons that were on offer. Women had similarly experienced change. They had had to do all the tasks that the men away at war had done before. They learnt they were equally capable of driving trucks, working and also managing a home. There was no way that they were just going to allow men to dominate as they had. My mother told me of cycling trips into the country where she had met Italian prisoners of war who were free to cycle the countryside. These encounters and the influence of the American servicemen opened hers and other women's eyes to a different way of living. They heard American music, learnt American dances and experienced American affluence, and they liked it. Some returned soldiers discovered that the British Isles they had left had changed and the old order was changing.

The music from the USA was wild, exciting, and teenagers loved the fact that their parents hated it. This hasn't changed over the time since and there have been music fads and genres that have risen in popularity, aided because the older generation don't get it, don't like it and won't listen to it. After the war there was comfort music for the establishment: Andy Williams, Bing Crosby, Joseph Locke, Jim Reeves, the crooners, but there was also more dangerous music: Frank Sinatra, Dean Martin, Sammy Davis Junior, where their rebel lifestyles matched with great voices, made them stars the young could like, but it was still adult music.

In the 1950s, US music was brought to the UK audience through acts like Bill Haley and the Comets, followed by Elvis Presley, and Buddy Holly and the Crickets. They hit world fame like a hurricane. The establishment hated them, wanted them banned for subverting the young, and refused to film Elvis from the waist down because of his gyrating hip movements. Rock Around the Clock, Heartbreak Hotel and Jailhouse Rock, the world would never be the same! The UK saw America as wild, exciting, the place to be and aspire to go to. It was wealthy and a leader of everything after the war. The UK musicians either tried to emulate their US counterparts or they lost popularity. There was a short period of skiffle music with Lonnie Donegan and other bands.

Television in the late 1950s and early 1960s was staid, with variety shows and family entertainment. It appeared to cater for children and adults and missed out the growing number of teenagers. British versions of the US stars appeared: Cliff Richard, Adam Faith, The Shadows, Tommy Steele, but it was the US stars such as Roy Orbison, Chuck Berry, Little Richard and Jerry Lee Lewis that really captured the youth of the time. They were wild, violent, sexually dangerous and everything that the parents of teenagers hated. 'Is it a man or a woman?' was a common comment from a father as they watched some of these performers when they appeared on television.

It was in the early 1960s that British music changed dramatically with the Beatles. They suddenly became the biggest band on the planet and were the inspiration for so many bands at the time and afterwards. Probably the biggest difference from other bands was that they wrote their own music and pushed the boundaries of the sounds that were current. By the summer of 1967, there was the Summer of Love and the birth of the Hippy movement. This was an even more dramatic challenge to the culture of adult America and saw the drug influence, free sex and alternative communes lifestyles appear. It spoke of peace, anti-war and creativity, but it spawned some dreadful cults, such as that of Charles Manson.

It was at this time that songs from California became popular and the Beatles produced music that was experimental and drug related. Sgt. Pepper's became one of the most influential albums of all time and bands such as the Rolling Stones, Pink Floyd, Led Zeppelin, The Doors, The Who and a host of others started experimenting. Progressive Rock, Hard Rock and Heavy Metal suddenly became the art of choice for students, and Universities and Colleges the major venues for band concerts.

My first interest was led by my older brother Andrew, who bought flowered shirts with accompanying bells in the late 1960s. He listened to and bought The Piper at the Gates of Dawn, Sgt. Pepper's, The White Album, Saucerful of Secrets and many others. Many of these I borrowed and took to parties to impress friends and irretrievably damaged the albums. Shortly afterwards, I started buying my own albums and Ummagumma, The Who Sell Out and the Small Faces album Ogden's Nut Gone, joined my collection. Then our circle of friends, led by Peter, started learning to play guitar and the nucleus of a band was formed.

The first song that I remember us playing was an unusual hit in the UK. It was called Neanderthal Man, by Hotlegs, who were later to become half of 10CC. It was incredibly simple, and we made a pretty ordinary version. The line-up of players altered and Peter, John and I became the nucleus, but others came and went over the years. Because we were captured by an interest in the hippy culture rather than the Mod, Rockers, Greasers, Pop trends, we started writing. Originally it was acoustic music, but bit by bit, when finances allowed, we became an electric band. Having limited guitar skills, I took over bass guitar duties as no one else wanted to. Being in a band gave you kudos and there were many high school bands around. As the youngest member of the band, I was happy to follow the lead of the others, and I took to the social side with gusto. Teenagers drank a lot, smoked a lot and many indulged in the drug culture that was being fostered by big name bands, cinema and television. Many artists promoted a drug culture and Timothy Leary's advocacy for LSD even led to David Bowie writing a song about him. Yellow

Submarine, I Am the Walrus, Magical Mystery Tour from the Beatles, fostered this way of life and films such as Easy Rider, Woodstock, Performance, with Mick Jagger and many others made teenagers aware of hallucinogenic trips. Crosby, Stills, and Nash, and bands from the USA similarly promoted drug taking.

At Roundhay School in the late sixties, I became aware that older boys were using drugs other than alcohol. There were rumours some were using hard drugs such as heroin, but that seemed to be a suicide journey to me and the one or two known addicts that hung around Oakwood, Moortown and Harehills did little to make anyone want to follow in their wake. Softer drugs, such as hash, were less harmful, and they appeared at parties. Wacky Baccy could be smelt at many gatherings and even more common at rock concerts at Leeds University or the Poly. The issue was knowing where to buy such things, but playing in a band with a large circle of acquaintances, eventually people appeared who could provide a supply. Many times, people were conned and Oxo cubes were passed off as drugs, but like many teenagers, we experimented. Some of my friends didn't smoke and so hash wasn't high on their lists, but LSD became the drug of choice for some. Long lasting, easily come by and seemingly an aid to creativity, it didn't take long for it to become common to see hazed out trippers and eventually I was offered the opportunity.

I was given half a tab prior to getting on a bus at Oakwood and going to a friend's house. At first it had no effect, but then it became a frightening. Daylight was brighter, I became disorientated, and could have wandered off if I had been on my own. We started to over-talk, senses became confused and overloaded and I remember sweating a lot. Half a tab lasted about four hours and it was a bit of a nightmare. I realised afterwards that it was not for me. I didn't like the lack of self-control. There was nothing particularly enjoyable and afterwards there was a genuine feeling of coming down. A few drinks were pleasant, but this was not. Clearly, others saw it differently and continued. In one or two cases, they became regular users and, bit by bit, they changed. There appeared to be a dullness about them, and it wasn't good to see. Now I am aware of the potential damage to mental health, particularly in teenagers, and I am glad I avoided that pitfall.

The late 1960s and 1970s saw the development of a wide range of musical styles. There was a coming together of relative affluence, technical ability and equipment, opportunities to play and watch music at the college and University circuits. They were new, fresh, challenging times of social upheaval that produced an environment where the younger generation had strong opinions. Youth found their voice and forced the world to listen. It was the birth of female emancipation, the pill, cheap fashion, free higher education, student grants, moving away from home to experience life away from our parents, overseas holidays and opportunities that might well have made our parents envious. It was a time when we had never heard of Aids, Pandemics, Global Warming and other portends of doom, when we and the world were improving.

Education was something to broaden the mind, not just a means of getting a job, and where we listened to other points of view and then argued our own without shouting others down, drinking wine into the small hours and feeling grown up.

I guess we were the lucky ones, but now the ills of the world are being laid at our doorstep and the generation of Baby Boomers who saw a brave new world are taking the blame for the current sick one. Probably it was ever so and will probably continue to be so for each new generation.

FANCY PANTS

As I have mentioned before, colour seemed to come in to my life at the start of the 1960s and the main exposure was through clothing.

Fashion was something that the working classes didn't really enjoy a lot of. Clothing was practical and free-standing wardrobes wouldn't have held a great range, so we never had much. As a young lad I never had more than one pair of shoes, maybe a pair of sandals and second-hand pair of football boots and the rest of my clothing was limited to school uniform and the odd T-shirt and hand knitted jumper for the weekends and holidays. My Dad wasn't a lot better, but he had suits for work and the rest was a few casual bits for weekends. This was much better than my grandparents had, though. Grandad had a cotton shirt with detachable collars that could be swapped during the week to keep him looking smart. With the new decade came major changes. Readymade suits, synthetic fabrics, nylon, rayon, appeared. The swinging sixties brought in mini-skirts that were cheaper to produce as there was much less material, and fabric dyeing and pattern printing really took off. Goods were imported from overseas and 'made in Hong Kong' became the byword for shoddy goods. Nobody cared, as clothes no longer had to last long, they just had to look good.

I remember my mum coming home after work and doing some shopping in Leeds market on the way. She would pull out a new dress, short with a very loud, bold print, but she was delighted with what she had bought for ten bob. Shoes were becoming cheaper and leather was replaced with cheap plastic pairs. I even had some plastic fashion shoes, but my parents soon learned that they didn't last the rigours of playground soccer, sliding on the ice in winter and that they were a false economy as they split, so it was back to the Stylo shoes and their guarantee to last six months.

Because my mother was building up a collection of clothes, my father got his next DIY project and that was to build fitted wardrobes into each of the bedrooms at Gipton Wood Crescent. This project took quite a long time, but produced wardrobes along one wall of each of the bedrooms. In the two larger rooms, there were wardrobes on each end with a small dressing table between. My father did a good job, and it certainly allowed us to accommodate the growing number of items.

I wonder if they are still there? They were a dark mahogany veneer and had a rail for hanging clothing. My older brother had the box room and so his wardrobe was smaller and just allowed the single bed to fit in. Being four years older than me, he was more into fashion of the sixties, whereas I was more the seventies. During 1967-8 he, along with almost everyone else, was affected by the Hippy culture from the USA. He was growing his hair and started attending St Wilfrid's Youth Club. As a teenager, he was interested in attracting girls and so music, fashion and image became important. The good thing about this was that I used to pinch his clothes when I started going to youth clubs. Black plastic shiny coats were the rage, and he had one that fitted me, but that was just the start. Whatever he owned was fair game for me, and I believe several fraternal altercations ensued. I also helped myself to his records. He went to Durham University in the late sixties and he couldn't take all his clothing and records with him and so I had a great time with what was left. His one claim to fame was assisting with the lighting for an early Pink Floyd concert at Durham, where projectors with multi-hued inks held between slides projected moving colourful patterns onto the band, stage, and audience.

My brother was also the first person I knew to buy a pair of desert boots. The soft, tan-coloured, ankle-high boots with a soft crepe rubber sole were very trendy and I know he had similar sized feet to me, as I purloined them frequently. These replaced the fashion for winkle-picker boots with elasticated sides and chisel shaped shoes and boots. I remember well my brother getting what were called rhino skin shoes. They were a grey leather, dull and rippled and they did indeed look like a rhino's skin, but I hope they definitely weren't. Speaking of endangered animals, there was a fad in the 1970s for elephant hair bracelets. These certainly felt very plastic, but maybe elephants had very wiry hair.

In the late 1960s, something happened that I am sure caused my brother great delight. I started a part-time job. Because of this, I could buy my own clothes to supplement the ones my parents provided the money for. My first fashion buy was a pair of Levi jeans for 37 shillings and 6 pence. There was the ritual of sitting in a bath of cold water, supposedly to shrink them to size. I don't think it did anything but shrink parts of my teenage anatomy. Jeans were the bees' knees, and I wore them with pride and a sense of being a man, which was a bit of a joke at 13. I bought them on an away rugby match where we were allowed a short stop at the shops. I believe it was Skipton and on the way back to Roundhay, there was the incident with the removal of underpants from a poor lad on the coach. His undies were cast out the window of the coach. Much, I am sure, the amazement of the local shoppers who probably commented on the virtues of a good grammar school education.

I managed to get a Levi jacket to match, a year or two later, when my mother gave me money to buy a jacket. She was a little surprised and upset with the aforementioned denim, but didn't make a fuss. I wore the jacket out for the first time when we had a five-a-side soccer match at the Judean Club at Moortown. We got changed for the match and when I returned afterwards, it had been stolen. I was heartbroken, and it took another thirty years before I replaced it, but not with a Levi one. There were only two makers of jeans that you would be seen wearing in the late 1960s: Levi's and Wrangler. Designer jeans were yet to make an appearance.

For most teenagers, having a bit of money meant wanting to buy what was in style. It is strange that as we wanted to be ourselves and express our individuality, we all dressed the same. I have noted over the years that each generation of teenagers tends to dress and look the same. True, there are subcultures: Teddy Boys, Skin Heads, Mods, Punks, Goths and the like, but within the group they look almost identical.

At Roundhay, being cool meant an ankle length ex-army or navy trench coat. We all had to have one, and the Army and Navy stores must have had the best years of their existence. To match, we had rough canvas haversacks. I remember my coat with affection. Despite smelling of years of storage, they were thick, well-made, and fabulously warm and waterproof in the cold, wet winters.

The Mods at school went for the fawn coloured canvas parkas, with the fringe of fur around the hoods. I envied them as most owned scooters. Scooters were not very practical, but adorned with chrome fairings, long, waving ariels, with tiger tails fastened and a hot chick on the back, I envied the lucky buggers.

As I was part of a school band image, and looks were important. Pete, the guitarist, had got spare bus driver jackets from his father and we frayed them in an attempt to look hippyish. He was the first person I knew who had the material inserts in his straight jeans to make them bell-bottomed. Within a short while, we all had them. Skin-tight jeans with enormous flairs were the vogue and to set them off, the new thing was platform shoes. As time passed, a slight platform became bigger and bigger until it was not uncommon for people to almost be stilt walkers. Accidents became common and ankles were broken, but who cared? If you attracted the right attention, that was all that mattered.

Other fashions that I sported during the late sixties and early seventies include Bags, probably based on Oxford Bags. These were very wide parallel legged trousers that were tight around the rear. Tie-dye grandad shirts, white brogue shoes, Ben Sherman shirts, tear drop collar shirts, kipper ties, a Norfolk shooting jacket, an afghan coat are just a few of the never to be repeated styles. Girls had skirts of various lengths, smocks, very long cardigans, flared trouser suits, ponchos, hot pants, dungarees, and many others that I can not remember.

A turning point, for me, came in 1971 with the TV series Budgie. Adam Faith was the star, and he was a really cool fashion icon, as well as being a pop star and actor. This coincided with the shop Boodle-Am taking off. It had started in 1969 and was near the university and it was trendy hippy heaven. Racks of multicoloured clothing at very cheap prices made it a real hit, and it then opened another store, upstairs in one of the Leeds arcades and later another shop in Leeds centre. It was from Boodle-Am that I purchased my first pair of loon pants. These were white cotton, very tight around the thighs and rear, but flared from below the knee. When I could afford it, I splashed out on a Budgie jacket, with maroon suede patches and tear drop collar. They were named after the style worn by Adam Faith in the TV series. It was an androgynous time and fashion became unisex. Roger Daltrey from the Who wore wooden clogs with leather uppers and suddenly everyone was sporting a pair and before long, so was I. I had all the appearance of a trendy rock star: long luscious locks and clobber but without the talent or the money. Little did I know that my hair was at its prime, and shortly the tide would go out, taking my hair with it. It was about this time that I attended a free rock concert on Woodhouse Moor, near Leeds University, and it was a mass of velvet, purple, wacky-baccy, hair, attractive ladies and way-out music. It was Hippy heaven! Did it ever get any better than this? Certainly the fashion did, but I think it was the best time for music. Those halcyon days!

SUMMER NIGHTS AND THE ICY KISS OF WINTER FROST

Youth clubs were all so well and good, but eventually we progressed beyond them and one local attraction was North Leeds Cricket Club. Now I never played cricket there, but many Roundhay School boys did. The club was ideally located on the edge of the Soldiers' Field and it had a wonderful rural cricket club feel to it. When you were there, you had almost no view of any part of the city and yet it was in the middle of bustling Leeds. From my recent ventures back home, it appears much as it did in the late 1960s early 1970s. The cricket club was a small single storey building and most of it was taken up by the barroom, changing rooms and toilets. I well remember that one of the changing rooms also housed spare kegs of beer for the bar. It was relaxed and welcoming and in order to raise funds, it used to hold regular disco nights for youths in the area. The chief attraction of these was that the bar would be open and there was a very, shall we call it, enlightened attitude to age regulations. The bar was always run by middle-aged members and wives, and certainly Roundhay students and guests were welcome. If you looked very young, which I never did, then the most they did was not allow you personally to buy alcoholic drinks, but they turned a blind eye to others buying them for you. The boys would mostly drink pints of lager or bitter. The girls tended to drink lager and lime, or lager and blackcurrant, both of which are a strange combination.

The big advantage of the cricket club for me and many others was that we lived locally. As it was, I could walk there in about thirty minutes and walk back home through Oakwood and Gipton Wood in probably forty-five minutes. Why the discrepancy in time, you may well ask? Well, by the end of the evening, my walking would be less direct and my wandering gait could probably add almost half the distance again. The other reason was that, if lucky, I may well have to go off my route and escort a young lady home and then head back. Oh, the days of chivalry! Well, that was how I hoped it appeared, but I may have had ulterior motives.

The events were always well attended by pupils from Roundhay Boys' and Girls' Schools and most people seemed to know each other, even if just by sight. Payment was made at the door, which was manned by a member of the club, usually a sixth former or two. After paying, the top of the hand was stamped so that you could wander out and back in without having to pay again. This was fairly essential, as the temperature inside the club, with a crowd of drinking and dancing teenagers, could reach levels only found in Scandinavian saunas set on overload. The heat was matched by the noise. The music and forced shouted conversations strained even the loudest patrons and eventually the quiet and peace of the outside world was a truly necessary break.

In summer the atmosphere was heavenly: soft insect calls and the gentle buzz of the traffic on Princes Avenue and maybe the occasional car on Old Park Road. There was the scent of cut grass and blossom from the flowering trees. Of course, you experienced this only if you mentally blocked out the thumping bass of whatever track was pumping out of the club. In winter, the air could cut the throat like a knife and clouds of mist escaped the mouths of any standing outside. The contrast with the heat of the inside couldn't have been any more extreme, and I remember gazing up at the myriad stars. Sometimes though, a thick fog would obscure the view of the road and the sounds were muffled and even more distant. Couples and groups would huddle together to maintain their core temperature, but certainly we boys never complained if it enforced close contact with the girls.

I cannot say whether this area is a place of staggering beauty, or whether it is in my memory of growing up there, but the seasonal changes to the trees on Old Park Road, the expanse of green playing fields, and the magnificent, very large houses, conjure up a way of life that was tremendously appealing and still is. I had many acquaintances and friends who lived in the area around the two schools and their lives seemed very different from those of Harehills and Gipton, where I lived and went to primary school. The canopy of wonderful tree-lined roads and drives, houses with grounds, not small gardens. Parkwood Avenue, Davies Avenue, The Drive, North Park Road and many others made this area special and were home to many of my school friends and families. It certainly opened my eyes to how the other half lived, but it never made me envious, as I was happy with my family and home.

I can't remember how it happened, but I was asked to DJ some nights at the cricket club. There was a double record deck, and it was just a matter of putting on the music that either the club had, or the more up-to-date records that people brought to play. It was good fun and there would be a stream of girls asking for requests. The evening would always start out sedately, but as time passed, and the alcohol was consumed, it became more raucous and the dancing wilder and noisier. There was one record that always got a great reaction and was in great demand towards the end of the evening and it was 'High Ho Silver Lining' by the guitarist, Jeff Beck. I thought he had written it, but when I checked, it was actually written by American songwriters Scott English and Larry Weiss and released in 1967. I did not know what the song was about at the time and after checking the lyrics, I am still not sure, but it was the song that always got everyone joining in with the chorus.

I didn't get paid in cash for my services, but got free drinks for the evening. As a result, my skill as the DJ suffered as the evening progressed, but no one seemed to notice or care. I am afraid to say that my friends and I didn't always behave as well as we should have, and I do remember a keg of beer being opened with the end of an umbrella. This resulted in a fountain of beer spraying around the change room, but there was no actual damage and no one seemed to know. Until now, that is!

They were good times, and I saw no aggression at any of these events and licensing laws meant that the evening finished fairly early. Everyone just wanted to have a good time and let their hair down. I am sure there would have been many sore heads the following morning. Our group of friends would tend to wander home together and we often cut through Roundhay School grounds. We would pass the weather station near the Mansion building and on the Monday the rain gauge would often show several inches of heavy rain, despite their being no rainfall in the area. Such was our teenage sense of humour, particularly after a few pints of beer, and I apologise for anyone who took the readings after the weekend.

Most nights I would have to choose between walking through Gipton Wood or take the longer route up the steps near what was Turnways' Garage. I almost always took the route through the wood.

It is funny how your mood affects how you see the situation. Some nights I never gave it a thought, and I took the most direct track, and in time I got to learn where every root was that could cause you to trip. Other nights it was a really scary experience, and you heard noises everywhere. I would often find myself walking faster and faster until eventually I was running. It was with a great sense of relief that I emerged out the far end and back onto the streets. The truth is that I never had any bad experiences, but I can't speak about how safe it would be nowadays and I probably wouldn't encourage my own children to take the same route.

We never listened to our parents, so I guess they wouldn't have listened to me. A friend of mine's printing work had a sign on the wall saying 'Employ a Teenager Whilst They Still Know Everything!' I guess there was, and still is, a ring of truth in it!

EXAMS AND THE DREADED RESULTS

To say that I have spent the whole of my adult life in education, I was far from a model student at Roundhay School. I entered the school in 1966, full of excitement and anticipation of what High School would be like, to find that much was not to my liking. I had loved almost every minute of Stainbeck Preparatory School and Harehills County Primary School and I assumed this would carry on.

The move from having a class teacher to a wide range of subject teachers was a bit of a shock, as was the wide spectrum of teachers at the school. Some teachers were inspiring and talented, but some were not, and some were vicious and probably should have been held accountable. But times were very different. I have always found that the subjects I did well at were the subjects where I liked the teachers and a poor teacher could mean that a subject I had done well in previously became a shocker. An example of this was mathematics. I did well at primary school and in the first year at Roundhay I had Deaf Jeff and he was kind, calm, spent time explaining before moving on and this approach suited me. Unfortunately, future teachers did not. The next teacher spent the whole lesson writing the homework on the blackboard, whilst we copied it down before he started wiping it off. For most of the lessons, this was the procedure and I don't remember any actual teaching taking place. The result of suffering this was that I was put off maths and did the minimum. Unfortunately, this wasn't the only subject that used this approach, and when combined with boring subject content, I turned off in quite a few subjects.

I know from my teaching experience that there are very different learning styles, and I benefit from understanding the 'why' and the bigger picture of how this knowledge fits into the real world. To learn about the Enclosure Laws in isolation was as dull as anything could be. Relevance in subject matter and explanation of its application makes sense to me, and as a result, I remember what we covered. Chemistry failed in this aspect for me, but physics was a winner.

I did have some misguided ideas, and I believed you didn't need to revise for Maths, English and, to a lesser extent, English Literature, as you either knew how to do it or you didn't. In English Lit, if you had read the work, then that was all you needed to do. Misguided as I was, no one ever explained this folly, probably because they were unaware. It would have been helpful to have had someone suggest how to study, how to prepare and revise for exams, but Roundhay had the Darwinian attitude of survival of the fittest and left you to your own devices.

I, and I suspect many others, have a low boredom threshold and if I am not gripped by the material and presentation early on then my mind blanks out, much like the soldier in 'The Naming of Parts' poem (Henry Reed 1942), as he stares out of the window. See, I must have paid attention during some lessons! Foreign languages fell into that scope for me, which is strange, as I married a linguist. Maybe my choice was because she complements the parts of me that are lacking, as well as being very useful when you visit foreign countries.

The thought of learning pages of vocabulary was as abhorrent as poking my eyes out and, as a result, I failed miserably. The Whitmarsh French Course didn't add a great deal to its relevance. Why would we want to learn 'the cat sat on the mat' in any language? I could make a good stab at translating French to English, but hadn't a clue the other way around. I chose Latin as the second language, as I wanted to become an archaeologist, but I was equally miserable at that. Amo, amas, amat, now there was something useful, or at least that was how I thought it to be so.

The result of my language difficulties was that we saw Roundhay School surrender. My classmates and I were so atrocious at French, which was compulsory to the 5th form, because of university entrance requirements, that they resorted to introducing CSEs. French was the only subject and where I can't remember who the lucky teacher was who got the poisoned chalice of taking us, but CSE we studied, though towards the end even that was given up on and he spent lessons reading La Peste (Albert Camus) in English to us and I now suspect that he saw us as the plague and the choice was deliberate.

In Latin, they realised which of us were the no-hopers and we were put in a new class to do Classics. Now this was wonderful! We suddenly started covering interesting things. We were set projects, and I did one on Roman Britain. Working at home (yes, I could do it when I enjoyed something) I produced a decent project with information and detailed illustrations. The resulting tome was so good that I won my only ever prize at Roundhay. I was allowed to choose a book, and I was quite thrilled. I selected a book on techniques of playing rugby and I still have it. I wasn't sure who was more surprised, me or the teacher, but my mum and dad were pleased.

Chemistry was too much like languages for me. Learning formulas with no obvious relevance was a real turnoff and our behaviour in labs became more extreme. I have spoken about some of our antics with Mr H, who I am sure was a wonderful fellow. Smoking in the lessons, John S pretending to faint, doing dangerous things with mercury (maybe the cause of our madness) and other disruptive and inexcusable behaviour meant that Chemistry was not going to become one of my O' Level subjects.

The problem was that we had to make certain choices for subjects and there was one group where you could have a choice, but the others were compulsory. Hence, CSE French was one subject, despite my having no hope of achieving anything. Maths, English Language, English Literature, Physics, Geography, Biology were my subjects. I would have loved to do art, history, woodwork, economics and music, but we could only choose one and I had chosen biology. I did start O' Level RE as an extra subject with Joe P, but I never sat for the exam in the end. Because I was only doing six O' Levels, it meant there were free periods and any such times were spent in the library, where a register was taken to make sure you attended.

Mock exams finally approached, and I did do some revision. This was centred on the subjects I enjoyed, so Geography, Biology, Physics and a little English Literature (I read the texts again), got a bit of a workout. I must say that I was lucky to be at school in the days when results were purely based on exams, as with a bit of effort just before the exams, you could make a decent attempt and pass. Nowadays, with continuous assessment, it doesn't necessarily meet a lot of boys' learning styles, but favours girls, and as a result, girls are now better performers than boys. Regardless, with the amount of effort I made, I was surprised that I did as well as I did in the mocks.

The actual exam sessions meant sitting at wooden single folding desks in the hall. I remember the horror of entering the room, knowing I was going to struggle and that everyone else was going to succeed in everything. I believe the exams were ninety minutes, and in some subjects it felt like an eternity, but in those I could make a good stab at, it was too short a time. I remember we could not leave the hall for any reason and even when you had finished, you had to sit in silence. The teachers would cross off the time on a board at the front every ten minutes and they would patrol, gown wearing, humourless and silent. The most you ever got was when they stood behind you and made the fateful sound of 'Tut-tut!' as they looked at one of your answers.

You were shown in just before the exam start time, and found your seat in alphabetical order, a challenge for some of us, during the stress of the occasion. Pencil cases were placed on the desk, and pens and pencils arranged neatly. At the start, you could fill in your name and details, and then there was a short time to read the paper instructions. After this came the dreadful words, "You can now open your papers and start! The time now is..." We were off. You scanned the questions to see if you could answer any. Usually, you had a choice of how many you had to answer from the selection and I hoped there would be some I could have a stab at. Sometimes I would jot down a few notes I had learnt, of dates, names, quotations, and then I was off. Panic often struck as I read the questions and realised there wasn't one I could answer, but then I worked out the one I could make the best attempt at and then worked through, attempting them in descending order of my knowledge level. All the time, we were watched like hawks as the black, raven-garbed teachers walked the aisles, arms clasped behind their backs. I guess they loved it. The quiet, the control, the power, something that some of them lacked in the classroom. Occasionally, one swot of a boy would raise his hand and wait. Eventually, an invigilating teacher would notice and slowly make their way over. There would be whispered words and then the teacher would walk to the front and return with extra paper, whilst the rest of us would look at the boy with hatred, envy, and loathing. I would cast my eyes on my answer booklet and realise there was no chance I was going to fill all the pages. If this wasn't bad enough, you recognised the back of the head of the boy with the extra paper and that you had discussed the exam with him prior to it starting and he had assured you he hadn't done any revision and that he was certain to fail. You knew now, "Lying toad!"

Even with the few words I was managing to scrawl, the top of my hand was aching with the strain. Added to this were the full bladder and the knowledge that there would be no relief until afterwards. It was hell, and we had to suffer in silence. More and more boys were now raising their hands for extra paper and you could sense their smug expressions, even from behind. I wonder if they could feel the wave of loathing flowing their way. Shortly before the end, one teacher would announce that there were ten minutes left and that if we had finished, we should read through our work and make sure we hadn't missed anything out, "As if!" I don't think I ever mastered the skill of going over my work, usually I either was struggling to finish, or I was getting into a panic on which of the two questions that I knew nothing about I should attempt. Eventually, we were told to put down our pens and not to speak until all the papers had been collected. Finally, we were allowed out.

Weeks later, we knew the results would be out. There was nothing private in these times. Results were pinned up on the notice board behind glass. All results were there, and we had to push our way through the smiling and smug faces of those who had excelled and the blank, zombie-like expressions of those who had not met their expectations. In my case, I did so-so. There was certainly nothing to dance home about, but then I was satisfied with the results. The reality is that once you get exam results, then they you start the next stage. O' Levels are replaced by A' Levels and then by a degree and then by higher qualifications, and no one really cares but you.

I take great pleasure in knowing that I will never take another exam in my life. This is one of life's pleasures and one of the few as we age!

LEARNING TO DRIVE

My mother must have finally passed her driving test by the time I was sixteen, as when my birthday came in December 1971, she paid for me to have driving lessons. Of course, the instructor of choice was Stan Waites, and she arranged for me to have two lessons a week. I can still remember the excitement of my first lesson. I had got my learner's permit and the afternoon of that day I was waiting in the front room for Mr Waites to turn up. He arrived and pulled up on the road outside and I went out to meet him.

    I wandered out, and he got out of the car and ushered me into the driver's seat. It seemed so strange to be sitting there. I was shown how to adjust the seat so that my feet could reach the pedals and push the clutch sufficiently to reach the floor. Next was how to adjust the mirror and to do this every time I got in the car as the examiner would look out for it. Seat belt was fastened and then I was introduced to the basics of the gear stick. I put the car in neutral and then was told to turn the key and start the engine. I can still remember the thrill. Hands at 'Ten to Two', I checked the mirrors, pushed down the clutch, put the gear stick into first, accelerated, released the clutch and the hand brake and then came to a shuddering stop. I had stalled. I noticed, out of the corner of my eye, my mother watching from the front room window. Mr Waites calmly took me back through the process and this time the car slowly, if not smoothly, pulled off.

    Learner cars were dual control in these times and I am not sure how much Stan Waites controlled the gear changes, but almost as soon as we started moving along the road, he had me changing to second. We drove to the end of the street and turned right, and then right again to Arlington Road. We then drove up to Easterly Road and turned left towards the Ring Road. Easterly Road is a dual carriageway and I think the speed limit is forty miles an hour. He got me up to fourth gear, and the speed seemed incredible. We hurtled along the road and I had the mixed emotions of exhilaration and fear. We went up Wellington Hill and this part was quite easy as there weren't many gear changes required, but I couldn't believe it when we turned left onto the Ring Road towards Roundhay Park and Moortown.

I am proud to say I had no difficulties with the steering. Maybe that was because of the time spent riding my bike, but getting the clutch changing smooth was much more of a challenge. We headed up by Roundhay golf course and back along Park Lane and Princess Avenue to Oakwood and then onto the streets near my home. We stopped in a side street and he explained the mechanics of gear changing, positioning in the road for turns and basic road rules. After that, we started off again, and we arrived back at our house. My mother was still in the window and she rushed to find out how we had done. Mr Waites said I had done very well, but was not overly gushing.

The next lesson followed a similar pattern, but this time he took me through Harehills and the streets around Chapeltown and Spencer Place, as he told me that was the usual area that the examiners would use. I was more confident the second lesson, and it went well and I looked forward to the next. Each lesson after that we went to more challenging areas, and he told me less and less and allowed me to drive. He had a quick way to remind you if you were doing something wrong. A swift slap on the hand if you rested it on the gear stick, or a curt comment to let you know you had made a mistake, gave you the impetus to improve and learn. It was always done with patience and good humour, and he was an excellent instructor. I never drove with either of my parents, and so the lessons were my total experience. After about twelve lessons, he told me he was putting me in for my test. I beamed with delight, but then the anxiety hit. How would I face everyone if I failed?

We did not practise along the test routes for the rest of the lessons and Mr Waites would quiz me on my road knowledge and Highway Code. I also did some practice at home and then came the dreaded day of the test. You still had to do hand signals then, even though every car had indicators, but I hadn't practised them with Mr Waites until the lesson before the test.

The time for the test was upon me. The driving instructor entered the passenger seat, and he barely said a word, apart from instructing where to turn and what procedures he wanted me to do. I was surprised that he didn't fasten the seat belt, something that would be compulsory nowadays. We set off from the test centre and I noted we were heading to the area that we had practised during the lessons. It was mainly Harehills and Chapeltown. This was a relief, and I was driving fine. We did the usual manoeuvres of three-point-turn, reverse parking and hill-starts. I knew that the emergency stop was coming, and he forewarned me that he wanted me to stop when he tapped his newspaper on the dashboard. The moment came, and I was pleased with the speed and control I maintained. I began to relax a little, and this was a fatal mistake. He asked me to use hand signals for the next period until he told me to stop. I wound the window down and we carried on. I managed the signals for a few minutes and then automatically returned to indicating.

"I thought I asked you to use hand signals?" he said in a stern voice.

"I'm sorry," I replied. "Using the indicator is just instinct."

He said nothing more, but my heart sank. I've blown it, I thought.

We were driving along Roundhay Road and approaching the Harehills Road Junction. It was late afternoon, and the sun was setting and the sunlight was dazzling. I had been told to be very careful with zebra crossings because if you drove over one and someone had stepped on it, it was an instant fail. The light was blinding as we approached the zebra crossing, and just as I was about to cross the black and white lines, I saw someone step onto the crossing. I slammed on my brakes and the examiner was thrown forward. His papers went flying and his glasses fell off as he hit the windscreen. If there had been any doubt I would fail, that quickly vanished. I almost cried, but carried on after the pedestrian crossed the road. It was nearing the end of the test and I continued in a dream-like state of misery and finally pulled into the driving school car park. The examiner was busy filling in his forms and then he turned to me,

"We're scraping the barrel here, Mr Cameron, but I congratulate you on passing your test."

I couldn't believe it.

"Just one thing. Why did you stop like that at the crossing?"

I explained I had been told it was an instant failure.

"Well, don't do it again! You'll have someone drive into the back of you."

With that, he handed me the form to get a full licence, got out of the car and had a quick chat with Mr Waites, who was standing there. Mr Waites then walked over and told me to get in the passenger seat and he drove me home. My mother was still in the window waiting and she rushed out. I was beaming at this point and waved the pass papers in front of her. I think she had mixed emotions, pride that I had passed first time, but a bit of embarrassment that she had had so many lessons and tests before she finally passed. I had done it in 24 lessons and despite the belief I had blown it on the test, I was raring to drive on my own.

My mum had the Morris Minor at this point and she let me drive over to my older brother's house in Crossgates. I must be honest, driving on your own was very nerve wracking. I was constantly waiting for someone to give me instructions and, of course, there was no one else there. I drove at night that first time and I hadn't ever driven the car before and it was quite a scary ride. I wasn't sure where I was going and got lost a bit, but eventually managed it.

It was a great gift from my mother. I think it is so much easier to learn when you are young. I became a good driver and partly this was due to the fact that my mum got me a job at Wraggs Motor Cycles on York Street as she was the wages clerk there. They wanted someone to drive the VW van to pick up and deliver motorbikes and scooters. They also had a shop on Lower Brigate and the workshop was on Brussels Street. I had to go in for an interview and they asked if I could drive the van and I said I thought I could. They sent me off to drive it around, and I was on my own, luckily. I did fine through Leeds City rush hour, but I made a mistake coming back and turned right at traffic lights from Duke Street into York Street where only buses were allowed. No one saw me and I got away with it.

I was given the job and on my first day, they wanted me to take the van home and the next day drive down the M1 to Birmingham to the Triumph motorcycle factory to collect a Triumph Bonneville. I had barely driven anywhere at this point and thought it good to take my friend David G along to act as navigator. It was a real learning curve, but it all went well and I dropped him at his house before taking the van and motorbike to Wraggs. I think it impressed them, but that was only to last a few weeks before I had a calamity.

THE UPS AND DOWNS OF WORKING FOR WRAGGS

So I picked up Dave from his house and we set off down the M1 to Birmingham. I was nervous, especially as this was my first time on a motorway. Now I must add that the road was not as busy as it is today, but it was still very challenging. We took our time and with some good map reading from my friend Dave, we arrived at the Meriden Triumph factory, near Birmingham, to collect a brand new Bonneville motorbike. I had the paperwork, and they were expecting me, so they directed me to the right section and the workers used a forklift to place the brand new bike on the tray of the van. They supervised the tying down of the bike and placed clothes where the ropes might rub and it all went smoothly, as did the return trip to Leeds. I dropped Dave off at his home before I returned to Wraggs. They were pleased to see the bike had arrived safely, and a little surprised to see me so early. It was still only mid-afternoon. They unloaded the Bonneville, and I was given a more thorough tour of the workshops and provided with work overalls. I worked for quite a long time and got quite used to driving around the North of England. The company was owned by partners at the time and one lived in a beautiful old house near Driffield. I would love the drive across the Vale of York and arrive at his large rural property, where there would be a collection of used motorbikes he had purchased, and they had to be taken to the Leeds workshop for preparation for sale. I would load up the van with a lot of motorbikes and occasional scooters and the machines would be hanging off the edges and the ropes criss-crossed to ensure they didn't move. I am pretty sure that it would not be legal nowadays, but it was never an issue then. I would leave the idyllic house and countryside and drive back to Leeds. The Yorkshire Wolds is one of my favourite places and the countryside is truly beautiful.

The drive down Garrowby Hill was always interesting, and the brakes used to get very hot before I safely reached the bottom. The hill is a steep, winding climb down and many either fail to make the summit of the highest hill in the Wolds on the long climb up, or come to grief on the very steep descent. The view from the top is magnificent on a clear day, as you look down on the vale that was a large glacial lake at the end of the last ice age. I was always relieved when I was safely at the bottom and the rest of the journey was straightforward. One of the mechanics, who used to do this trip before I started, was most displeased when I returned in the afternoon. He had apparently taken the full day for the same trip and I was making him look bad. He insisted I didn't do it again. Another lesson that I never took any notice of! The work became quite routine but, bit by bit, various staff asked me to do things for them. Now, I have never really worked in businesses much in my life, apart from as a student, but there did seem to be a lot of underhand dealings going on. I was asked to deliver bikes to workers' houses. One manager would have me do deliveries for them that were not actually work-related, but private. I would be instructed to fill up jerry cans with petrol when I was filling the van and they would then take the cans and fill up their private cars with petrol that was meant for the van. There were a multitude of small fiddles going on that together must have cost the business a lot. None were major and no one actually explained that they weren't work-related business, but a number of employees seemed on the fiddle in one way or another.

Wraggs had two shops in Leeds and one in Chesterfield at the time. I had to do a lot of work between the shops and often on a small moped. I would shoot around, taking parts and documents from one shop to another. Sometimes, I had to go to stores for parts. This was one of the most amazing experiences. You would arrive at the service desk and a man would saunter over to you. They never hurried. "Yes?" he would say and I would show him the written part I was to collect. He would look at the note and stroll out back into the warehouse. I would wait and wait. Five minutes later, he would return, look at the note again and saunter off into the back. Another five minutes and he would return. He would pull out a parts catalogue, flick through the pages, appear to find what he wanted and then he would turn around and disappear again. He never once spoke to me during this time, but he would occasionally mumble something to himself. Eventually, he would return like a successful bounty hunter with his prize, pass it over, get me to sign for it, and then I was allowed to leave. This experience has stayed with me, as it seemed to reflect the general attitude of many workers in the UK at the time. Don't hurry, don't put yourself out! Unfortunately, it was the attitude that saw Britain lose its manufacturing industry to countries where people would do the work cheaper and in a fraction of the time.

I worked there for the whole of the summer. I had to drive quite long distances, and it really developed my driving skills and knowledge of Yorkshire roads. I experienced a number of strange things and one that I have never forgotten, involves a cat. I was returning to the workshop in the van and it was about four in the afternoon. I was following a double-decker bus, and I was just about to stop to turn right into the workshop. One of the mechanics was standing in the entrance and was trying to start a very large old motorbike. He kick-started the bike and there was a very loud backfire. A stray cat was standing next to the bike, and it was suddenly startled and ran straight across the road. It missed the oncoming traffic, but unfortunately for it, it didn't miss the bus. I watched in horror as the bus's front right tyre ran directly over its head. I was totally shocked and sat stationary, indicating right. To my amazement, the cat got back on its feet and, I can only think through some reflex memory, ran back across the road to the very spot it had started from. The poor creature then keeled over, twitched a few times and finally lay still. I managed to get the van back, but I was in a state of shock. I think this was the first time I had seen anything killed. The mechanic seemed oblivious to what had happened, and I don't even think he saw the cat. The poor creature had used all its nine lives at this point.

One other memory, less horrific this time, but still shocking, was when a young lad came to collect a scooter. Now these were still the days of Mods and Rockers and Lambrettas were still popular and had chrome fairings. He had bought a second-hand scooter, and he had never had one before. They had serviced the scooter in preparation for his collection, and the excited lad had paid for the machine days earlier, and it was his time to collect it. There was a bit of waste ground at the back of the shop and the mechanic brought the machine up. He spoke with the lad and explained how the clutch and throttle worked and I stood watching with interest, which was more than could be said for this youth. He had a look of, 'Why are you telling me this?', written all over his face. Anyway, at the end of the pre-delivery run down, the mechanic asked if he was OK to drive the scooter up to the showroom office to sort out the insurance papers. The lad said he was fine and had driven one before. Clearly, he was lying! He sat on the machine with an air of confidence and joy. He kick-started the scooter and throttled hard. The engine raced, as did my heart. He let out the clutch and the scooter almost took to the air. It flew across the side road and he panicked, and fell to the side as it struck the corner of a brick building. He lay in the dirt, his hand still clutching the throttle open and the rear wheel spinning alarmingly. The mechanic ran across and took his hand off the throttle and helped pick the boy and the bike up. The mechanic had a definite smirk on his face. As far as he was concerned, the lad had learnt a hard lesson. I don't think there was a lot of damage to the rider or the scooter. He had a bruised ego, and the scooter had damaged fairings and had lost some paint. Probably more devastating for him was the fact that the damage would not have been covered by insurance, as the papers had not been signed. On reflection, it was probably a good lesson for him and maybe had taught him how dangerous driving scooters, bikes or any motor vehicles can be, for that matter.

    My time passed at Wraggs and I enjoyed the work as much as one can at seventeen. I got quite good at getting the heavy bikes onto the back of the van. You had to run hard up one plank whilst pushing the bike up the other. I learnt to park facing downhill, so the gradient wasn't too steep. Occasionally, a bike would slip off, but I always managed to control them and get them up without any damage. One day, I was delivering bikes and scooters to people that had bought them. The van was fully loaded, and I set off on my rounds. It was to be a long day and so I was to take the van home with me when I finished. The bikes were all second-hand, apart from one that was a brand new Honda 250cc machine. It was good looking bike, but quite heavy. The day went on and I was down to my last two deliveries. I dropped off the last second-hand bike and went back onto the back of the van to tie in the Honda and then set off. I noticed that it was not quite in position, so I shuffled it across tight to the side of the tray. For some reason, it tipped a bit, and somehow the hook that held the side of the tray in place was not locked in. The rest all seemed to happen in slow motion. The bike toppled, the side fell open, and the Honda appeared to stop, poised, and then it fell. The drop was onto its top from a height of at least three feet. There was a crunch. My heart stopped, and I realised I was doomed. The handlebars were bent, the speedo broken, but the rest seemed ok. I felt like dying. Why hadn't I left it alone? What was I to do? Someone was waiting for it. I got the bike back onto the van. I then drove to a public phone-box and spoke to the manager. He was a young, mid-thirties, cocky man. He was not impressed. He told me to take it and show the man who had ordered it. I did this and the man was as good about it as could be expected. He was waiting for a new bike, but clearly he wasn't getting one that day. He knew he would have to contact the shop the next day. I had to take the damaged bike and van home overnight.

The next day was my first, and only, time I have been sacked. It didn't take long and I suppose I can understand it, but I felt hard done by. My mother still worked at Wraggs and she let the manager know exactly what she thought about it. I can only imagine what she would have said and how he suffered, as I had been at the receiving end of her tongue-lashing on many occasions. I guess I got off lightly compared to him, but I was sorry to lose the job and income. As it was, it was almost Christmas holidays, and I then applied for Christmas post work at the Harehills delivery office.

David M Cameron

THE GIRL IN THE SHORTS

Cars were relatively few in number at the end of the 50s and early sixties, but I can still remember several incidents that have stuck with me all these years. Some of these I have mentioned before, but others tell of how engineering, public safety and awareness have changed, and of the folly of youth.

For those of us old enough to remember, the road layout at Oakwood used to be very different, partially because trams used to run. The Oakwood Clock used to stand at the very edge of where Princes Avenue joined Roundhay Road. The road took the shortest sweep around the clock and avoided the current lights with Weatherby Road near the library. The bend around the clock was interesting as it had a camber away from the turn and, to make it more interesting, originally the tram lines used to run behind the clock, leaving it on an island where the car park is now.

I must have been at Roundhay School and the trams had long since gone, and I was sitting at the clock when a Morris Minor came tearing down the road from Roundhay Park. It took the bend around the clock tower at speed. There was a screech of brakes, a sudden tearing of metal and sparks flew as the front wheel of the Morris just bent over and the front of the car tilted, and came into contact with the road, amidst a fountain of sparks. Luckily, there were no pedestrians in the way and no other vehicles, and the car skidded, eventually coming to a standstill. It certainly grabbed the attention of those of us waiting at the clock. Some adults ran over to check on the driver, and after a bit of ogling someone's misfortune, we got back to whatever we were doing.

I used to walk to Roundhay School via Oakwood and one morning I remember reaching Oakwood and was just passing the clock when I noticed a grey squirrel. I can't remember if it was startled by a car backfiring or some such incident, but I clearly remember watching it run across Gledhow Lane. This wasn't particularly noteworthy as there were a lot of grey squirrels at Oakwood in the trees near the clock and the public toilets, but what it did was. The squirrel ran past a double-decker bus going up Gledhow Lane and suddenly jumped onto the open platform at the back of the bus. It all happened quickly and I think the squirrel was as surprised as the conductor and passengers and it turned and then fell backwards and lay on the road. There were lots of Roundhay boys about and one of my classmates, Roger, went over and picked the squirrel up and put it into his hold-all. This was an altruistic gesture, and he meant well, but grey squirrels were frowned upon for putting their red brothers in danger of extinction.

He carried it to school, probably to seek assistance, but when he opened the bag up, the creature had recovered and as his hand went in, the squirrel's large, sharp teeth went into his thumb. The squirrel beat a hasty retreat and probably returned to the trees to tell a tale that the other squirrels wouldn't believe, whilst Roger had to seek medical attention as he was losing a lot of blood. He was taken to hospital, given a tetanus injection and several stitches and carried a bandaged thumb as proof of his ordeal. I imagine that both he and the squirrel learned from their encounter.

I passed my driving test at seventeen after about twelve weeks of learning and, as I have mentioned before, much to the thanks of Mr Waites and his skill as an instructor. When I passed my test, my mother allowed me the use of her car. Her car was also a Morris Minor, and it was a reliable, if not fancy, car. The steering wheel was very large and the gear stick long, and changing gear was quite a challenge. The interior was very sparse with a metal dashboard and the seats very upright, but when my mum allowed me to take it out on my own, the evening I passed, I couldn't have been happier or more elated.

I set off to visit my brother in Seacroft and it was a real shock to be driving with no one giving instructions. I now had to learn to make all the decisions, as well as picking my route. I managed it though and also got back home again afterwards. I was very quickly employed as the van driver and general dogsbody for Wraggs Motor Cycles. This was only part-time holiday work, but it was a crash course for my driving skills, and luckily didn't involve any crashing. Having use of a car and the ability to drive provided a wonderful amount of freedom. I no longer had to wait for buses, or cadge lifts off my parents and it is something I have never taken for granted. I love to drive and I know that many share that feeling, but I also know that many struggle to drive and are not confident drivers.

Some of my friends were older than me and they already had licences, but many were learning. I must have driven long enough to supervise learners. A friend of mine, John L, had bought a car, a mini I recall, and he wanted me to supervise him driving. Now, on this particular occasion, a group of us were going on a day trip to the Yorkshire Dales and there were three cars. Another friend called John had a new Ford Capri with a brown vinyl covered roof and he and his girlfriend had maybe another couple of friends in the back, Peter, I think, had his own car and I was accompanying John L in his mini with David G in the back. There was one particular feature about minis in these days and that was that the sub-frames had a tendency to rot and the suspensions come adrift. I had never seen his car before and certainly never been in it, or I might well have refused.

The three of us squeezed in and John got in the driver's seat and, I think it had front seat belts, so we put them on. I don't remember David G in the back having one though and as he was tall, he had to sit sideways and had his head of tight curls bent down. I think he chain-smoked most of the journey, for reasons you will understand.

John started the car, and we set off. He jumped the clutch, and there was a bit of kangaroo bouncing, but eventually he got going. He over-revved the engine and when we approached a junction on a slight hill, he informed me that the handbrake didn't work so could I put my leg over to the foot brake whilst he got the car to hold on the clutch. This came as a bit of a shock and was certainly nothing I had been taught, but there was no alternative. The tangle of legs was interesting and David in the back had no means of escaping as the car rolled backwards. Another cigarette was instantly lit, which didn't help us in the front. I held the brake down and when the lights changed, John heavily revved and slipped the clutch and I withdrew my foot. It may not have been orthodox, but it worked. We followed our friends in the other two cars and headed out of Leeds along Harrogate Road, and soon we were in the countryside. John had clearly grasped the basics of driving, but his car seemed to have given up on most of them. Every bump in the road produced a loud bang from one shock-absorber and David's and my comfort and security weren't helped when we looked down at the floor. We spotted a few areas of light where we could see the road below us. David G lit another cigarette, hands shaking, in the back seat.

John's car would have failed any MOT test, but I don't think they had been introduced. If they had, someone must have been bribed to get it through. We were managing quite well at this point. I had perfected with John the ability to reach over to hold the car on the brake whilst he put it into first and controlled it on the clutch. We were well out into rural Yorkshire and the views were stunning, but the roads were narrow, twisting and bordered by dry-stone walls. It was a warm sunny day, and we were relaxing. Life was good! John was always interested in the girls and he had earned the nickname of 'Screwer'. I can't say why, but he had, and I can only guess it was because he was good at woodworking. Anyway, we were approaching a sharp turn that rose up a steep hill. There was a stile in the wall and, on the far side, a copse. A group of hikers were trekking down the hill and some were climbing over the stile. One of the party was a teenage girl wearing short shorts and clearly John noticed this too. But he failed to notice that the road turned at ninety degrees and carried straight on. John's eyes were glued to the displayed young female flesh. Fortunately, I was not so distracted, and I just grabbed the steering wheel and yanked it over so that we continued on the road, avoiding ploughing into the group, the wall and then into the trees. David, in the back, was equally aware of the situation and hurriedly lit another cigarette, but John's eyes and head just turned, following the girl's legs. I am sure that the young lady in question was oblivious to how close to death she had been.

"Screwer!" I yelled. "You have to watch the road!" I think he just smiled as if nothing had happened. The rest of the trip continued and, despite the unorthodox gear changing technique, we eventually returned to John's house. The car was left on the road, in gear and with the wheels turned into the kerb so that it couldn't run down the hill. We piled out, David climbed out of the back and he lit another cigarette. I don't think he ever volunteered to go with John L again.

Leaving the car, we headed up to Moortown Corner and to the Chained Bull, where we enjoyed a pint to steady our nerves, and David lit another cigarette.

THE COW AND CALF

Many of my teenage activities were both inspired and facilitated by my older brother, Andrew. I have no memory of how he got into rock climbing, but somehow he did and he became heavily involved for a while. It was an activity that appealed to me as it met my youthful need for danger and I fancied it made me highly visible.

The Cow and Calf

I suppose I was assisted by my kind brother, inviting me to go with him and a friend to climb at the Cow and Calf Rocks at Ilkley. I can't have been much more that about thirteen at the time and I had visited the Cow and Calf before with my parents on one of their day trips. The Calf is a separate enormous boulder that is part of a land slip after the last ice-age, but the Cow is a larger cliff of millstone grit and there is a quarry within it, creating a horseshoe of climbable vertical slabs and chimneys. There is a very large pub/hotel nearby, and it has always been very popular with day trippers, tourists and rock climbers. The path up to the rocks is well-trodden and in the sixties, cars were just parked along the sides of the steep road up from Ilkley. One thing that sticks out in my visual memory is that Ban the Bomb protestors had painted the large symbol and the words Ban the Bomb across the rock faces that faced the road and the tourists. Nowadays, everyone would be outraged at the defacing of the beauty spot, but I don't remember that at the time. Maybe that was because I was young and the oldies were outraged quietly and without the means of making it public.

My brother, his friend and I went by bus to Ilkley. Andrew had climbing breeches, special PA climbing shoes/boots, a large coil of climbing rope, screw gate carabineers (karabiners) and other assorted equipment. All in all, it looked quite impressive on the bus. There was a lot of chatter and a lot of nerves on my part, and the trip was long and uneventful. We arrived and trudged up the steep path to the Cow and into the quarry. My memory tells me it was a warm and sunny day and it was quite busy with sightseers wandering into the quarry watching the rock climbers and those just scrambling over the boulders. The slab we started on was on the right as you had entered a little way. I can't remember the name of the climb, but I remember my brother telling me it was graded VD, which meant very difficult. I felt this was a rather challenging grade for my first go, but they seemed to know what they were doing. I do now wonder if my mother knew what they were doing. She might not have been too keen if she had.

Andrew's friend climbed up the very steep slab of rock and I think it was about thirty feet to the top. His friend sat at the top, fixed a belay, and then threw the rest of the rope down. Andrew then tied himself on and did the climb and then returned by descending the rear path and coming back into the quarry. The waistband in those days was a twenty-foot length of number one or two climbing rope wound around your midriff, tied off with a knot. A screw gate carabineer was then fixed around this and the main rope was tied with a figure of eight knot and then clipped through the carabineer and the screw gate closed. Sounds impressive, and maybe it was.

One problem was that the main rope was not the maximum gauge for climbing, but had a 2000lbs breaking strain and it was not the covered rope that was more common, but more expensive. Tied on, I was nervous and very visible, as I was clearly not wearing suitable clothing. I believe I wore jeans, T-shirt, jumper and, I can only think, my school shoes. Now I could be wrong, but I don't think that I would have looked much of a seasoned climber, but the word 'Ready?' was shouted down, 'Ready' was shouted back by Andrew. I said nothing. 'Taking in the slack!' was barked down from above. I was almost lifted off the ground by the rope pulling tight and I was left with no alternative but to climb.

The rock face was smooth, but there were obvious points where there were foot and hand holds. The problem was trying to reach them, whilst your heart is hammering, your jeans are restricting movement, your shoes are not really getting any friction and your older brother is shouting what he thinks are helping words of encouragement and guidance, but are in fact confusing and intimidating. I was surprised and delighted when I managed to reach up and then place my foot on a small knob of rock and lever myself upwards. The rope remained tight and was quite painful, but I didn't say anything, as it was quite reassuring. A voice from below told me I was doing well, and that there was a handhold to my right. Similar advice now started coming from above and was quite useful and I slowly, but steadily, made progress up the rock face.

After a while, the quarry bottom was now well below me and Andrew's advice, 'Don't look down!' had the immediate effect of making me look down. The quarry bottom was boulder-strewn and also full of seemingly tiny visitors who were intrigued by the youth, dressed unlike any other climber, who seemed so unsure what he was doing. I was hanging like a spider, spreadeagled against the rock. The rock offered comfort and security, as it had been there for millions of years, but I could not just hang there for the remainder of my life. I had to continue and the only way was up. There was no way that either of my climbing stalwarts was going to allow me to go back down. I was getting a little tired by this point and I started to get what is known as the shakes. It is called the shakes because your muscles are so tense they begin to twitch uncontrollably. The only way to deal with it, I was told from above and below, was to relax. Relax! Great advice! How are you supposed to relax when death is staring you in the face, or at least, in the imagination?

This was one of those moments when you surprise yourself. I was about three quarters up the climb and somehow I did manage to relax my leg sufficiently for the shakes to pass. A voice from above gave encouragement, but it was the belayer holding the rope, not God. I carried on and found the going easier.

Within a few more minutes, I was at the top, pulled myself over the edge and sat next to the lad who had supported me. I felt a million dollars! I was unclipped from the rope and I sat there and stared down into the quarry. There were shouts of encouragement from my brother, and a couple of elderly visitors clapped. I can't really explain the feeling of achievement that I felt at that moment, but I'll try. It felt as if I was sitting on the top of the world. The sense of achievement, of beating your own fear, is a sensation that leaves a permanent mark upon you. The first time is probably the most important. The first time you walk, ride a bike, swim, or anything where there is a sense of danger, remains with you, somehow etched into your brain, waiting to be drawn out so that you can relive it, or it is with me.

After this climb, we did a couple of others: another climb in the quarry and then one on the main crag, just to the right of the entrance and in full view of all the visitors. Afterwards we just messed about on the Calf. There are low overhangs where you can test yourself without ropes and you are only a yard or so off the ground.

This was a bit of a baptism of fire, but it whetted my appetite for climbing. I think I went once or twice with my brother, but then he was away at uni and I started with Roundhay School friends.

DANCING WITH DEATH

There have been occasions when the Grim Reaper has approached, but not tapped me on the shoulder. One such occasion occurred when I was in the sixth form in high school.

There was a real interest in rock climbing amongst some of the staff and some of my friends. We had quite a bit of experience in Yorkshire on the abundant crags, Ilkley Cow and Calf, and Almscliffe to mention a couple. We had also climbed in the Lake District and North Wales, so we were no novices. A friend of mine and I decided we would head into the Yorkshire Dales to do a bit of exploring. He knew about Trollers Gill and that there were old lead workings, so we decided to venture there with ropes, torches, etc. to try our hand. Now these were different times from today and neither of us had access to a car and so we did what many did and that was get a bus. Not very glamorous, but not a problem when you are young. Anyway, ropes and other equipment, packed lunch, fags and high hopes, we made our way into the Dales. The weather was good. One of those warm days, where matched with a keen sense of humour, made one feel good to be alive.

Now I can't quite remember if the bus passed the Gill or how we got there, but we arrived. It was about 1971/72 and everything, apart from the countryside, seemed to me to be in black and white. Trollers Gill is a very steep sided limestone valley, so steep it is almost a gorge. It is seldom visited as there are more well-known attractions in the area. I had never been there, but I had heard of its legend. Similar to the beast in the Tinder Box, Trollers Gill was supposedly haunted by a giant dog with eyes the size of saucers. The beast was called the Barguest! To put your mind at rest, the monster was not the reason for my near death experience, but being in the Gill, it was easy to imagine how you would feel if you were there after dark. It had a foreboding and mysterious atmosphere, even on a bright, sunny day.

The only company we had was Dales sheep, and they were dotted around the valley sides grazing on the thin Yorkshire grass. As you entered further into the Gill, the valley narrowed, the sides became more precipitous and shadow filled the valley floor. The rocky outcrops were limestone and their structure gave the impression of castle ruins, skeletal white against the green. As we walked the trail, we saw evidence of mining. Workings opened into some of the cliffs, like open mouths, they spewed a scree of white rubble down the valley sides.

Advancing further into the valley, we saw signs of more recent activity. A larger adit entrance was covered by a metal gate and clearly someone had started reworking the mine. It was obviously a small scale working, probably someone's hobby, and the gate had been built to prevent anyone from wandering in. As we approached, we saw the gate was open and the lock missing. There appeared to be no one inside, but there were some tools and old rails led into the mine. A small cart straddled the rails, but it appeared not to have been used for a long time.

Looking at each other for confirmation, we decided to explore. We had originally thought about climbing some of the crags, but this was always another possibility, and we had come armed with the basics of torches and a few candles. Looking back, it was clearly not one of our best planned adventures. We entered the mine, and the darkness became complete when we turned a bend and the entrance disappeared. At first, the floor was smooth on either side of the rails, but as we advanced further into the valley side, it became increasingly uneven and wetter.

Working only by torchlight, we advanced carefully as we noted that sections of the roof had collapsed and the space above opened out to a height of many feet. We could see tunnels running parallel to each other and realised that what we were seeing was the result of parallel adits cut one above each other to extract the lead and that over time they had collapsed. We stood gazing upwards to the maximum the torch beams could reach. Our breaths hung as mist in the cold, damp atmosphere as we contemplated what we were doing. Further on, the rails disappeared almost vertically as the floor had collapsed and we assumed into lower adits. There was an open space of approximately fifteen feet. We shone the torches downwards, but all we could see was a floor of rock twenty feet below us. I am not sure which of us dropped a small rock down, but one of us did and rather than the crump of rock striking the floor below, there was a whoosh of the rock entering deep water. This certainly confused us. We shone the torch beams along the rails, following them downwards. The sleepers had long since disappeared, but the rails looked solid enough and stopped at the visible floor. I dropped another bolder and this time there was the solid crunch of rock striking rock. My partner followed with another, and this time there was another splash as the rock hit deep water. I sat down on the side of the chasm and wondered what was happening. The ground below seemed solid enough, but the sound of the water contradicted that.

"I'll go down and have a look!" I said.

We unravelled our climbing rope, and I fixed one end to my carabineer, whilst my friend found a metal post a little way back and secured this to act as a belay. I took a couple of candles with me and slid down the tram rail. The angle was about eighty degrees and the rusty rail was about five inches deep by three wide. He took the slack of the rope and, using the friction to prevent me from sliding too quickly, I edged my way down. At this point, I was in the dark, as I couldn't manage the climb whilst holding the flashlight. My heart in my mouth, I began to wonder the wisdom of what I was doing, but since I had started, I could not turn back. The descent was accomplished without mishap, and I sat on a rocky surface. I breathed a deep sigh of relief and took out my torch to see what was about. It then hit me! On either side of me, the rock walls were a similar width to those in the passage above, and where I was sitting was a solid platform of rock that extended about ten feet in front and behind me.

I discovered I was sitting on a rock jam that was lodged within a vertical drop. I shone my torch down and saw the black surface of deep water. I knew the answer to my conundrum. The rock I was on was the remains of the passage floor from above. When it had collapsed, some of it had wedged itself in the space below and formed the platform I was now sitting on. The walls on either side were smooth and offered no means of an escape by climbing. The opposite ends to where I was sitting had no walls, and the cavern just opened out in extending blackness. The only means of escape was along one of the two rails that had collapsed when the floor had given way. I calmed myself and explained what was happening to my friend. I told him to keep the rope tight as I wasn't sure how stable the rock jam was. I lit the two candles so that he could get a good look.

This was probably not the shrewdest idea, as we had no idea if gas was present. I can only assume this was not the case, as nothing happened apart from the ghostly illumination of my dilemma. I was a lone figure, stranded like some character from Lord of the Rings in the Mines of Moria, huddled on the rock jam. To make matters worse, if that was possible, I realised that the rail I had climbed down hung over the open space above the water. If I had fallen, I would have hung over water and not over the rock and there would have been no means of getting out, unless my friend could have pulled me up, which was very unlikely. A cold clammy sweat came over me. Luckily, I had been totally unaware on the way down, but I had only one way out and that was back up the rail, knowing my fate if I lost my grip, or couldn't make it up the steep angle. We discussed the problem, and I gathered my thoughts. There seemed little point delaying. We knew it was unlikely that there was anyone else in the Gill, so we prepared. He checked his grip, and I turned off my torch and stowed it in my backpack. The candle light was all I had, which was probably a blessing. My potential fate was partially hidden from me, and I was thankful for small mercies.

Needless to say, the grip I took of the rail was tight, almost to painful point, and the moment I pulled my feet off the not so solid rock wedge, seemed to take an eternity. I was grateful for the rust, as it gave me better traction and I was so aware of my balance. A wobble too far and I would have overturned and been suspended like some giant spider over a black bottomless void.

Just writing this brings back the fear from so many years ago. My friend ensured there was no slack, and I worked my way up the rail like some giant inchworm, breathing heavily with the exertion. Painfully slow and painful, I got further up the rail. Probably because of tiredness, I began to get the shakes. It is a feature of rock climbing. Sometimes when you are physically tense, the muscles go into a spasm of shaking. It doesn't have a direct link to fear, but the timing in this case added to my dread.

When there is no alternative, it is surprising what the human body can achieve and finally I made the top and, with help, pulled myself over and just lay on the damp muddy tunnel floor. At this point I thanked all possible gods, fortune and even my friend. It took a while, but eventually I looked back down and saw the subterranean void lit in the ghostly candlelight. It took even longer to compose myself, but we continued our exploration. In a side passage, we came across a seam of quartz. The crystal glittered magically in the torchlight and veins of bluish-black crystals laced through the white majesty. Galena! The lead that was sought by the miners. There was evidence of recent work in the shaft and this vein was a new find and offered the hobby miner or miners some reward for their effort. For our own efforts, we took a couple of small samples of the quartz-galena. Geological hammers in hand, we cut out a couple of pieces, felt satisfied with our day's exploration, and made our way out to reward ourselves with a packed lunch and smoke.

Sitting in the daylight, I reflected on my fortune, my foolishness and how wonderful the world was. The crystal I had taken became a prized possession and a reminder of my mortality. I guess I never really learned, as other stories will prove, but I loved that rock.

As a footnote, my galena and quartz rock were stolen from my classroom in a school in Yorkshire when the school was broken into years later, but it reappears in my novels in The Moondial Series.

ALMSCLIFFE CRAG AND SNOWDONIA

After my initial ventures into rock climbing, courtesy of borrowed equipment from my older brother, at the Cow and Calf and Hetchell Crags, I began to venture further afield. One favourite jaunt was Almscliffe Crag on the way from Leeds to Harrogate. The crag was a very popular site for picnickers and my parents had taken me there on a number of occasions and I loved to scramble over the boulders. Almscliffe had a number of advantages and the main one was that it was accessible by bus. My friends and I, along with our ropes and equipment, would board the bus and sit chatting as it took us slowly to our destination. We would similarly use the bus service to wind our way to Ilkley or Otley Chevin for climbing trips, but Almscliffe was a favourite. The Millstone Grit crag was high enough to provide interesting and not too challenging climbs. As you reached the steep hill that led down to the Wharfe Valley, there were Harewood Castle ruins on your left. The castle was a fourteenth century ruin and I have always been intrigued, but never ventured into it. It is now protected and preservation work has taken place. If you looked ahead whilst travelling down the hill, Almscliffe Crag was visible across the valley, standing proud above the fertile land.

Harewood Castle

Arriving at the field and stile over the dry-stone wall that led up to the crag, there would often be an ice-cream van, if the weather was warm and crowds expected. It was a bit of slog up the path, surrounded by sheep, but they never seemed to take much notice of our passing and seemed content to chew the grass. Weighed down with the ropes, gear and climbing shoes, we would drop everything at the base of the crag and decide what we wanted to do. One of my favourite climbs was a chimney on the back of the crag called Parson's Chimney and that allowed quite a long climb, whereas others were quite short. One of the most enjoyable, easy, but quite impressive feats for the picnickers gathered around was to abseil off the top. We got overly confident and would race down, cigarette held between the lips, but sometimes we would stop mid-descent and take a leisurely look at the wonderful views and hoped that any teenage girls present would be suitably impressed by our daring and doing. I can only say that, if they were, they never approached to share their feelings. That didn't stop us, as we were eternally resilient, hopeful, and stupid! On a really warm day, and there were many at the start of the 1970s, we would abseil without a shirt, and our blindingly white skin must have stood out like a beacon against the dark grey rock. After the harder climbs, there was nothing more satisfying than sitting at the top and enjoying a cigarette. Now, I can't believe how foolish we were to smoke, but most people seemed to do it. (Almscliffe Crag below)

In 1971, Mr H, a Roundhay School teacher, took a group of us to Snowdonia for a climbing trip. I am very sure that the trip would not be permitted nowadays, as health and safety would have put a stop to it, but times were different. We set off on a Sunday afternoon and a group of us were in Mr H's old van, most cramped into the back without any restraints. Accompanying us was Mr H's friend, Gel, and he drove a Triumph Spitfire. It was a very relaxed, and can I say, un-Roundhay like excursion with the boys and staff smoking freely. We were staying at Tyn Y Maes near Bethesday in Snowdonia, which was the Manchester University cottage. It was very basic with water from the stream, paraffin lamps and a gas bottle fired stove. We didn't care, and it was a great place. For many of us, this was our first time climbing in Wales, and Gel and Mr H led all the climbs with any novice climbers. On the first day, we started with Milestone Buttress at the base of Tryfan Mountain. We did some easy climbs and got a feel for climbing in Wales. The Buttress was fairly easy, and it was a good place to gain confidence and then we moved onto Tryfan itself.

The climbs on Tryfan were much harder, much longer, and much more challenging. I was climbing with Elson and started Grooved Arête, which was a 700 foot climb. Both Mr H and Gel were excellent climbers, but Gel was hesitant and it made me nervous watching his progress.

Idwal Slab at Cwm Idwal Snowdonia

Elson was great, and he started off and we worked well as a team. I seem to remember at one point there was a move called the Knight's Move as it resembled the chess move, forward and across. At the end of the horizontal traverse, I had to belay Elson as he moved onwards.

Me (top) climbing in Snowdonia

The spot where I stood was the most amazing one. It was a little shelf of rock, maybe six inches deep, and a foot long, that jutted out on a corner promontory. I was fixed to the cliff by a loop of rope fitted through my waistband and clipped into a piton that someone in the past had hammered into the rock. Everything had gone well and Elson had disappeared around the edge and vanished out of sight, but I gradually let out the rope that was attached to him. I had time to just take in the surroundings. We had climbed through the clouds to get to this point and there were breaks that opened up the valley floor and I appeared to just be standing, facing outwards on top of a cloud. It was quiet, apart from the odd seagull that flew below, when suddenly the tranquility was shattered, as there was an almighty roar from down the valley and, as the cloud cleared, a fighter jet shot below me at tremendous speed, barely above ground level. It cast a black shadow on the land below and it weaved through the narrow valley at breakneck speed. The sound followed on behind the fighter jet. Moments later, another appeared and I couldn't believe my luck witnessing such a thing. I had never thought I would be looking down on such a sight. The ability of the pilots was amazing. The planes almost scraped the valley floor and their wings appeared, but clearly weren't mere inches from the rock faces.

The aim for the pilots was to fly below radar and the narrow valleys were ideal for practising their skills. There was no room for error and they would be lucky to eject if they miscalculated. The nearest thing to it was the x-wing fighters in Star Wars as they flew around the Death Star. If I gained nothing else from the trip, that single memory was worth it and has lasted all my life. Elson and I made the top of the climb well before the others and we rested and had a cigarette. I am now really anti-smoking, but at the time there was nothing more pleasurable than having a cigarette at the end of a challenging climb. I was elated and life was good.

The next day, as is often the case in Wales, it was raining, and so we decided to go to Tremadoc and climb the old sea cliffs. On the coast, we found the weather was good and there were lots of climbers about. Many had a similar look: bearded, wild and woolly, and often accompanied by very attractive wild and woolly young ladies. The men often smoked pipes and, intriguingly, so did some women. Climbers are a separate breed, who feel the need to challenge themselves. Two of us were paired with Gel that day, and despite the climb being quite fascinating as you were often climbing rock through trees and so not exposed in the usual manner, I found Gel's slow, dithering method unnerving. Climbing, like many sports and activities, is as much about confidence and mental hardness. If you are following someone who seems unsure, this affects you and your confidence. The reality was that he was leading and a fall could be much more serious for him, whereas I was always belayed from above and so a fall would be almost instantly halted. When it came to my turn, I did the climbs in a fraction of the time, as did the other boy.

We did several climbs over the day before we went back down and had a few drinks with other climbers in the village nestled at the base of the old cliffs. On the return to the cottage, the Triumph broke down, which meant everyone had to squeeze into the van.

Next day was a Wednesday, and the weather was fine, and we went to Idwal Slabs. The slabs are very popular with climbers and easy to access, with a very enjoyable walk from the van. The slab is very impressive. Elson and I were paired together, and we started with the Subwall Climb, which Elson said is the hardest on the slab, which we followed with Tennis Shoe.

Much like Almscliffe Crag and the Cow and Calf at Ilkley, there were lots of spectators, which added to the enjoyment and resulted in the odd bit of posing. When the top of the slab was reached, the ropes came off, and we had to make our way down to the base to start another climb.

Climbing the face looks dangerous, but the way down is much more so. The walk down is graded VD, very difficult, in the guides and facing outwards, relaxed and chatting, you were far more likely to slip.

Tremadoc Cliffs

We had lunch at the bottom and then climbed all afternoon. Towards the end of the day, a small group appeared in brand-new climbing gear and there was someone with a movie camera. We ate and watched the drama unfold. They started one of the easier climbs, made very slow progress and were filmed every inch of the way. Pitons were hammered in, which was unnecessary and, really, vandalism. Climbers around were tut-tutting and eventually the lead got stuck and had to abseil back to the base. The rope was pulled loose, but the pitons, carabineers and other bits and pieces were still left on the rock. There was a hush from the climbers around the rock and as soon as the group walked back to their cars, other climbers ran at the rock with no ropes and raced each other to get to the expensive equipment abandoned on the slab. The group that had left it must have felt devastated with shame and the watching crowd applauded when the equipment was recovered.

We then went back to the cottage, and Thursday was the final day. It was raining heavily, and it was too bad to climb, so most went up Snowdon, but I stayed with one or two and rested in the cottage. On the Friday, Mr H had to ferry us back to Leeds as the other car wasn't fixed. He took half back and then turned around and returned to Wales to pick up most of the rest. Elson remained on his own overnight and then, according to his report of the camp, he hitchhiked back the next day.

It is experiences such as this that have stuck with me, and I don't suppose the others involved would know the impact that their kindness and camaraderie had on others. I have taken many opportunities to assist with my children's scout camps, caving excursions, and been part of, and led many school camps where children learn new skills, overcome doubts and fears and realise whether a certain activity suits them or not. Some people love team games and sports, whereas others don't. Finding what you enjoy is part of growing. My lifetime activity has been running, but that is a different tale.

WHAT STRANGE TEENAGERS

I don't know if my friends and I were particularly unusual or not, and I suspect you will let me know, but being a teenager for me was an opportunity to show off, try new things and sometimes learn from my mistakes. Early on at high school, we boys wanted to impress others, and this started for me in a decision that has never made sense to me afterwards.

I somehow came up with the idea that drinking Quink ink and eating chalk would be my way of achieving status in the class. Now, I really had no idea whether this was potentially dangerous or not, and seeing as probably very few would deliberately try it, even the manufacturers would have not considered this when producing their products. Anyway, I know I performed this feat frequently and, seeing as I am still around, I can only assume it was safe. Whether the act impressed my classmates, I can only guess. Why wouldn't they be impressed with someone with a blue/black tongue? Luckily, this was a brief phase, but I changed it to eating cigarettes.

I developed another innate skill that I didn't know I had until I blew my nose hard one day. The pressure as I held my nose forced air out through my tear ducts and, apart from making my eyes water, the ducts made a clear whistling noise that was quite loud. I still can be encouraged to perform this feat for adoring crowds to this very day, but it isn't in great demand. I have only seen one act where this skill is taken to greater heights and that is the Tokyo Shock Boys. This group of four Japanese men perform dangerous stunts such as juggling working chain saws, but they have a stunt called the Milk Man where one takes a drink of milk and then holds his nose whilst blowing hard. Instead of air, as in my case, the milk comes out of his tear ducts. I guess if he is ever out of action, I could probably stand in!

Of course, it wasn't just me, and people had a range of tricks that were introduced to the groups of friends at parties or when round at each other's houses. One trick was supposedly easy for girls, but almost impossible for boys. A dining chair was placed against a wall and you stood directly in front of it. You then had to rest your head against the wall and then take hold of the chair and lift it off the ground. The task was then to stand upright. I have seen girls do it easily, but almost all boys fail. The explanation at the time was that it was due to body shape and pelvic differences. I don't know if that is true, but we boys just floundered at it.

Another similar trick was played at parties. Someone had to sit on a dining chair and four people then had the task of lifting them and the chair, using only two fingers each. This task started with the four pressing down hard on the top of the head on the person on the chair. At an agreed time, probably ten or twenty seconds, the four had to remove their hands and place two fingers from the same hand, as if pointing under the seat of the chair and, at the count of three, lift. The effect was quite stunning as it was quite easy to lift the seated person, hold them and them lower them safely back to the ground. I have no idea behind the science of this. Apart from that, four people focusing their strength through two fingers creates considerable force, at least sufficient to lift and chair with someone sitting on it. I can't see what pressing down on the head does, apart from making it seem more magical.

One simple challenge was the Jacob's Cream-cracker eating challenge. The task was to eat two plain crackers and swallow them in a minute. The only stipulation was that you couldn't have a drink of water. To most of us, this appeared to be simple enough and one we were confident we could achieve, and we started with great gusto, but the dry cracker quickly removed all moisture from the mouth and made swallowing very difficult. Needless to say, the first person to bring this to a group with no prior knowledge could make a killing with small wagers.

Whilst I was at Roundhay School, breaks and lunchtimes, when in the early years, were often spent playing Chicken. Chicken involved penknives, and the two combatants stood facing each other with their legs wide astride. Each boy then took turns to throw the knife between the opponent's legs and stick it in the ground. If it landed correctly, the boy had to bring in one of their legs to the place where the knife was and therefore shorten the target area. That boy then took his turn and each time the space between the legs narrowed. This carried on with the gap getting smaller and smaller until one of the boys gave in and admitted defeat, rather than being prepared to have their foot impaled to the ground by the knife, hence the name Chicken. The most scared surrendered and was the Chicken! In most cases, this was fun, but sometimes it was quite a serious business with kudos on the line. I don't remember any genuine accidents, but some wayward throws came very, very close to piercing human flesh and bone.

One stunt that I was once introduced to at my house. Chris M and Roger H were present. It was potentially very dangerous, so can I add, 'Do Not Try This at Home, Folks!' We were in my parents' lounge and we must have been about thirteen, maybe fourteen, and either Roger or Chris knew this trick where you could knock someone out. To perform it, one person had to bend over and take forty quick deep breaths in and out. The other two stood, one at the side and one directly behind. At the end of the breaths, the person stood up quickly. The person behind put their arms around the chest of the one standing up and squeezed tight.

I was told what to do, and I thought I would try it. I did what I had been told and, as I stood up, Roger's arms went around my chest and the next thing I knew I was lying on my parents' carpet, with a dizzy throbbing in my head. The result was so marked and quick that it was frightening. It took me a little while to get my wits back. Some of you will be questioning whether I ever had any, but Chris wanted to have a go and I wanted to do the squeezing to see if it worked. Chris followed the routine and when he stood, my arms went around his chest and almost instantly he became a dead weight and I had to support him and Roger and I lowered him to the floor. I can only think that with hyperventilating and then suddenly standing upright and blood flow being restricted, the brain becomes depleted of oxygen and the victim is rendered unconscious. Luckily, this was an experience that we only ever wanted to do once. I can see so many dangerous aspects to this, one being the possibility of someone hitting furniture or not regaining consciousness, that it truly frightens me now. Fainting is quite common in teenagers and I have done it at Roundhay School assemblies and seen many others do it, but it's certainly not something you should deliberately do.

Somehow we survived, but I am sure that many others were not always so lucky. There was almost an attitude that you had to learn how to fend for yourself and make the right choices, knowing that sometimes you wouldn't. Now, almost all risk is removed from children and we cocoon them in a safe world, but really, the world isn't. How can you judge danger when you drive, if you have never ridden a bike too fast and fallen off, scraped your knees when running and tripped, or fallen out of a tree? We learn our limits and develop our skills through challenges whilst we are growing up.

My last example has more to do with our mental wellbeing, and that was having a séance. Fashionable was the Ouija Board game by Parker Brothers. Maybe it was the enlightened times, but it was not strange for a séance to be seen as a game, but I am sure it would raise a few eyebrows in current politically correct times. Now I don't believe in the supernatural, but that doesn't mean I can't be frightened by old houses, woods at night, cemeteries or other classic scenarios. During our teenage years, we had several séances and often they were instigated by girls within the group.

This may be provocative, but it has been my experience that girls gravitate more to believing in the supernatural or spiritual. Wind-catchers, crystal healing, candles, scents, holistic medicine, clairvoyance and others have a higher number of female followers. My suggestion is that maybe they hope that there is more to life than the men they have come across. Who can blame them? Certainly, the teenage boys left a lot to be desired, as these examples show.

One memorable example was a night held in a friend's house. There was a group of us and there was Pete, Kim, Anne H, Anne W, Dave G, possibly Caroline and me. We were late teenagers at this point and one of the girls suggested getting the Ouija Board out. I know several of the girls had one, and I didn't know one boy who did. The board came out, and we sat around the table. A Ouija board comprises letters and numbers, yes, no and goodbye, and there is a pointer (planchette) that everyone has to place their hand on. The lights were dimmed, there might have been a candle, and we all touched the pointer. One of our group became the host and called the spirit with, 'Avante, spirit'. I believe this is Spanish, but it was supposed to call a spirit of a departed person into the room. The host asked if a spirit was there and the pointer moved to yes if there was. Questions were asked with subdued voices and, if there was a spirit, the pointer moved presumably of its own volition and spelled out answers to questions.

Now, on this occasion, a few spirits in the alcoholic form had been consumed, which seemed to add to the mood and atmosphere. The spirit in the séance seemed quite responsive, and messages, names and answers were provided dramatically and produced the odd tingle of fear down my spine. We stopped after a while and there was questioning of the participants. Had you been pushing it? You must have pushed it? But how would they know that answer? I'd never told anyone that!

It did spook a few of the group out and some were convinced the spirits had been present, whilst others assumed it was a hoax. I wonder if that night confirmed some present that the spirit world exists, or whether it was just a passing evening of fun? If someone was cheating, then they have kept that secret for nearly fifty years! For anyone easily influenced or scared, then I certainly wouldn't recommend taking part.

Oh! For the record, I did push the pointer, and I have kept the secret until this day!

RUINING A WEDDING

Our rock band, Atlantis, was starting to put together some decent concerts. Rough, yes, but audiences were approving of what we did. Subtlety was never our forte up to this point and we were limited in the vocal area for the want of a PA system and decent microphones. Lack of money for equipment was always a problem and the amount we raised through our performances was very limited. 50 or 100 Watt amps were cranked up to ear-bursting levels, distortion was provided not by effect peddles, but by overloading the speakers. The advantage of this was that the audience was hit by a wall of sound and teenagers seemed happy to enjoy the vibe, more than subtle lyrics or virtuoso playing. We shared a lot in common with the Punk Movement that followed several years later, but without the spiky hair and safety pins.

There was always a tension within the band and that was both good and bad. The chalk and cheese were Peter and John. John was thorough, methodical and liked a more gentle sound to his music, whereas Peter was more eclectic in his tastes and had a restless side. I was just happy to play, and I enjoyed all aspects of being in the band. We had finally got a good drummer at this point called Reg. He was from Alwoodley and his parents were happy to allow us to practise quietly at his house. Elton John's Rocket Man sticks in my head as the song that was the hit of the time, so it was 1972. Playing bass along with Reg was a dream. He kept good time and played great rhythms and could put together a decent solo. I found him easy-going and a positive band member.

Another Cup of Tea – The Teenage Years

We had played quite a few gigs by this point and were getting a small but supportive following, and we slowly added to our repertoire of rock numbers. Peter was the primary source of the material, but the rest would chip in and add their mark to the songs and often the lyrics. After the last gig, which had been our best received, I thought we were starting to go places and that we needed to keep the momentum going. At the next band meeting, however, Peter had definite plans. He wanted to dump most of the material and replace it with as yet unwritten numbers. He felt we needed an additional guitarist and suggested Chris. Chris was a good friend of mine, but I really didn't see the need to throw everything out. John tended to agree with Peter, and Reg was non-committal. I was overruled and Chris joined and, looking back, it was possibly a good move as when Peter played lead, the rhythm loss was quite marked. We had a gig booked at the modern synagogue at Moortown and so we had to have material to play, therefore we couldn't drop everything.

We had a rehearsal at Reg's house and Peter and John had an idea for a new piece. This was to be an instrumental that had quite an interesting piano start. John and Peter played this to the rest of us and there was agreement that it was a good idea and that it we should work on it after the gig. John and Peter had different ideas. They wanted to add this to the set, and I was filled with horror as we hadn't really played it at all. Reg seemed to share my concerns, but again, we were overruled. It was to form part of the show, with a central part of improvisation built around the rhythm section of the drums and bass, before returning to the main theme for the ending. We tried it at Reg's house in very quiet form and I was quite nervous about this, but the others were adamant.

The day of the gig came, and we were told we could set up and do a sound check in the afternoon. The room we were taken to was upstairs with a small low platform stage and we were quite impressed as it was a large, modern venue with good acoustics. We had to lug our heavy speaker cabinets and amps up the stairs and it was one of the many times I was glad that I didn't play the drums. The drums were always heavy and difficult to carry and set up. I think Reg's dad had a large estate car, otherwise it would have meant several trips. Finally, we were ready to do our sound check and in particular to try out the new piece, called Atlantis 2. Tuning was always a bit hit and miss, but eventually we were ready and we ran through our set.

We had noticed that there were other people in the building, but we didn't really give it much thought, as we had permission. We started our set with gusto and underlying nervousness. It was clear this was a step up in venues and we wanted the performance to be successful. This, along with the untested and tried Atlantis 2, added to my anxiety. The run through went pleasingly well, and we then tried the new number. It started well and then we entered the long improvised section. I think I had a basic bass pattern of about four notes, whilst Peter and John improvised over the top in a similar fashion to early Pink Floyd. I played the bass with my fingers rather than a plectrum and I often suffered with sore finger ends and by the end of the run through, they were particularly sore.

I don't think we had quite finished before a very irate middle-aged lady burst in. She was livid.

"You've ruined my daughter's wedding!" she yelled.

Apparently, there was a wedding taking place below us, but we were totally unaware. We apologised, explained that we had permission and that we would stop. It struck me at the time that I couldn't see why she had waited so long. If any of the wedding party reads this, then please accept our apology and we hope that the marriage was very successful. We had never been wedding singers before that time!

This incident did not bode well for the evening performance and the omens made me even more nervous. We took a break, much to the joy of the wedding party, I assume, and returned in the evening shortly before the evening gig was to start. We checked the equipment, did a quick tune-up, and the audience began to arrive.

The room had a low ceiling and was wider than it was deep. This gave the feeling of a larger crowd, as the stage was only a foot high. It was a very intimate atmosphere. The small stage pushed me back very close to Reg's drums and made hearing the others difficult, but I felt that if we played together, then the others would follow and we'd hold it together. My playing wasn't anything fancy, but it served its purpose and the gig started and the audience listened attentively and this was quite intimidating. In the past, many in the audience didn't pay great attention, and our music served more as a background to teenage courting rituals, but this time we had their full attention. I seem to remember that John started off with a solo number again and it went down well and then we hit the band set and again the response after the first number was generous applause. This took me aback, and I just hoped we could keep it up. My fingers were beginning to really hurt, but the adrenalin kept the pain at bay. Despite the difficulty in monitoring the rest of the band, we held the numbers together and reached the crunch moment, Atlantis 2. I really didn't want to do this. We had gone so well so far and it seemed a risk we didn't need to take. Peter and John, though, were having the time of their lives and there was friendly banter between the numbers, with each other and the audience. I think it was Peter that introduced Atlantis 2 and he may even have referred to the fact that we had never performed it in front of an audience. There was a central part of the audience sitting before the low stage enjoying the performance as if we were really good. This just shows how you can fool people who want to have a good time and was probably helped along by our band of supporters who were always enthusiastic about everything we did. Their enthusiasm was clearly contagious and I am not sure we ever really showed our appreciation.

The moment came. The electric piano started, and we were off and running. Once we had started, the nerves disappeared, and I just had to focus on Reg's drums and my playing. The opening theme was tight and impressive, but then we entered unknown territory. The improvised section started, and I had to maintain the regular bass pattern. There was no opportunity for me to join in with anything different, and those four notes just ran on and on. The audience gave us their full attention. I could see the looks on the faces of the nearest and they seemed almost mesmerised. I wasn't sure if that was because they couldn't believe what they were hearing, or whether they were moved by it.

My fingers were killing me at this point and it was a struggle to maintain the pattern, but I did. John and Peter seemed quite inspired, or at least lost in their own worlds, and the number ran on and on. Finally, the signal was given, and we ran back into the main theme and we came to a dramatic closure. The audience went relatively wild. It was the best received number of the evening and I was flabbergasted and ready to eat humble pie. We finished the set and turned off the instruments and congratulated each other. I accepted that both John and Peter were right.

As we were turning off, someone I recognised came up and spoke to me. He was the Head Boy of Roundhay School and I am not sure now of his name. He was very encouraging, loved the 'Floyd-like number' and really dug what we were trying to do. This was about the most positive thing anyone had ever said to me about our music up to then and really made up for the agony of my first two fingers of my right hand. Bass strings are very thick and they had turned the end of each of the two fingers to blood blisters. I guess everyone has to suffer for their art!

Of course, the rest of the evening was our packing away after celebrating the success. As usual, it was late by the time parents had come and collected the gear and we finally got home. Was this to be the start of greater things? Well, not really, but that is another tale.

BOATING, PIRACY AND A NEAR DROWNING

As a young lad, I spent a lot of time in Roundhay Park and I have many good memories of the wonderful place. In particular, the lakes were an opportunity for adventure and misbehaving. I have spoken about my grandma nearly sinking a little paddle boat on the small lake, but the large lake held more possibilities of fun. After saying that, I have very early memories of feeding the ducks and swans on the little lake. I also remember having my cane fishing net and a jam jar where minnows and sticklebacks were scooped out of the lake around the edges and deposited into the jam jar. Usually we let them go back into the lake, but at least once took them home, only to find that they died within a day or two. The boats on the little lake were not challenging once you got a bit older, and that is where the big lake (Waterloo Lake) came into its own.

In the late 1950s and early sixties, there were two motor launches that took trips around the lake, and this was a must for families. The boats had names, but they escape me at the moment. Was one called The Mayflower? I think about twenty or thirty people could fit on one and they would take a tour of the lake. The boat area was fenced in and there was a large metal turn-style gate that allowed access. You bought tickets at a kiosk and then you lined up to wait for the boat to arrive back, whilst the people disembarked and then you got on. It was always exciting when you were little.

As you got older, there were other options, and they were the rowing boats. These were much more interesting. The boats were wooden and sat low in the water. They had a seat with a back at the rear, but the oarsman or woman sat on a bench adjacent to the rowlocks. Courting couples would often hire these and the men would try to impress the ladies with their smooth rowing and ability to steer around the lake. About four adults could fit in, so some families or two couples could share a boat. In this case, two men would sit next to each other and use one oar each. The rules were quite strict, and you were not allowed to stand or deliberately rock a boat. If anyone was seen fooling around, then staff would appear in a small motorboat and give a warning or get the people on the boat to throw the mooring line to them and they were embarrassingly towed back to the quayside and evicted.

You hired the boat for a set time. I think it was thirty minutes and each rowing boat had a number. Every so often, the motorboat would appear and, using a megaphone, the person in the boat let boat numbers know it was time to head back. Because the lake was so big, this could take quite a time, particularly if you were at the end near the castle and the fenced off island. The tricky part was getting on and off the boat. The helpers had boat hooks, and they held it firm until you got in and out. They always had a certain swagger as they tried to impress the young ladies with their skill.

I have seen the lake drained on at least one occasion, whilst it was cleaned and repair done to the dam wall near where the outdoor swimming pool, Lido, used to be. There was a rumour that bodies were removed, but I don't know if that is true, but the lake was quite deep and I believe there were drownings. I have also seen both of the lakes frozen in a thick sheet of ice and walked on them. Lots of people were on the ice at the time and it must have been very thick. I have also been there when the ice was thin and warning signs told people to keep off. I am not sure when was the last time the ice covered the lake as the climate has changed.

As teenagers, though, the lake offered much more excitement, and our main focus was the big lake. We were immortal, or so we thought. We were full of surging hormones and wanted to impress everyone with our skill, courage and bravado. This is not a good recipe for health and safety, and we assumed the rules were for everyone else but us. Groups of about twelve of us would hire the rowing boats and, of course, there would be every attempt made to outdo our friends in the other boats. Races from one end of the lake to the other would take place and two teenagers on the oars could get up quite a pace and would frighten other rowers and wildfowl as we careened across the water, leaving a wake behind. The no standing rule was seen as a challenge and standing and rocking the boat until water came in over the sides was the usual pastime. Hopefully, you weren't spotted by the boat workers or you would suffer the ignominy of being towed back to shore.

My friend Peter was on the lake with others from Allerton Grange School and the usual tomfoolery was taking place. It was a hot summer's day and spirits were high. I wasn't there on this occasion, but Peter has recounted the experience many times. One boat with about four lads was being rocked, but this time it really filled with water and the boys ended up in the lake. My friend's rowing boat headed over and one boy was missing in the water. Peter gazed down into the dark depths and caught sight of the boy's head. He was floating below water and not moving. Peter reached down and grabbed hold of the lad's hair. Thank goodness for long hair in those days. With a handful of hair, he pulled the boy upwards and got his head above water and they manhandled him into their boat. Luckily, there was a lot of coughing and spluttering and the lad was none the worse for the dunk.

What I was told was that if he hadn't been spotted, then he would have drowned, as he was not moving or trying to get to the surface and was just immobile, suspended under the water. I am not sure the boy ever truly realised what my friend had done for him.

You would have thought that this cautionary tale would have limited our behaviour on the water, but not in the least. One Saturday afternoon, we were rowing and there were four of us on the boat and we ended up near the island near the folly castle. The island was about four or five yards from the banks on its nearest side, covered in trees and thick undergrowth. The surrounding water was shallow and more mud than water. It was fenced off from the lake with a wire strand and we chatted as we rested against the fence.

We must have been bored as we looked at the lake, the fence and the boat and seemed to all come to the same idea. We would take the boat under the fence and hide it on the island, so that we could come back the next day and sail free of charge. Now, why we thought this would be a good idea, I don't know. We didn't want to damage the boat. It was just a prank, I suppose. I seem to remember there was

Peter, Chris, John and me, but I could be wrong.

Somehow we manoeuvred the boat under the wire fence, and we got onto the island. The lake was full of boats and I have no idea why no one reported us, but they didn't. We dragged the boat onto the island and covered it in branches. It wasn't a brilliantly hidden boat, but from a distance, it was difficult to see. We were watched by a family on the lakeside, but they said nothing as we smiled at them and waded ashore. We put our shoes back on, rolled down our trousers and set off on the walk home.

We had arranged to meet the next day to release the boat from the island and enjoy our prank. It was fairly early when we returned the next morning and there was a light mist over the water. The island was shrouded in it, and we wondered if the boat would still be there. To our surprise, it was, and the mist helped cover up our getting the boat back into the water and under the fence. Once done, we headed out onto the open lake. We had the only boat on the water and this was a bit of a problem. We assumed the authorities must have known that a boat was missing, or maybe they didn't. I would have assumed that they would have counted them back in, but maybe somebody was slack and just missed it. If they were aware, then goodness knows what they thought had happened. Anyway, we rowed about a bit and then chose the sensible option. We rowed to the lake edge; put the oars back into the boat and beat a hasty retreat before our misdemeanour was discovered.

As wicked deeds go, it doesn't rank very high, but I was very pleased that we had got away with it. I wouldn't have wanted to face my parents if we had been caught. In the end, no harm was done, and the boat was later towed back by the motorboat. It wasn't uncommon for boats to be abandoned if the crew didn't want to walk from the boathouse, as it was a much longer distance. Maybe they thought it had been similarly abandoned. I don't suppose we will ever know.

FINAL YEAR AND GROWING OLDER IF NOT WISER

I have spoken in a previous tale about taking A Levels and I must admit that I did not know what I wanted to be, or to do with my life, but I knew I wanted to be grown up and enjoy the privileges that came with it. I can't say I knew the responsibilities that it involved, but that didn't matter. If I had an aim, it was that I wanted to become a student and to enjoy student life. This was something that had all the positives. You were paid to study, you didn't live at home and you had freedom to do what you wanted. The only difficulty I had was that I couldn't see myself getting good enough grades to go to University, and I certainly would not work hard to address this problem. The obvious option was to either do a degree at a Polytechnic or go into teacher training. I applied to do a Business Studies degree at a poly, but I chose to do teacher training. After all, I knew something about schools, having spent the last fifteen years in three of them. I had loved primary school and thought that would be a good way to go.

   I based my knowledge of student life on my older brother's experience at Durham University, the Tyke magazine, Leeds University Rag Week, Leeds Poly and Leeds Uni concerts and the Skyrack and Original Oak, student pubs in Headingley. My belief was that they did little, if any, work, were drunk most of the time, had lots of sex and got to listen to and watch great bands. It certainly seemed to be the case for the hundreds that packed out the two pubs every night of the week. There was a heady exuberance in both places, and the university/college scene in Leeds was in its heyday, and I wanted a piece of it.

Roundhay School took little notice of anyone not going to university and their star pupils were those getting places in Oxford or Cambridge. Teacher Training Colleges were never on their list. Luckily, 'Holy Joe' Pullen was more enlightened and ran some sessions at lunchtime for anyone considering the teaching profession. I went along.

It was easier to get into, trained for a job and offered a lifetime of fourteen weeks of holiday and a short working day. The pay wasn't supposed to be great, but it was clearly far more than I had ever earned before. I was sold, particularly when you only needed five or six O levels to gain entry. There was a form of clearing places, but it was not like UCCA for Unis. We were given some guidance on how to find out about colleges and the process of applying, and I decided on two criteria. The first was that it was not to be in Leeds. I did not want to live at home and, secondly, I wanted to apply for as good a college as possible. I looked at the lists and sent off for prospectuses from several colleges. I had read about PE Wing colleges and they were for elite sports people and seemed interesting, so I wrote my letters asking for them to send a prospectus and application forms.

I waited a couple of weeks and then large envelopes started to arrive and I opened them and studied them. I must add that my mother was delighted I wanted to become a teacher. I hadn't the heart to explain that it was more a necessary option, rather than a burning vocational ambition. She had loved school and I am certain that she would have loved to have become a teacher herself, and I am certain she would have made a good one. The other reason that she was delighted was that I think she had severe doubts about my aptitude for anything other than being a wild child, or hopefully she saw where my future would lie.

I received replies from several colleges and these included York, Carnegie in Leeds and Borough Road College in London. There were others, but I have cast them out of my memory. York was tempting as it was away from Leeds, but near enough to drop back home when it suited, and Carnegie I discarded for no other reason than that I wanted to move away from home in a hall of residence. Borough Road, I read, was the first teacher training college in the world.

Founded by Joseph Lancaster, who started the monitorial system of teaching. This was where there was a teacher and a large group of multi-aged children were sub-supervised by monitors and the teacher supervised the whole operation. The college sounded great. The photos of the facilities looked good, and I was impressed that most students had two A levels. The clincher was that it was in London. The 'big smoke' was an exciting prospect and if I couldn't have fun there, where would I?

We could apply for up to six colleges and we had to put them in order. If you were offered your first choice, then that was it. I was called for an interview and, within a few days, I received an offer of a place based on my O levels. That was it then, decision made and future planned!

There was one snag. I had a steady girlfriend, and we had been together for several years and she was not too pleased, but the decision was made. The other tug on my heart was that I was still part of the band, Atlantis, and clearly I was going to leave. Now this really was an emotional pull, but the die was cast.

The date for leaving Leeds seemed a lifetime away, but like most things, the future comes surprisingly quickly and catches us off guard. Bold decisions have played a part in my life and this was the first major one. I discovered an older Roundhay boy was already at Borough Road and he chatted to me one evening at Roundhay Cricket Club, when he heard I was going. He was very positive, so I was set.

This out of the way meant that I could get back to enjoying my last year at Roundhay School. In the Upper Sixth, we no longer had to go to the library during free-periods. We could now spend our time in the Upper Sixth common room, in the Prefects' common room, or on the grounds. The summer of 1973 was a long one with day after day of warm sunny weather. We spent our spare time on the volleyball court playing a game where you kicked a soccer ball over and it was allowed one bounce before the opponents had to kick it back over. Heading the ball was permissible and by the end of the school year, my skill level had improved considerably. Roundhay School was transiting to co-ed, starting in the upper years and we lazed around, listened to music, chatted and generally had the most relaxing of times. I did a little work for Geography, but English was a bit of a disaster that even Les Lees couldn't fix. In the end, I got two

A' Levels and my future was set.

Before one could be a student, a number of formalities had to take place. Applications for a grant had to be lodged and my parents had to fill in their income details and so on. Most students didn't get a full grant and parents had to contribute. I believe my parents had to give me fifty pounds a month. That was quite a lot of money in these days. The Government provided the rest of the grant and that covered the cost of tuition, board and accommodation, food, money to purchase equipment and to cover recreational costs.

The other formality I had to do was to have a medical. I believe this was to check I was physically fit enough to teach, but I didn't give it much thought. I know I had an appointment at Leeds Infirmary and that I had to take a urine sample. I was quite naïve at the time and I took a Rose's Marmalade jar to hold the sample. I don't know what I thought they were going to do with it, but I had filled it to the top. I attended and was nervous, handing it over to the nurse. She seemed totally uninterested, or impressed, and I am sure she had seen far worse, but I could have died of embarrassment. I had to go behind a screen and take off almost all my clothes. My chest was listened to, reflexes checked, and then a hand was thrust down the front of my underpants and I had to cough whilst she held me. I still do not know what that was about, unless it was just to see me squirm with shame. I think I was tested for colour blindness, but I knew I was fine, although my father couldn't differentiate between red and green. Next, I had to get dressed and go for a chest X-ray.

I was escorted into the room and placed in front of the machine, and the technicians went behind a lead screen. There was a pause and then they said that I had to wait on a seat in the corridor. After a few minutes, they came and asked me to go back and they did it again. Afterwards, I was in the corridor and once again, they called me back in. Apparently, there was something wrong with the machine. I seem to remember they tried about thirty or forty times. I can only assume it wasn't working at all, otherwise I would have glowed in the dark by the end. Whatever the case, eventually I must have passed the test, as I was allowed to go home. Several weeks later, I received approval for the grant and my future at Borough Road was set in stone.

It was this year that I got the job at Wragg's Motor Cycles and so I managed to save up some additional money to take with me. I also bought a copy of a Gibson Hummingbird acoustic guitar to accompany me to London. I have covered the drama of my work and ultimate dismissal from Wraggs in a previous tale but, apart from that, the summer of 1973 was a glorious one. The day of the exams came and went and I was delighted to say that what I had learnt for the A' Level Geography came up and I had no problems answering the paper. I believe we had to answer four out of nine questions, but a friend who sat the same paper had not read the instructions properly. I will not mention his name, but he will know if he reads this, and he answered all nine questions. I believe that the markers only marked the first four questions, regardless of whether they were his best answers, and, of course, he was at a real disadvantage. I don't suppose he ever made that mistake again. My English Lit exam was a bit of a disaster and several of us failed to get what we wanted, but luckily General Studies came to the rescue. This paper suited me as it tested wider knowledge, opinions, writing and logical skills, with some political thoughts thrown in.

After the exams, we still were asked to remain at school and that was it, even greater fun and games. School was wonderful and a pleasure to be at. We lounged around and just basked in the sun. Even the weekends were heaven. I remember spending most of the time playing casual soccer on Roundhay Park Arena with a wild group of reprobates and then venturing down to the Lakeside Cafe, which is no longer there, having ice creams and watching the mods on their scooters lined up outside, mixing with some Rockers on their motorbikes. The maze was still there. I loved that summer. We went on the boats on the Big Lake and frequented the Phoenix Bar, at the Roundhay Mansion, in the evenings.

Focus was **the** band at the time, Crocodile Rock was a massive hit, but my least favourite Elton John song. Other notable songs of 1973 were: You're So Vain by Carly Simon, Frankenstein by the Edgar Winter Group, That Lady, the Isley Brothers, Stuck in the Middle With You, Stealers Wheel, Long Train Running, the Doobie Brothers, Daniel, Elton John, Smoke on the Water, Deep Purple, Higher Ground, Stevie Wonder, Reelin' in the Years, Steely Dan, Angie, the Rolling Stones, Money, Pink Floyd and Space Oddity, David Bowie. What a soundtrack for a year and the start of a new phase of my life!

David M Cameron

Roundhay School Upper 6th Form 1973

ABOUT THE AUTHOR

David M Cameron was born in Leeds, in Yorkshire. He is married with four sons and two grandchildren. David has lived in England, Papua New Guinea and Perth, Western Australia, where he has been for the last twenty-nine years. He has written two novels for children, Wickergate and Soulmare and the Moondial fantasy series for adults, and the thriller Dead Men Don't Snore. David also has a weekly blog and podcast of his 'Cup of Tea Tales' that tell some of his life's stories on growing up in Leeds during the 1950s.
More information on both David's music and books can be found on his website/blog:

http://davidmcameronauthormusician.com